World History of Erotic Art

Editor: Alex Comfort MB BSc

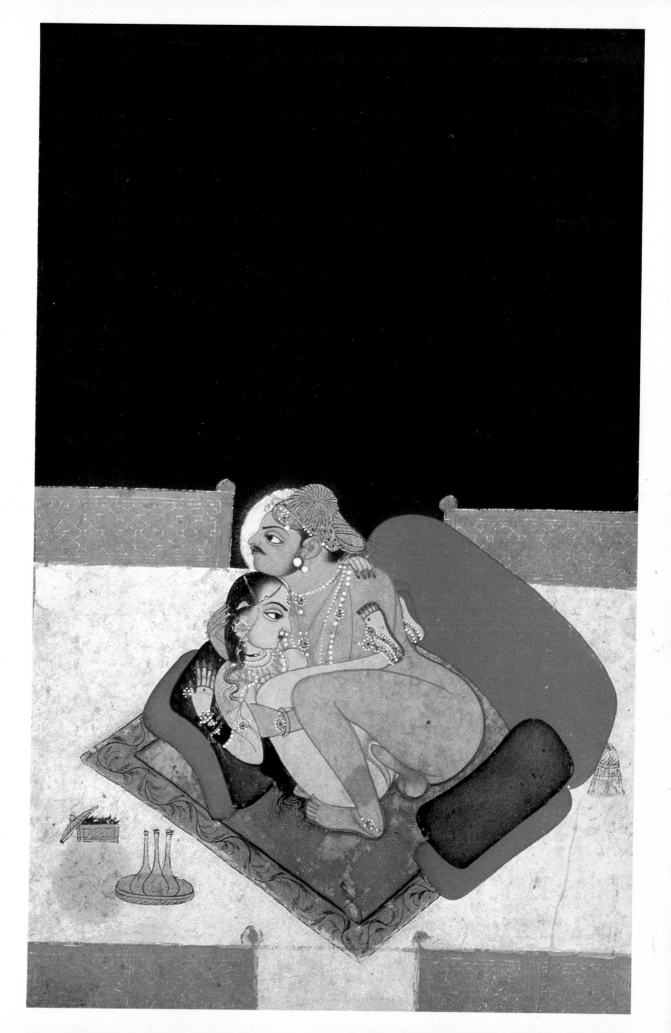

Erotic Art of the East

Philip Rawson

Erotic Art of the East

The Sexual Theme in Oriental Painting and Sculpture

Introduction by Alex Comfort

G. P. Putnam's Sons 200 Madison Avenue New York

Contents

ISLAM by David James

CHINA by Philip Rawson

JAPAN

Acknowledgements

The author and publishers wish to thank the following for permission to reproduce the illustrations in this book. In particular they would like to express their thanks to M. Roger Peyrefitte, C. H. Mitchell, Kiyoshi Shibui, Tetsu Takahashi, Robert Vergez and the owners of important collections in Japan who have allowed unique objects in their collections to be specially photographed for this book.

M. H. T. Hodson, XIX; the Rt Hon Malcolm Macdonald, 152, 153, 169, 170, 175 and 179; Roger Peyrefitte, 8, 37, 120, 126, 137, 138, 140, 166, 172, 179, 180 and 183–194; Nicolas Thompson, 174; Department of Archaeology, Government of India, 15, 21, 45, 46, 48, 49, 53, 54, 63, 64, 67, 72, 73, 75, 80, 81 and 90; Asutosh Museum, Calcutta, 26, 96, 97, 98, 115, 118, 119 and 122; Bibliotheca Ambrosiana, Milan, 130 and 131; Bibliothèque Nationale, Paris, 129; British Museum, London, 135 and 136; Edinburgh University Library, XVII; Fitzwilliam Museum, Cambridge, 141; Freer Art Gallery, Washington, 142; Gulbenkian Museum, Durham University, 150, 151, 154–165, 167, 168, 171 and 172; India Museum, Calcutta, 6, 17, 31 and 33; India Office Library, 19; Nationalbibliothek, Vienna (former Archduke Ranier Collection), 128; Crafts Museum, New Delhi, 113; Patna Museum, 35, 38 and 99; Sarnath Museum, Benares, 32; Victoria and Albert Museum, London, Crown copyright, 101, 117, 123, 134, 138; V and XIII; Victoria and Albert Museum, Salting Bequest, XX, XXI and XXII; Archaeological Survey of India, Western Circle, 19 and 32; Bans and Bans, Chadha, 22, 55 and 56; Ian Graham, 60 and 68; J. C. Harle, 41 and 42; Sunil Janah, Calcutta, 30, 82, 88 and 106; Ajit Mookerjee, 24 and 91; K. L. Syed, Palanpur, 18.

List of Colour Plates

Introduction by Alex Comfort

A Hindu carver of erotic groups would not have needed Aretino's swagger, because he would have lacked Aretino's anxiety. In any case, the suggestions for phallic celebration which Aretino makes jocularly had already been literally adopted in a large section of the Hindu religion. We are nearer to Aretino today. Most educated people would now agree with him, even if they did not think it politic to say so. At the same time, although – because of the notoriety of the *Sedici Modi* – 'Aretino's Postures' are one of the few pieces of Renaissance erotic art which they will know by name, precious few will have seen them.

There is point in editing a book of the world's erotic art which goes beyond the putting down of the Ghibertis. Sexual representation in art, and society's reaction to it, go to the roots of what art is about – its magical function, its privileges, its significance and our attitude vis-à-vis pleasure and fantasy, and droves of other matters which it is extremely hard to put into brief order. Now that we are starting, willy-nilly, to look at the origins of our attitudes towards good taste, the forbidden, and the disturbing, the artist's dilemma is becoming public property: in popular mythology he is a privileged person, like a wizard or a buffoon – he is given license in exchange for some operation he carries out on our behalf, but at the same time his privilege is restricted by arbitrary rules – usually described as conventions of taste or morality, but actually, now, representing matters or symbols disturbing to a small, vocal minority of legislators. The significance of some of these taboos can be understood, as the artist's own psychosymbolic preoccupations can be interpreted, in Freudian terms – otherwise they are quite arbitrary. In China he may decently depict nakedness and coition but not the female foot, in Meiji Japan, coition but not as a rule nudity – in Victorian England, nudity provided that it recalls that of a Greek statue (which excludes the female pubic hair – the Greeks shaved it off) but not coition.

The point about imposed conventions is that they look natural from inside a culture – one grows up with them, and even when, like the clothing of furniture because it has legs, they approach the paranoid, enough people will adopt them through fashionable imitation to preserve the illusion of rightness and propriety. It is quite vain for artists, robust individuals like Aretino, or the *homme moyen sensuel* to argue against such taboos: they are maintained as much by the force of habit as by the vigilance of professional taboo-makers: the whole thing becomes a conspiracy, in which the 'ordinary man' – who likes nudes and coital pictures, for if he did not, it would not be necessary to spend endless man-hours in smelling out and suppressing them – at the same time tacitly assents to the view that they are 'dirty'.

II Leaves painted in miniature illustrating the postures of intercourse. Other sets based on the same designs are known. Eastern Ganges, mid 19th century

19

It is when conventions are set side by side cross-culturally that the fiction of reasonableness breaks down. Most of the reassurance which eventually broke down the Victorian *terror sexualis*, making possible a dispassionate study of its origins and, eventually, the psychoanalytic study of human behaviour in general, came from such a juxtaposition between cultures – with the Greeks, who were culturally respectable; with Martial, who was not, but was read in schools; finally with Burton and the Arabian Nights – by then the Djinn was out of the bottle, and nobody held a Symposium on the Ethics of Imparting Insight to get him back in again. Public taboos do not quite match between cultures, so that neither the neurotic's private police activity against himself, nor his public police activity to suppress the frightening liberty of others, is ever one hundred per cent effective; this fortunate fact is the nucleus of every libertarian renaissance. Sometimes it generates too much anxiety, fears get the upper hand, and books and pictures are burned again. This ice-age-like oscillation is rather typical of cultures whose religion is basically father-centred; the two responses to infantile anxiety, patricidal self-assertion and submission to being castrated gaining the upper hand alternately. What is more interesting is that they 'gain the upper hand' in a relatively small proportion of people – the decencies of the majority are determined imitatively, which gives the castrators, relatively the noisier party, a small advantage. Their expeditionary forces can influence adjacent cultures – 'Westernization' in India or Japan has meant the simultaneous export of yesterday's prudery (which nearly succeeded in banning Indian classical dance because it was associated with prostitutes) and today's tradition of prurient compromise, exemplified in the comic book or the bunny club. The waves are somehow out of phase: art in the modern Orient is subject to the sexual attitudes of the nineteenth-century English missionary now seen as Western and modern rather than Christian and foreign: meanwhile in the cultures which sent the missionaries out, Hinduism and psychoanalysis have, eclectically speaking, joined hands.

It is an odd picture, but one for which we can be thankful. There is always something we can set against our own cultural prejudices, as we set the opinions of our fellows against private bees in our own bonnets. It is difficult, in the face of a knowledge of human natural history, to describe, for example, homosexuality as 'unnatural', even if it is undesirable. Books which one can read in Denmark are hard to prohibit on grounds of imminent public catastrophe in England. If one may bathe without a costume in Sweden, it is hard to point to any moral peculiarity of Brighton which renders it distinguishable in this matter. Of course it is not as simple as that – Hindu erotic art or Japanese shunga has grown in its own soil, shock is no part of the artist's intention, and our fear or enthusiasm at his choice of subject would be beyond his understanding. But by making these subjects actual, even in a different culture, he has made them permissible. In a process of censorship based on infantile anxieties about parents, permission is highly important.

And not only to the artist; he is himself a giver of permission – which is why the prohibitors regard him with anxiety; by dealing with matters they would rather exclude from consciousness he helps others to admit them, thereby threatening the prohibitor's own defences. The real distinction, apart from aesthetic flair, between live and dead art is that the live variety conveys the sense of permission

'After I had persuaded Pope Clement to release Marcantonio Bolognese, who was in prison for having engraved the *Sedici Modi*, I felt a desire to see the pictures which set off Ghiberti's complaints that this brilliant artist ought to be crucified, and when I had seen them I felt the same spirit which moved Giulio Romano to draw them. And since poets and sculptors both ancient and modern have from time to time written or carved erotic things . . . I rattled off the Sonnets which you see at the foot of each page. Their wanton memory I dedicate to you, *pace* all hypocrites, for I renounce the bad judgment and dirty habit which forbids the eyes to see what pleases them most. What harm is there in seeing a man on top of a woman? Must the animals have more freedom than we? It seems to me that the you-know-what given us by Nature for the preservation of the species should be worn as a pendant round our necks or a badge in our caps. It has created you, one of the first living surgeons: it has made me, who am better than bread. It has brought forth the Bembos, the Molzis, the Fortunis, the Franchis, the Varchis, the Ugolin Martinis, the Lorenzo Lenzis, the Dolcis, the Titians, the Michel-angelos; and after them the popes, emperors and kings; it has produced the pretty children and the beautiful women with their *sancta sanctorum,* and for this reason we should decree holy days and dedicate vigils and feasts in its honour, not hide it away in scraps of cloth and silk!'

Aretino (1538) to Battista Zacchi,
surgeon, of Brescia.

I Album miniature. Prince and lady on the terrace at night. Bundi state, Rājasthān, c. 1775

and the danger and insecurity that freedom implies. In man, where such repressed matter is so largely sexual, at least in its origins, erotic art is a highly important index. In fact, since the artist is by vocation a permission-giver, allowing us to share his fantasy, all liberating art is 'erotic': if it depicts an apple, it still exemplifies the degree of sensual appreciation, of pleasure, acceptance or rejection, which the artist feels towards roundness, colour, scent and taste. A landscape can be sensual or puritan in its brushwork without a single human figure in it – which explains why some art wholly without genital reference provokes from the prohibitive the epithet 'obscene'.

At the same time, the depiction of the old, sore foci of the neurotic's anxiety, the genitalia and the primal scene, does differ enough in kind from other permissive acts of the artist to merit a separate title. The anxieties here are cross-cultural and are usually reflected in the depiction, but the strength of the love-hate relationship towards these subjects in our own culture is specially intense. Much of this intensity comes from the intensity of past prohibition – sexual subjects are popular in all cultures, but not all have acquiesced in, or even attempted to achieve, the English paternalist posture – 'these things are not only wicked but bad for you, and you must be protected from them'. Few sons have submitted to symbolic castration with the docility of the Victorian Englishman. His assessment of erotic art, perpetuated today in the legislative voice which still signs international conventions against obscenity, and argues that sexual representation must earn its keep by being meritorious in some more refined way, has its ancestry in the Victorian small boys who slept with their hands tied to prevent masturbation, and awoke to cold baths and hard exercise to keep their minds occupied with what Dr Kurt Hahn calls the non-poisonous emotions.

Art does indeed have moral effects – not so much in what it shows but in the way it handles its matter. The emphatic coitions of Japanese prints 'accept' sex so far as depiction is concerned, but show deep anxiety over it (so does much modern art; one needs to be driven, perhaps, to paint – what one paints may show only the anxiety or its resolution). Hindu art, by contrast, is an art of acceptance which comes close to the ideal of the new psychiatric humanism – lack of fear or surprise at one's own impulses, coupled with rational control. Exciting as this work may be to the artist at the purely formal level, it is still more interesting to those who value and wish to further this humanism. It gives us – without falling head over heels into bogus Indophilia – a real insight into our own cultural problem, and – more important – into potential ways of dealing with it. This art is part not only of a plastic architectural technology, but of an emotional technology, a therapeutic process. Unlike ourselves, the ancient Hindu lived in a world which was not polarized between Black to be shunned and repressed, and White to be arduously sought. In his iconography Black and White are two faces of the numinous, both present in himself, and, for the sage, neither to be viewed with fear. In his technology of release, sexuality occupies, with art, the position which Christianity has always denied it – and which it now grudgingly takes over from humanism. A sage may avoid it in the interests of self-sufficiency, a rigid man (*paśu*, literally a tethered beast) may accept it only hedged about with obsessional observance, but for some – especially the spiritual 'hero' (*vīra*) – it is in itself the road to enlightenment and the experience of divinity. The vīra is in some attributes not far removed from the intellectual 'hero', the scientific man – now conspicuously lacking in transcendent experiences compatible with rationalism – whom the modern European artist addresses; and here is art, in a deeply sophisticated culture, serving as a fullscale technology of emotional expression. The attention of the artist may be less riveted by this than by the formal effect, but not that of the human biologist with an eye to social psychotherapy.

It is perhaps the most striking feature of our culture that we lack a technology of the emotions. We have extensive technologies for dealing with our bodies as mechanical systems and our environment seen as external to and apart from ourselves – but we have nothing approaching the highly sophisticated technology for self-management and self-reconciliation, to internal needs and those of the culture, which we see in 'primitives'. This is the original function of both art and religion. In the process of getting the 'objective' realism necessary for science, our religion has lost most of the use it ever had in this field, and has become a paler competitor of science, offering pseudofactual accounts of the universe and of human behaviour against the realistic accounts given by the scientific method. By this literalism it has lost both appeal and intellectual integrity, so that even emotionally valid rituals which it perpetuates have become unavailable to educated people. Primitives by contrast have an active and time-consuming non-factual 'religious' life, which is concerned through ritual, symbolism and corporate ceremony, not with external Gods viewed as objective facts like the manganese atom or the Eiffel Tower, but with the integration of processes wholly within the human head and the interaction of human heads. The aborigine's attention to the Dream Time is not factual (he does not confuse the ancestral Serpent with real snakes and look for its fossil bones) nor practical at the level of improving hunting or making rain – or not this alone. It is far more concerned with the expression of needs, the acceptance and taming of unacceptable drives, and the appreciation of self-hood; its materials are the boundaries of I-ness and us-ness, which concern us as social animals, and of I-ness and that-ness, which concern us as practical or scientific animals – both of which, like ourselves, the aborigines and all human beings undoubtedly are.

The terms I have used here belong rather to Hinduism than to ego psychology or to philosophy because Hinduism is possibly unique among systematized religions in having kept at least the potentiality of such a function. It is not working as a fully adequate 'integrative' technology of feeling for the modern Indian, partly because he has become influenced by Western and Judaeochristian ideas, but it is still a comprehensive shorthand for almost all that we now know discursively about the unconscious mind. Hinduism also goes further than the relatively simple emotional technology of the aborigine and his Dream Time rites, which we should find it hard or impossible to take over culturally, beautifully as they are fitted to his way of living, and much as they resemble the imagery we all experience in actual dreaming and fantasy. The Hindu canon of techniques comprises everything from the most recondite metaphysics, some of them directly applicable to scientific topics like those of modern physics, to orgiastic magic; its versatility as an emotional tool-kit is staggering. Much of this versatility comes from its bisexual orientation. Historically, it has assimilated both goddess worship, which is commonly, though not always, orgiastic, and paternalism, which is puritan. This is something which with rare exceptions among heretics Christianity has never managed to do, its goddess worship and its family trinity (father, son, mother) being solidly rooted in a paternal and largely prohibitive God; so that its excursions into sexual mysticism all start with a piacular rejection of the physical – the Goddess is a virgin, the love of Christ for the Bride can only be acted out in human relations against a continual background of abstinence and expiation, embodied in the two chief icons, the child at the breast of a virgin mother, and the same child dying as an offering to placate the father: love is expressed as death. This is an icon which, for our culture, is out of date as well as unedifying.

The Hindu diversity (which made it look morally equivocal to past Christians) is much closer to human needs – gods are one or many, male or female at the need of the worshipper; orgiasts and ascetics, puritans and antinomians are equally orthodox, the chosen deity or deities of any man's *sadhana* (chosen ritual) are the familiar denizens of his own Dream Time like those of the aborigine, uncomplicated by historicity. The simple will objectify them as an image (*mūrtī*) – he needs some manifest object to get hold of; the philosopher will idealize them as the Whole (*paramātman*) – the Tantrik initiate, who comes perhaps nearest in his primitivism and his psychoanalytic insight to our own fragmented culture, acquires the insight that all Gods are within his own psyche and govern his relations to himself, his body, the outside world, and his fellows. Discursive psychoanalysis has at last begun to turn the weapon of objective self-awareness to cut through this confusion and to describe its structure, but in many ways the Hindu, oblique presentation of the same material is emotionally more digestible: we have to get psychoanalytic insight *against* the trend of our natural way of thinking, while Hinduism is far more the kind of insight-giving for which man, who evolved his brain through long selection at the aborigine level, is probably programmed.

The nearest we come to a technology of the emotions, psychotherapy on a one-by-one basis apart, is through art. This is a very shrunken and truncated thing in its individualist form, compared with the patness and economy of its use in primitive, or social, societies, but it has been less castrated than has religion by the growth of logical objectivity, it is less intellectually dangerous in contexts where religion hinders us by confusing emotional needs with our assessment of external objects and relations: in fact, starting with real objects which the artist re-creates and re-experiences, it provides about the only effective emotional technology we have left. It has undergone its own form of evolution, making up in the grandeur of the individual liberty which we see in masterpieces what it has lost in common language and cultural effectiveness. In fact it has gone right back to the earliest human manifestation of individual exposition, the makings and sayings of a possessed and partly dissociated individual whose internal strains cannot be soothed by the culture, and who has to break out of its normal rules to express them – thereby acquiring 'inspiration', the power and the right to put such unmanageable material to socially profitable use. In primitive societies, the accepted rituals are sufficient emotional technology for most people, but the shaman, the possessed, can step outside them and as it were take them over, instituting his own rituals and communicating them to others with what his fellows treat as supernatural authority.

We split this function. Artists are the possessed and imaginative half of the primitive shaman; his healing functions we depute – rightly, in view of the fact that the mind can be studied – to the psychoanalyst, who does not himself dissociate or break down in order to acquire the knowledge to help, and who offers us the rational explanation which, in our culture, is the most helpful aid to self-acceptance. Yet when it comes to social rather than one-by-one communication of insight, the artist's language is the more economical of the two.

The relevance of erotic art to this argument (or of this argument to erotic art) is as follows. The function of an emotional technology, whether it be analysis, primitive dance, art, drama or any other *sadhana,* is to make conscious or at least manageable the unacceptable unconscious forces in our own minds and in our interaction with others or with 'the world'. That many of these unacceptables are derived from sex is a natural consequence of what we know of the development through the primates of human family-pattern and character-structure; where in their overt form they are not immediate derivates of the father-mother-child situation, they can be reduced to, or expressed as, their origins in that situation. This is the basic insight both of Freudianism and of modern work on human evolution. In the same way, however (and this is less widely emphasized and realized), the most effective techniques by which cultures deal with them, relevantly to our present situation, are themselves sexually derived. Sexuality and aggression are the most unmanageable as well as the most powerful human emotions; both require domestication for our own development and our social survival. The expression of these, and the ability to accept them, in forms which do not make life intolerable is the chief object of all the complex emotional skills which primitive ceremony reinforces. It is also the most powerful medicine, in the Redskin's as well as the psychiatrist's sense – real as opposed to symbolic discharge of aggression is, however, destructive, while love is not, and we probably owe our precarious survival to the fact that aggression can be expressed as sexuality as well as killing. Art expresses both these unmanageables: Art as violence we already have in full measure. What we need now is a corresponding art which is truly erotic.

Now in order to tame unwelcome emotions we commonly need, like the shaman, to undergo a process of dissociation or disinhibition. We may do this individually, by working over our dreams and attitudes, and by vehemently expressing ('abreacting') those things we cannot on practical grounds act out – some patients, and some therapists, need help in doing this, or shorten the process, by the use of 'psychedelic' or intoxicant drugs. Whether obtained by persuasion or by pharmacology, however, some release of inhibitions is needed.

Primitives, whose technology operates not couch-wise but in the society at large, use other stimulants to 'let go' – suggestion, ritual, overbreathing, isolation, dancing, rhythm, meditation and acting-out; the last, where aggression is concerned, in primitive warfare or the destruction of a devoted animal, object, or person. This last ritual erupts individually in our culture as aggression expressed in sport or in the Bomb, as burglary, or against public property such as telephone boxes and railway carriage fittings – unfortunately such symbolic expressions are too unorganized to be controllable. Their undisturbing counterpart is personal fulfilment in sexual love. Violence apart, the most physiological form of un-

24

conscious nakedness, of self-transcendence, is precisely in sex: where this is fully mature, it involves loss of identity in fusion with another person and in mutual orgasm, while old residual anxieties may be placated ritually by details in the manner in which the act of coition is performed. Normal sex seems to combine the moral nakedness of the psychiatric situation (we say in bed things we would nowhere else admit), play therapy, abreaction, realization, identification, aggression and submission, and a built-in electroconvulsion therapy to reinforce them. Primitives may use sexuality in this way, as do Tantrik mystics, but in our culture, apart from irrational violence, *it is almost the only transcendent experience we have left.* As it is perhaps the paradigm and original of such experiences, this may be as well, and it is beneficial even though not all of us can surrender so fully.

Our other surviving transcendent experience is that of art. The production of art is itself, in its shamanistic context, a kind of intoxication; on canvas, as in bed, we communicate implicitly things we cannot or would not say, or even admit. Better still, what the artist makes, unlike an orgasm, persists as a tangible communication to others, though at a lower level of energy.

I question whether any artist in our culture can now make an icon as widely effective or as powerful as in a primitive culture – our diversity is now too great, and our most emotionally effective cultural icons have come rather as by-products of the purposive – trains, bridges, planes, ships and mushroom clouds – all nominally functional, but having the faces and roles of ancestors, war-gods and the like. In trying rather haltingly to devise an emotional technology of our own without going outside our culture, drama, in which all can participate, seems the most likely candidate for development – indeed psychodrama is already a therapeutic technique. But in erotic art two powerful magical or emotional tools are combined. Some of this power is evidenced by the extreme fear with which our culture views it, by the use made of it in Hindu iconography, by the oscillations of Chinese or Renaissance society between prudery and enjoyment, and so on. At any rate, viewing society as it is today, it is hard to resist the conclusion that of the medicines capable of doing for us what the rituals of the Dream Time do for the aborigine, and which our religion emphatically does not, only sex and art – formal psychotherapy apart – really qualify as feasible. Indeed when minorities such as amateur 'witches' or naturists devise or discover a lay sacrament, it is the sexual and the ritual factors which are the effective agents in producing inner release. The art of sexual fulfilment, genuinely erotic art, is a ceremony of this kind, and is wholly salutary – even the depiction of sexual deviation helps, for such deviation is a private ceremony for the banishing of anxiety, and by depiction reduces its charge of guilt, rendering the ceremony less private. Indeed, the art of virginity, chastity, and love-as-death is itself the making concrete of a deviation quite as much as, or more than, the depiction of a coital fantasy – which is why our own religious iconography has had its positive effect on us. But by all counts, acceptance of love as love, pleasure as pleasure, is surely better.

We shall examine the Western and the modern artist's dilemma more fully in a later volume. But it is in the attempt to get this in perspective and use this – to our culture – unbiddably powerful reagent that the erotic art of other cultures is important. For them the reagent is not so powerful. Just as torture as an artistic subject has been blunted by centuries of Christian iconography, which, blunt as it now is, still whispers 'love means death and suffering' – so for the Hindu tradition sex has its place in religious iconography from which not even the imitators of Western moralisms can quite displace it: for the Japanese artist it was an unremarkable branch of naturalism – yet here, in the vehemence of the lovers, the emphasis on huge genitals, exhausting women, copious secretions and what George Moore calls 'furious fornications' we can trace some of the explicit anxieties of Japanese culture which the good-mannered naturalism discharges.

Even so, perhaps, none of this would be so remarkable if our own peculiar cultural situation had not caused it to be concealed. Many great artists have produced 'erotic' art as naturally and as fruitfully as any Hindu or Japanese – that is to say, they have painted sex as they have painted still life, landscape or portrait, with little sign of the cultural irritation which their audience has been conditioned to show in face of it. These works are scarce, however, and the public has not seen them, because they have been militantly destroyed or hidden by disturbed people. Few Victorians knew Millet's 'erotic' pictures, and Gosse burned all those of Turner which came into his hands as trustee. There is an analogy in the violence of public love–hate towards erotic art from other cultures in the case of nudity. Complete habitual nudity is rather rare in human societies, though many accept it casually and some permanently; in others, because it is prohibited, it has *mana* and becomes a psychological tool – witches, shamans and rainmakers in such cultures may strip naked because they thereby canalize the power of the unusual, the uncustomary, as if nudity were a medicine dress, while modern nudists experience social nakedness as a symbolic release of anxiety, falsity or inhibition. Thus the pharmacological effect, if one may call it that, of nudity depends less on its lock-and-key releaser effect than on its rareness in the given situation. In exactly the same way, though erotic art deals with a powerful psychosymbolic releaser and symbol, the 'primal scene', its power to excite, disturb, anger, express or interest depends even more on secondary cultural taboos. Artists and publics who have been excluded from it by the activity of paternalist anxiety-makers may initially react with an enthusiasm as great as the prohibitors' anxiety, but this will pass, unless we oscillate like the Chinese, and the next oscillation makes us clothe the legs of furniture once again – thus keeping up the intensity of the stimulus.

It is for a combination of all these reasons that it now seems reasonable to redress the balance. Western erotic art is the product of the attitudes and limitations I have described, affecting both what has been produced and what has survived. In these books we shall be putting it side by side with that of other cultures, with enough parallel comment to make clear the differences in situation and intention between them. This is of use to our understanding, and with a complex iconography like that of India it is essential, but I doubt whether the cultural background will make much difference to its effect upon one major section of the public we have in mind, namely the artists. It took little appreciation of the intellectual basis of Japanese art to make Whistler, Bonnard or the Art Nouveau movement adopt its purely visual lessons. I think it quite possible that the full exposure side-by-side of the relatively unseen erotic art of our own past tradition with that of other cultures could have considerable effects on contemporary painting – not by setting everyone to the production of posture-books, but by bringing to the surface a number of relatively buried trends in European visual art through contact with what is, even to artists, unfamiliar. One of these is the balance of tension, which Lessing saw as the Baroque ideal, and which feels its way inexplicitly towards the tensions of embracing rather than struggling bodies (it has been said that sexual activity is a basically unsuitable subject for composition, but this rationalization hardly stands up to the Indian or Aretine examples). We see this in Rodin, but one needs to examine a whole sequence of 'primal scene' studies by various hands and in various styles for the underlying allusion in non-sexual art to be fully obvious.

Since the authors of the individual studies are orientalists, anthropologists or art critics, the emphasis of my preface as editor has been rather on setting the scene into which the books are to be projected than on repeating their detailed comment, e.g. on the meaning and use of Hindu or Chinese sexual representation. Artists who are enlightened or educated by this material will be so, primarily, for its formal and evocative quality, but at the same time they, and their audience if they transmit any of it, are as open to the power of this emotional tool as any – indeed, one cannot study Hinduism or Hellenism objectively without undergoing some operation upon one's own unconscious machinery, and it is for the likelihood of some such operation in the context of present-day art and society that I chose to edit these volumes. It will be interesting to see what, if any, the effect of them, and of the general availability of artistic treatment of the sexual elsewhere, will be upon figuration and the search for a modern style.

INDIA

1 The Divine Couple

Love as ritual

India, that vast burgeoning subcontinent, fertilized by sacred rivers of stupendous size and by monsoon rains of devastating power, has become for Europeans the legendary country of erotic fulfilment. For out of India we have received the *Kāmasūtra,* and *Kokashāstra,* two of the sacred classics of the technique of love. We have seen, if only in photographs, the fantastic erotic sculpture of her great temples. The verses of her poets, devoted to the unstinted and uninhibited praise of the beauties of God's own sexual partners have reached us through excellent translations. And India is indeed what one nineteenth-century English writer called 'the land of the liṅgam', to whose service the troupes of Devadāsis or Bayadères were dedicated.

We are not wrong; and yet a merely romantic image of Indian love can never be true. The reality is far more emotionally complex and more interesting than the legend suggests. At the same time we must beware of writing down Indian eroticism into the kind of bio-therapeutic sport which accords with our Western rationalist mythology. To the Indian, as indeed to every Oriental mind – *pace* Kinsey – mere orgasm is never the goal of love. For to an Oriental every act of love partakes of ritual, and is carried out adorned with, bedded in, to consummate a luxuriant garland of imagery. The East knows well that what distinguishes the art of human love from bestial acts of mere procreation, or relief of tension, is the psychological consummation which it represents. If one so wishes one may perhaps put the case in another way, and say that in Eastern eroticism ideas and sensation are vital correlatives, enhancing each other, and producing out of their mutual relationship, by a kind of synergy, an experience which is far more than transitory. It is regarded as so exalted as to be called by divine names. In fact the whole story of Indian eroticism begins at every point with God. This, we may say, *1* is the Indian way of attributing to it the highest possible psychological value. So that when, as we must, we discuss the divine names, transcendent types and ideas, in connexion with Indian sexual love, we must not dismiss them as mere theosophizing. They represent the indispensable root, the ultimate principle of value from which Indian eroticism springs. And not all of them will actually turn out to be unknown to Western myth and value-systems.

Visual art is in India one of the prime vehicles for erotic imagery, for the ideas which combine with and enhance sexual sensation. Art forms a vital part of the science of love. Certainly there were in India, as in China, Japan and Persia, illustrations whose function was simply educative. Just as the *Kāmasūtra* devotes many pages to explaining the possible variations in the performance of the sexual act which lovers may learn to employ to enhance their love, and keep it green for whole lifetimes, so there have always been pictures whose purpose was visual instruction of the same kind. It is characteristic of India that all kinds of variations of such educative sets were made. Their background was not usually coldly clinical. For all Indians freely accept that love is a most interesting topic, and they do not have the spasmodic guilt-response to thoughts of sexuality which Europeans have acquired as a consequence of many centuries of Christian myth and theory. So it was common enough for educative manuals to include by the way interesting or amusing folklore, or to incorporate stories which everyone knew. At the same time many illuminated manuscripts of well-known literary works, at some suitable point, where say, the happy reunion of lovers was described, would incorporate a set of educative postures. Thereby the educative set was given a special value by being presented as illustrating the practice of gods or heroes – proper patterns for the behaviour of the natural man. Many manuscripts of India's heroic epics, the *Rāmāyaṇa* and *Mahābhārata* of the Purāṇas, where the lives of gods are described, and of the works of vernacular poets were so illuminated. We know too, from literary sources, that many houses contained as wall paintings educative sets, some based on the amours of the gods, which no doubt served as incentives to erotic invention and variation by the inmates. All this art thus retained a solid basis of reality which saved it from becoming mere fantasy.

The substance of the educative illustrations will be discussed later. But here the point to be made is that in India even the most factually educative illustrations tended to have qualities which made them fit to serve as the ideas correlative to and enhancing sensation. The reason is that they were never mere diagrams, as Western illustrations would be. The Indian sets, however modest, were always works of art. That is, they set out as all works of art do, to convey feeling. They were executed in that Indian style which was always fundamentally erotic in flavour. As well, their actors were conceived as types based upon the heroes and heroines of romantic legend. So that even the crudest educative sets convey, as intensely as they are able, a feeling of the sweetness of love and its fulfilment. From the very beginning visual style portends delight. And erotic images represent the final consummation of all the formal tendencies of Indian artistic styles.

Underlying the whole of Indian eroticism is one fundamental idea. Down the centuries of India's cultural evolution this idea may have been overlaid, combined with others, sedulously reinterpreted. It may have been hidden, inverted or at least kept wrapped up. But it has always been there. The idea is that sexuality is intrinsically divine, and that the sexual afflatus in man and animals is the sensible presence of creative divinity. For from very early times, in the most sacred literature of Hinduism, there has lain embedded this germinal image. The great *Bṛihadāraṇyaka Upanishad* for example, the earliest of the Upanishads, composed probably during the early first millennium BC, says:

> In the beginning this world was the Self (*ātman*) alone in the form of a Person (*purūsha*). Looking around he saw nothing else than himself. He first said 'I am'. Thence arose the name 'I' . . . Verily He had no delight. He desired a second. He was indeed as large as a man and a woman closely embraced. He caused that Self to fall (√*pat*) into two pieces. Therefrom arose husband

(*pati*) and wife (*patnī*). Therefore this is true: 'oneself is like a half fragment' as Yajñavalkya [a great sage] used to say. Therefore this space is filled by a wife. He copulated with her. Therefrom human beings were produced. And then she bethought herself: 'how now does he copulate with me after he has produced me just from himself? Come, let me hide myself.' She became a cow. He became a bull. With her he did copulate. Then cattle were born. She became a mare, he became a stallion . . .

The passage then continues in the typical manner of the 'pursuit songs' of many literatures and concludes:

He knew: 'I indeed am this creation, for I emitted it all from myself.' Thence arose creation. Verily he who has this knowledge comes to be in that creation of his.

Another passage from the ancient sacred canon of the Brahmins is illuminating. It is from the *Chandogya Upanishad,* and deals with the analogical bases of one of the sacred liturgical chants, and its successive phases.

One summons. That is *Hiṅkāra*. He makes request. That is *Prastava*. Together with the woman he lies down. That is an *Udgītha*. He lies upon the woman. That is *Pratihara*. He comes to the end. That is a *Nidhāna*. He comes to the finish. That is a *Nidhāna*. *Nidhāna*. This is the *Vāmadevya Sāman* as woven upon copulation. He who knows thus this *Vāmadevya Sāman* as woven upon copulation comes to copulation, procreates himself from every copulation, reaches a full length of life, lives long, becomes great in offspring, and in cattle, great in fame. One should never abstain from any woman. That is his rule.

Probably older still than these passages is a yet more condensed image of the form of the universal origin, before it appeared as double sexed. Hymns of the *Rigveda,* composed probably during the second millennium BC in archaic Sanskrit, refer to the Golden Germ from which all creation sprang, the ultimate unit of the universe. The parallel is close between this Indian imagery and that of the Greek Orphics, who imaged the origin of the existent world from chaos as a gigantic egg, from which a double sexed being emanated.

Another passage in the *Bṛihadāraṇyaka Upanishad* gives the first account of the sacred nature of sexual intercourse, transforming the woman into the sacred site of Vedic sacrifice:

Her lap is a sacrificial altar; her hairs the sacrificial grass; her skin the soma-press; the two lips of the vulva are the fire in the middle [a reference this to the fire generated in the slot by the rubbing-stick used in ancient times; for the sacrificial fire so generated is holy]. Verily, the world of him who practises sexual intercourse knowing this, is as great as the world of him who performs the great *Vājapeya* [strength-libation] sacrifice.

These old Indian canonical expressions of the idea of the metaphysical significance not only of the sexual relationship but of sexual 'delight' help to explain why sexual love has been so highly valued in India, whereas in the West similar vestigial notions were expunged as 'heresy'. Certainly these particular passages will not have been known to most Indians. Before modern times, when European scholarship and publication broke down the barriers of secrecy, only certain Brahmins will have known of them directly. But a wealth of folklore conveyed the same idea; and there was always the liṅgam – the phallic emblem of stone which serves as the main focus of worship in thousands of temples.

Accumulating vital energy

The idea of the spiritual significance of sexuality expressed itself in a myth-based attitude towards the bodily functions and secretions, especially the male semen. It is clear that from early times Brahmins have regarded themselves as personal vessels of the Brahman, that supporting and creative power informing the whole universe which is stored in the head. So in common with other Indians they have also identified the semen and its generative 'power' as the concrete form of this metaphysical power. Dr M. Carstairs's recent investigations support other older evidence that this identification of spiritual vitality and semen is still widespread – also among non-Brahmins. Amongst modern Indians loss of semen, either by intercourse or spontaneous emission, is a constant cause for anxiety, and is viewed especially by Brahmins with dread. It is felt that in losing semen men are losing part of their limited store of 'vitality'. And this is of special importance to the Brahmins, whose life's profession it is to *be* vehicles of the divine. Dr Carstairs' Brahmin informants, who were villagers whose nutrition was probably not ideal, even went so far as to avoid intercourse with their wives, except on specific occasions when the wives had a right to require it of them.

Conversely, this mythology indicates that anyone who is able to retain his semen, and store it up until his body is filled with it, at high pressure, becomes a paragon of radiant spiritual energy (called *tejas*), a saint, able to accomplish tremendous works, even a magician. Folklore is full of significant stories. Some for example, concern a great saint attacked by robbers and cut with a sword, who bleeds not blood but semen. In fact the Indian conception of spiritual achievement of all kinds rests firmly upon this mythical idea, and we shall explore some of its ramifications in later chapters. There cannot be much doubt that Gandhi's well-known sexual squeamishness, seeming so perverted to the modern Western mind, was based upon this same myth – which in turn made it acceptable to his Indian followers.

It is interesting to compare these ideas with very similar myths which seem to have prevailed in the classical Mediterranean world. Most important inferences may emerge from the comparison. Professor Onians has isolated the evidence, and characterized the implied beliefs. In fact, of course, what are here called mythical ideas or beliefs are really unconscious assumptions or images so deeply rooted in people's minds that they are rarely given conscious expression. They appear always by implication, as a basic pattern of thought which is taken utterly for granted. In Homeric and post-Homeric Greece it seems quite clear that the *psychē*, the main spiritual faculty of the body, was thought of as contained in the head and spinal marrow, escaping as semen, and somehow related to the breath. It was figured in art as the winged phallus, or phallic-headed bird, which appears so frequently in all the later erotic art of Europe. Aphrodite's phallic-headed goose, which classical sculptors and seal engravers often represented her as nursing on her lap, is one of its chief forms. It is very naturally associated with the Goddess of Love. This is probably the true image behind the story of Leda. It may very well be that the hitherto unexplained use in the Upanishads of a goose as an image for the human 'spirit' goes back to a similar conception. Although so far as I am aware there are no actually phallic geese in Indian art, the comparison is illuminating, and helps to explain the forms of many goose-like birds that appear in erotic paintings in *XIV* India.

It is interesting, too, that in Greece and Rome castration seems to have been believed not to destroy the source of the vital fluid – for medical knowledge was not then so precise – but merely to interrupt the channel whereby it flowed out from the head via the spinal marrow. Such interruption could only have the result that the *psychē* was retained and stored up. Priestly castration as practised in temples of the Mediterranean goddesses, and European priestly continence may thus have the same mythical bases. The head, of course, is the focus of this myth of vital creative energy. Professor Onians has amply documented the significance of many beliefs and rituals associated with the head in the Mediterranean world, which will be found to throw a great deal of light on comparable Oriental ideas and rituals. They can show the coherence and vital sexual basis of many seemingly disparate ideas and customs which are given artistic expression, and act as paradigms to remote, unverbalized but potent ideas.

Outgrowths from the head are specially significant. The horned animals are the most sacred, because they carry about upon them visible evidence that their 'head-stuff' is developed to the point of extrusion. Bulls, rams and he-goats are especially well-endowed. So too are deer. There is ample linguistic evidence in the West for the association between horns and male sexuality. In Indian miniatures and ivories of the seventeenth and eighteenth century AD horned deer are frequently used as symbols for the desire of a lovely girl in the forest, for example in illustrations of the *Toḍi rāginī*. Head hair comes in for special attention in both West and East. Priests who wish to conserve their vitality, to 'cut off their outflows' to use a Buddhist term, shave it off. His long hair was the repository of the Biblical Samson's vital energy. So is the Sikh's. The Indian god Shiva, who is the personalized representation of the creative and sexual vitality of the universe, is always represented as having a mass of long, tangled, piled-up hair upon his head. Yogīs who are his devotees imitate their divine pattern in this respect. Abundant hair represents the abundance of divine energy, in the same way as Shiva's erect phallus. It is also interesting that even today the ordinary Indian believes that the way to avoid 'catching cold' and stay healthy (i.e. preserve his vital energy) is to wrap up his head, even if the rest of his body is practically naked. Hence the turban.

Golden haloes and golden crowns also represent visible manifestations of the spiritual energy in the head, transmuted into the form of light, or the concrete radiance of gold and gems. This idea is common both in East and West. Crowned and haloed figures are very common in Indian art. In India, however, we find two special visual images reflecting similar ideas. The first is the third eye of wisdom in the middle of the forehead, which is based on a kind of verbal pun. For in India knowledge and seeing come from the same verbal root $\sqrt{vid}$, to see. And the sacred Veda is that which is seen with the eye of wisdom. The second and most important is the prominence on the top of the head, called the *Ushnisha*, which all statues of the Buddha display. We shall have occasion to discuss this more fully later on; but, briefly, this signifies the actual physical presence of the vital energy of the body, symbolised by the semen, concentrated in the top of the head.

Now, this mythical complex, whereby sexual vitality, creative energy, and the creative force of the cosmos are seen as cognate, and manifest themselves in concrete form in the bodily secretions, lies at the root of the whole of Indian thinking about sex and love. Even where it is not expressly stated, it is implied; and many works of art bear obvious marks of its influence. It is even implicit in the opulent, inflated and colourful styles of Indian sculpture and painting. We can see how there are two possible attitudes towards it, not exactly mutually exclusive, but responsible when taken together for the ambivalent, or what seems to us ambiguous character of Indian culture and art. In our encounters with many Indian cultural facts we have to be prepared to see that two interpretations are always possible, the two points of view having become almost inextricably interfused during the evolutionary history of Indian art and thought.

16   The first of these two attitudes is expressed in the cult of personal restraint and asceticism, proper to the individual Brahmin. Because of his profession as the vessel of sanctity he is supposed to develop his inner content of brilliant vital energy (*tejas*) by withholding it, stopping its outflows with all sorts of deprivations, prescriptions, yogas and rituals of which the texts are full. This mode of religious life and expression is the one pursued by the heroes of Brahmanical thought, the sages, magicians and royal ascetics of literature and legend. And since the Brahmins were also usually the littérateurs and learned men of India, the sole agency for the preservation of the literary heritage, their outlook has been steadily fostered and gradually imposed as the 'official' cultural view, especially during the last two centuries. Brahmin explanations of many cultural phenomena are nowadays universally accepted in India, where old authorities still tend to be more highly revered than new thought. The 'official' explanations for the existence of the erotic sculpture on the temples of India, still sedulously repeated by Indian authors, are often tendentious interpretations of Brahmanical tinge, as we shall see. For centuries Western culture has lain under the same sort of handicap. In India, however, the original imagery and rationale underlying the Brahmanical conception can still be deciphered from the available sources.

Strictly speaking, the official Brahmin view is theoretically more liberal than often it actually is. For since ancient times it has recognized that the life of a man should be divided into four stages, to each of which particular activities are appropriate. After childhood is over comes studentship, then the stage of 'householder' (*grihastha*), during which the acquisition and owning of property, the pursuit of pleasure and the propagation of children (male if possible), were perfectly appropriate and permissible. At its worst, this idea can authorize all sorts of practices which we could call immoral, such as oppressive trading monopolies. After a third stage of 'forest' life with the family came the fourth, reached when the family was grown up, and the wife's consent had been given. This was *sannyāsa*, the

III Album miniature. Prince and lady on the terrace at night. Bundi state, Rājasthān, *c.* 1790

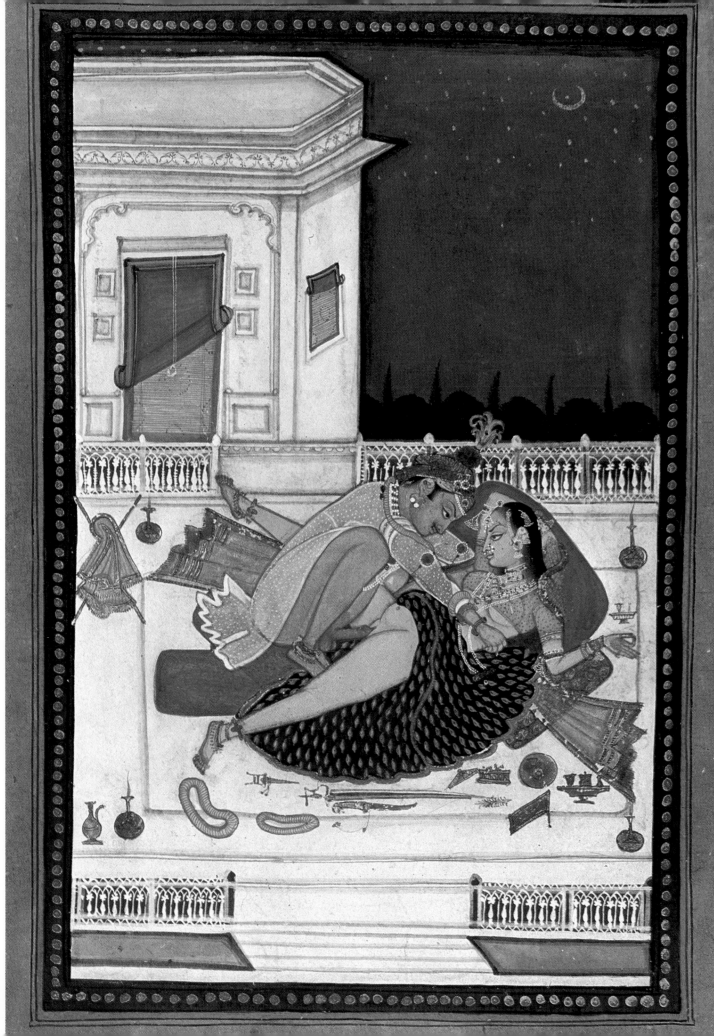

abandonment of home, possessions and desires. It is to this last stage, the wandering homeless life, that the rigours of ascetic energy-compression are fully appropriate. But it is interesting to remember that even up to the early centuries AD forest-dwelling hermits are described in the *Rāmāyaṇa* and *Mahābhārata,* and in the work of the great Gupta poets, as living with their wives and children. The utmost rigours of asceticism were only meant for those to whom they specially appealed.

Nowadays we should indeed suspect psychological reasons for the self-mortifications practised by so many ascetics. Such practices as the *pañchadhuni* (five-fires) – sitting between four blazing fires with the sun the fifth – starvation, loading oneself with chains, standing for months upon one leg, gazing sunward until the eyes are destroyed, were intended most forcibly to drive the vital energy inward, away from objects of the outer world. We might today interpret them as a violent direction of aggression against both the body and the outer world which sustains it, the supreme act of violent hatred and negation, deeply satisfying for all sorts of reasons. This the Buddha and more moderate sages fully recognized. The middle way avoids the *other*, the black kinds of pleasure. But one may legitimately query whether the cult of aversion from the world, even when adopted as a cultural norm as it is today in India, does not in fact still represent a means of satisfying deep-rooted aggression against a dreadful environment, producing a pleasure more intense than any other available. Numberless religious treatises in India take as premise *Sarvam dukham* – 'All is misery'. In Chapter Four we shall discuss a number of sexo-yogic practices, as a background to the art which they inspired.

Diffusion of erotic energy

The second of the two attitudes to which I referred is probably older, popular and more deeply rooted where erotic feeling and vital energy are abundant, constantly renewed, and not restrained by Brahmin theoretical inhibitions. It fosters a spiritual generosity, an opulence of emotion, a cult of communal delight, a positive spreading abroad of vital energy. Without it Indian art and life would be gloomy indeed. In fact it represents the solid basis of all Indian artistic achievements. For art is above all concerned with feeling; and in India art has always devoted itself to the extremes of feeling. Brahmin intellectualism succeeded in reducing even the Indian delight in art to a theory – the theory of *rasa* or 'sublime flavour', crystallized by the Kashmiri Brahmin Abhinavagupta in the eleventh century, about which I have written elsewhere. And it is characteristic that later writers used *rasa* as a schematic technical term, to replace an older term used by the fourth- to fifth-century writer Bharata in his *Nāṭyashāstra* – a manual about drama and the dance. Bhārata's term was *Harsha* – 'joy'.

Everywhere we will encounter this opulent physical and emotional generosity in Indian art; in the ornament of temples, in the sensuous volumes of the human body, in the flowering landscapes of later Indian painting, in the voluptuous excitement of Indian music. And everywhere there is sex. Sexually sensuous appreciation, either overt or oblique, is demanded. The icons of sublime deities appeal

IV Album miniature. Prince and lady. North-western India, late 19th century. The border of flowers recalls the symbolism of temple vegetation-carving

to sexual and sensual feelings as directly as pictures of any handsome man or pretty girl. And this confirms my most important point about all Indian eroticism.

Since the image of the divine was conceived *ab initio* as imbued with sexual feeling in one way or another, and since this image was deeply rooted in the imagination of the Indian people, even the most commonplace sexual relationship benefited. For every sexual act, every manifestation of love, was automatically interpreted as a paradigm of the divine original idea. Wedding songs sung in various parts of India expressly call upon the bride and groom – in intimate physical detail – to repeat the loves of the gods continually their whole lives long. This, perhaps, is the most powerful 'correlative idea' to reinforce the 'sensation' of sexual love that has ever been conceived – the image of the transcendent deity dividing itself to copulate for the sake of delight, as well as for creation. All the manifestations of Indian erotic art amount to an exploration of the visual expression of this same germinal idea.

Many of the primary sexual images of deity are, of course, autonomous images generated in the minds of all men, a natural psychological – some may say biological – function of organic humanity. The great virtue of Indian culture is that it has given these ancient autonomous images pride of place in its psychological-religious scheme, whereas other cultures have repressed them, or driven them into the wilderness of neurosis. There are a fair number of images too, of some degree of apparent sophistication, which are probably related to forgotten cults. They may have survived in forms adapted to later cultural expressions, and been assimilated into discursive versions of legends in which originally they had no place.

The most obvious, fundamental visual image in which the 'cosmic' or divine aspect of sexuality is expressed is the lingam icon, and its further development, the lingam-yoni altar. Lingam images are of great antiquity on Indian soil. During the period of the Indus valley civilization of the third and second millennia BC it seems that the idea of the erect phallus as the embodiment of creative energy flourished. Surviving seals which illustrate a horned divinity who has been associated with the later persona of Shiva-Prajāpati show this feature most markedly. Indeed there survive into modern times standard iconographic representations of the god Shiva *ūrdhvaliṅga*, with erect penis, strikingly resembling the figure on some of the seals. Also at Mohenjo-daro, one of the Indus cities, were found a number of images of the male organ of different sizes and patterns. They certainly appear to be the prototypes of what are known in later historical India as lingams. It has been noticed that some of the smaller Indus Valley phalloi strikingly resemble the amulets carried in small boxes strung round their necks by members of the present-day sect of Liṅgāyats, widely diffused in the south of India, whose religion may be of immemorial antiquity.

Lingam-worship is ubiquitous in India today, and has been throughout her history. Although it is usually associated with the god Shiva, it is not always. The lingam is in fact a symbol of the penis, or phallus, which in its turn must be the emblem of the potency of divinity. But so stylized and unrealistic have the normal representations become, that there are even modern Brahmin apologists who declare that there is no reference to the penis involved in lingam-symbolism. This, of course, is impossible to maintain seriously; for a symbol without reference to feeling, beyond mere verbal belief, is without real meaning. It is worth remembering the custom, once probably more widespread, which still survives at the present day among certain groups of yogīs, of worshipping their own erect organ; only the sexual afflatus can make the actual member into a true emblem of Shiva. To try and dissociate the lingam from its roots in reality is to destroy its validity as symbol, which can only depend on the individual's own direct experience of the afflatus of sexual desire.

Lingams are of many different types and materials. Some Lingāyats, for example, employ a quickly squeezed mud pillar for their daily worship, and destroy it when they are finished. Anthills, boulders, dead trees and broken bases of old pillars are often revered as lingams by the country people, and such simple hallows when they are sanctified by age, may be incorporated into a temple. But generally any household of substance and each Shiva shrine has its own properly made lingam. *44* The various types have been systematically formulated by Indian tradition, and prescriptions for making them and setting them up have been carefully preserved. They may be large or small, and are either kept in the innermost sanctum of a temple, or form part of a small domestic shrine. They are worshipped in the normal Hindu fashion, with offerings of rice, flowers, lights, and incense, are anointed with melted butter or milk, and perhaps painted with vermilion or plated with gleaming metal foil. In certain areas a sacred lingam was used in the customary pre-marital defloration of brides, or they were merely seated upon it. It is considered proper that all women should first belong to the deity. Amongst tribal peoples defloration may be performed with a special terracotta lingam, in which *12* a light burns.

The commonest type of lingam is a round-topped cylinder, which may have the outlines of the glans and fraenum denoted by incised lines called *sūtras*. It may be chamfered first into an octagonal section and then into a square and set on a plinth. Instances too are known in which the surface has been worked into continuous bands of smaller lingams in relief. This, of course, represents the religious idea that all lingams are versions of the Great Lingam. But perhaps the most interesting variants are the *mukha* (face) lingams. These bear one or more masks of the god on their surface, sometimes even an entire figure. These are obviously meant as images of the indwelling divinity, who is often identified as Shiva by the *18* horizontal Shaiva sect-marks on the forehead. The oldest surviving instance of this kind, dating to an early century AD, is probably the Gudimallam Lingam from the South, which is at the same time one of the most naturalistic. It is of stone, about five feet high, and bears the figure of the god on its under surface. There is with this fine work no possibility of missing the clear double symbolism. The organ, emblem of the divine, is larger than the personalized deity.

There survives in Southern India – though it may once have existed in the North as well – a practice of maintaining at a temple a pavilion or lean-to building which contains a collection of lingams. Some of the large Southern temples have hundreds. These do not appear to be of any particularly great age; but it is probable that since, as the texts tell us, the prosperity of a kingdom depends partly on the quality of its temple images, it may well also depend on the quantity. Two lingams may be considered better than one, and twenty better still. For the temple is regarded as a sort of reservoir of spiritual power in the countryside upon which the people, crops and herds draw for their well-being.

Purely anthropomorphic sexual icons also play their part in Hindu imagery. Representations of Shiva with erect penis have been mentioned. This kind of image has practically the same significance as that attributed to the *mukha* lingam; the relative proportions of lingam and person are simply naturalized. Medieval temples bear many examples of these, and a number of different legends developed which express mythically the idea of sexual vigour on a cosmic scale. One such is recorded in several Purāṇas. Brahmā and Vishṇu, conversing in the vast emptiness of space, are surprised by the appearance beside them of an apparently endless lingam. They fly off in different directions to try to reach its ends, but cannot. Finally the lingam opens to reveal Shiva within it, who by this means has asserted his superior power over the other two. There are also syncretic legends recorded of Shiva propagating other lesser deities – who historically may be as old as he – by means of his seed escaping and falling on the ground, or passing down the stalk of a plant. This conveys the idea that such lesser deities share in the single divine nature of Shiva. Occasionally these images appear carved on temple cars, or in the folk paintings of Eastern India.

Female symbols

In all the lingam types so far mentioned the male, phallic emblem stands alone. But in the other type of icon it is combined with a symbol of the female organ, called the yoni (vulva). In this icon the lingam, of one of the normal types, stands in a shallow circular or elliptical basin with a spout running out to one side, which represents the yoni. When an offering of milk or ghī is poured on to the lingam, it collects in the basin, and runs off along the spout, where it may be gathered for a variety of ritual uses. This icon refers, of course, to the abstract notion of the cosmic dyad, the double-sexed divine. The feminine component of the dyad has perhaps a more ancient history than the masculine. At Mohenjo-daro ring-stones were found, which, like the lingams, were probably religious objects. Modern ring-emblems are used to refer to the feminine aspect of the divine dyad in religious ceremonies. In fact the goddess is possibly more highly regarded in India today than the male deity. For it is she towards whom, as mother of all things, the ordinary person feels the greatest affection. Sometimes she is represented as mother-earth, Pṛithivī, exposing her fertile genitals; sometimes as the metaphysical principle of creation by stylized emblems of the female genitals such as the open lotus flower. Again the actual female genitals may themselves be the object of worship.

Sculptured images of the vulva play another role. At many shrines there are female figures carved generally near the doorway, which spread their legs apart and expose the yoni to view. Visitors to the shrine habitually lick a finger as they pass, and touch the yoni 'for luck'. This practice, continued over the centuries, has resulted in many of the images acquiring a deep hole where thousands of fingers have worn the stone away, so that the modern pilgrim thrusts his finger deep into the touch-hole. Other feminine images on a temple may also acquire these touch-holes. One, quite frequently reproduced, is on the Kailāshanātha temple at Ellora (now, apparently, chastely cemented over).

1 Shiva and the Goddess, as Prakāsha and Vimarsha. Two-thirds life size stone sculpture. Khiching, Orissa. 12th century AD

2 and 3 (*above and left*) Painted
panels from an interior door in a
house. South India. 19th century

4 (*left*) Leaves from an erotic
posture-book on palm-leaf. Orissa.
Modern

5 (*opposite*) Pages from an Orissan
posture-book. 19th century

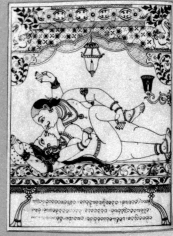

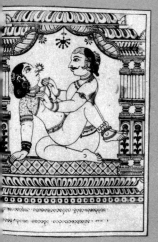

6 (*left*) The deity as half male, half female. Black stone sculpture. Two-thirds life size. Bengal, *c.* 1200 AD

8 (*opposite*) The divine hero holds multiple sexual intercourse with his women. Carved wooden panel from a temple-car. South India. 17th century

7 The deity as half male, half female, flanked by emblems of masculinity and feminity. Etching by Laxman Pai, 1964

9 Male and female stones, used both for grinding grain and as an emblem of deity. Bastar state. Modern

10 Phallic crocodile. From an Indus Valley seal (*Harappā*). 3rd millennium BC

11 Female figure in intercourse with a phallic crocodile, possibly a fertility emblem. From an Indus Valley seal (*Harappā*). 3rd millennium BC

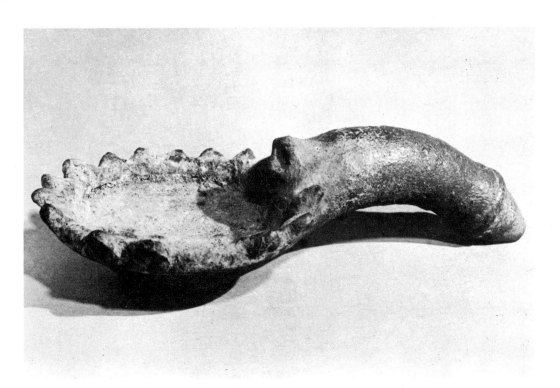

12 Lamp, of terracotta, used in the defloration of girls.
Bastar state. Modern

13 Emblem of the creative feminine orifice. Painted
wood. Eastern India. Modern

14 Lingam-yoni altar. Stone. Eastern
India. Modern

15 (*opposite top*) Fragmentary image of a female deity exposing her genitals for reverence. Stone relief from Nagārjuṇakonda, a Buddhist site near Amarāvatī, Deccan. 3rd century AD

16 (*opposite bottom*) Dancing ascetic. The ring through his penis indicates that he can never have sexual intercourse. Stone relief on a temple at Vijaynagar, Deccan. 14th century

17 (*right*) Divine couple; the man's phallus is erect. Ganges Valley. 3rd century AD

19 (*below right*) Terracotta phallus. Indus Valley. 3rd millennium BC

18 (*below*) Relief representing the lingam of Shiva, with the face of the deity on it, flanked by worshippers. Stone, from Badopal, Western India, *c.* 400 AD

20 (*opposite*) Ushas, as an Apsaras, causes by her
beauty the seed of the fire-god Agni to flow out.
Wooden panel from a temple car. South India.
17th century AD

21 (*right*) The God Ganesha, with his wife. He
caresses her with his trunk. This illustrates the delight
of a divine couple. Stone sculpture from the Deccan.
14th century AD

22 (*below*) Cloud-elephant coupling with the Earth
Goddess. Boundary stone. Baroda. *c.* 1000 AD

23 (*opposite*) Girl putting on her jewels. Her sexually attractive feminine attributes are much emphasized. Small Indian ivory panel. Begrām, Afghanistan. 1st century AD

25 (*above*) Miniature ivory carving of a girl, with female attendants; her genitals are emphasized. Indian, from Pompeii. Early 1st century AD

24 (*left*) Part of the railing of a shrine at Mathurā. An early image of a heavenly Apsaras. Pink sandstone, about two-thirds life size. 2nd century AD

27 (*opposite*) An Apsaras unfastening her skirt. On the heaven-bands of the Kandāriya Mahādeva temple at Khajuraho, Bundelkhand. *c.* 1000 AD

26 Collection of miniature terracotta plaques bearing erotic reliefs. From Chandraketugarh, Bengal. 3rd-2nd century BC. Chandraketugarh seems to have been the site of a factory for such terracottas

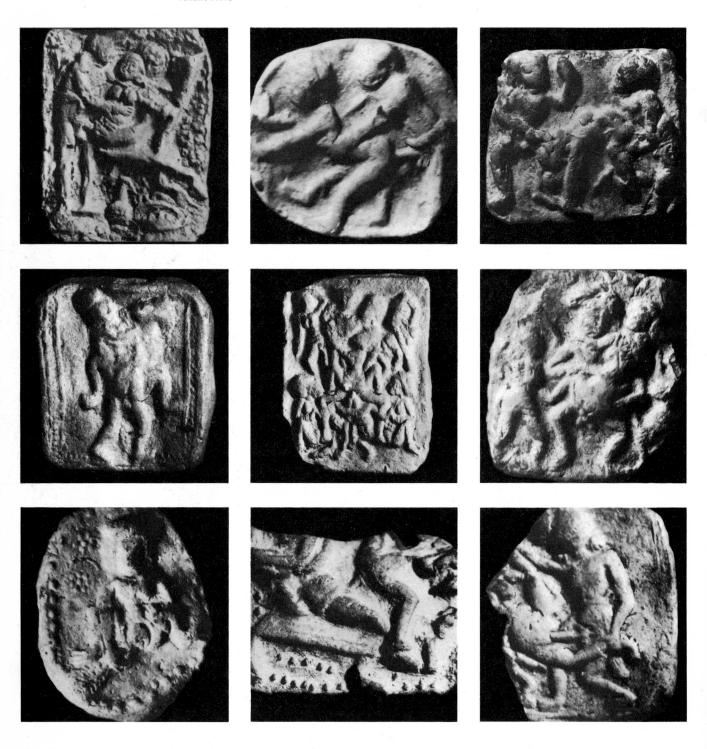

28 Music and dance by
Apsarases. From a shrine
gateway. Central India.
c. 400 AD

29 (*below*) Pair of lovers in
a garden pavilion. Wall
painting on plaster at
Ajanta. 5th century AD

That the custom is old we know from the beautiful, weather-worn snake goddess, in the style of early second-century AD Mathurā, found bricked up in one of the Buddhist stupas at Sānchī, with an enormous touch-hole at her yoni. It may be that the custom in Europe of putting a horseshoe, itself a female emblem, 'for luck' at the house door is a survival of a similar long-dead practice. But we do know that many Christian churches, even into the early nineteenth century, used to have obscene female images by the door. Possibly the Indian custom, whereby the visitor has a symbolic intercourse with a temple female, is related to the institution of temple prostitution which we will discuss later, in Chapter Two.

There are, of course, numerous images in which both the male and female deities are represented together anthropomorphically. Often the two stand side by *17* side, as Shiva and his wife Pārvatī, Shiva being *ūrdhvaliṅga*. There is a type of icon, dating from the tenth to twelfth centuries AD, in which the goddess sits upon the *1* knee of the god, and holds up a mirror. This icon is a direct representation of a metaphysical doctrine which appears in many of the tantras, which we will discuss later in Chapter Four. It is that of the phenomenal world brought into being through the cosmic dyad conceived in terms of light as Prakāsha and Vimarsha, light and its reflection. The god represents the radiating forth of existential energy, and the goddess its reflective working out. Again the male deity is represented as filled with the energy of sexual desire, *ūrdhvaliṅga*, whilst his wife holds a mirror to point the idea. The conception is an Indian form of that expressed by St Bonaventura in Europe in the thirteenth century, which presents the glory of God as reflected back upon his central being from the created world. At the popular level, Indian mythology has many legends which convey the same sort of idea. For example, the goddess is described as quenching a blazing liṅgam in her yoni to save the universe from its destructive radiant energy. It must be obvious that the meaning of such images goes far beyond the reach of any verbal commentary, however subtle it may be.

One particularly interesting erotic image is related to a legend about Vishṇu. But it is likely that here, as in other places, the image is older than the legend, and it appears in other versions (Chapter Three). The image represents a female deity, *80/108* as beautiful as the artist can make her, with exaggerated primary and secondary sexual characteristics, to whom male devotees with erect liṅgams pay fervent court. This, as a pure image, no doubt represents the vigorous sexual affection with which the divine idea of the feminine is pursued by men. But religious syncretism has incorporated it into the legend of Vishṇu. He is represented as changing his sex, and taking the form of a divinely beautiful woman called Mohinī, 'the be-wilderer of the senses' to seduce certain demonic characters from their claims upon the ambrosia of divinity – a typical piece of pious iconotropy. It does, however, make the point that the deity has not merely a feminine aspect, but plays a feminine role.

Perhaps the most important autonomous image of the divine unity in duality *6* is the Ardhanārīshvara. This shows the anthropomorphic deity with the right half *7* of his body male, usually with erect member, the left half female. The meaning of this image should now be clear, for we have reached the crowning artistic repre-sentation of that ancient image of divine sexuality contained in the Upanishads with which we began. From about the fifth century AD onwards numerous sculptures of this icon were made. Psychologically it was profoundly important. Both man and cosmic deity here contain the double sex within the single body. The state *before* creation, when man and wife had not fallen apart, is here vividly conceived. The full implications of the account of creation in the *Bṛihadāraṇyaka Upanishad* are drawn, and the most profound original state of deity beyond the created world is represented in the image of bisexuality. Typically of India, this state is envisaged as attainable by man, at one level by marriage – a union whose end is not only orgasm or progeny but permanent engagement – at another level, psychologically, by the discovery of and union with the *persona* of the opposite sex within each sexual human. It is impossible to refrain from recalling Jung's theories in this context, which rest upon the traditions of medieval Alchemy with its bisexual *prima materies* and its Hermaphroditic *Adam philosophicus,* upon the earliest of the Gnostic mystical texts, *Poimandres,* and upon Iamblichos' account of Pythagorean beliefs, with their images of the ultimate divine Hermaphrodite.

2 Love in Society and Poetry

The ideal wife

As in so many other societies, it is the masculine idea of the proper roles of the
sexes in society and love that has been best recorded for us in India. Once again,
there is a conflict, or rather ambivalence of outlook revealed. Woman as wife, and
woman as lover are virtually irreconcilable. And it seems that society was organized in such a way as to cater for both images. For in the great epics, the
Mahābhārata and the *Rāmāyaṇa*, which set the ideal patterns for conduct through
the centuries, and in many other literary works, we find the two images, the social
and the erotic pushed to their ideal extremes. There must be elements of fantasy
in both, for not all women could possibly be as chaste and totally submissive as
wives are supposed to be, nor yet as vividly and permanently erotic as women who
are not ideal wives are supposed to be. And yet it has often been supposed that
somehow, by the alchemy of love, the ideals might find themselves combined.

The ideal wife is rarely the obvious subject of visual art – at least overtly – but
at the same time she is the indispensable half of man. However, her whole aim in
life should be to efface herself completely, and minister with total dedication to
her husband. She should look upon him as a god, treating his lightest whims as
divine commands; she must eat only what he leaves uneaten and bear him as many
sons as possible. She must observe total obedience to her mother-in-law, fear her
father-in-law; she must never speak to her husband unless he first addresses her.
She must never speak to another man, never stand at the door gossiping,
always walk a few paces behind her husband, and sit on a lower seat than him.
She must not complain at, but rather glory in his amorous adventures. She may
never display any public tokens of affection towards him or her children, nor may
he to them or to her. 'To a woman at her wedding', says the *Mahābhārata,* 'one may
lie'. So all the promises the wedding ceremony may offer that a woman should be
queen in her own house can be hollow indeed. When her husband dies the widow
should if possible follow him to the next world as faithfully as she followed him
in this, burning herself upon his funeral pyre as a *satī* – a good wife. By this means
she will stay close to him when both are reborn. If she fails in this duty the only
life to which the widow can look forward is miserable indeed, for only widows of
the lower castes may remarry. A respectable widow will only be someone else's
burden, and a prey to the sexual appetites of all and sundry. A woman whose
husband leaves her has no hope of heaven.

On the other hand, the obligations of the husband towards his wife are considerable. He must cherish her to the utmost, never dispute with her if she so far
fail in her duties as to abuse him. He must never chastise her, be generous and soft

spoken – never over-severe – to her. It condemns him to undying shame and even to a posthumous hell if he cannot provide for her properly and protect her. He heaps his wealth upon her in the form of luxuriant jewelry. Anyone who kills a woman, especially an *atreyī*, one who is bathed after her menstruation, commits an unspeakably abominable crime. And an *atreyī* has an inalienable right, her *ṛitu*, to sexual intercourse with her husband. Indeed the epics mention that warriors leave the battlefield to fulfil the *ṛitu* of their wives. But all men must remember that no woman, including one's wife, is ever to be trusted. She is a fickle child at heart. Secrets are never safe with her, and one cannot carry on a serious discussion with her. One has continually to protect her against her own inherent weakness and folly. Finally, her pleasure in love greatly exceeds that of her husband.

Such is the ideal image of the wife and her status. No doubt there have been people, especially of the highest castes, who have succeeded in imposing the image upon life. Indeed high caste to a great extent depends upon strictness of marital behaviour. But life is always far larger and more polymorphous than any image. And the truth of marriage in India has always eluded convention in one way or another. And certainly women have often earned distinguished status as other than wives. A woman of character would have plenty of means of bending a husband to her will other than tears – although the *Rāmāyaṇa* envisages delightful provision for the exercise of this kind of pressure. The hero's palace might contain a 'sulking room' to which the wife resorts to tear off her ornaments, weep and threaten suicide. Her husband must then hasten to stroke her, speak softly and pacify her.

It must be mentioned that in India there have always existed forms of marriage different from orthodox Hindu monogamy, which give variety and flavour to erotic relationships. Usually marriages were carefully arranged by the parents of bride and groom long before the partners reached puberty, so the element of erotic choice and romantic love played no part at all in most marriages. Love has always been expected to grow after marriage. Thus married love has always tended to be thought of as an amalgam of duty, sex and affection, rather than romance. Sexual technique would thus be very important in converting such marriages into true consummations of the self. Certain kinds of runaway romantic marriage-by-exchange-of-garlands were, however, recognized by law. They were called Gandharva marriages – a most significant name, as we shall see. Fear of the social disruption caused by such marriages may well have been one reason for the common Hindu custom of child marriage. Caste, of course, played its role in all marriages. Normally husband and wife would be of the same caste. A husband could marry a slightly lower caste wife, and elevate her to his caste; but a woman who married into a lower caste would suffer loss of her own caste. A man, of course, suffered nothing from mere sexual connexion with a woman of any lower caste – save only the really low defiling castes (an important point this).

We cannot go here into the actual ceremonials of marriage, and all the anthropological implications of the various Indian wedding customs which have been so exhaustively studied. But there are certain facts which have a bearing on our subject.

V Album miniature. Prince and lady prolong their intercourse. Kangra style, Panjab hills, *c.* 1790

Polyandry and polygamy

The first of these is the survival of matrilineal and matrilocal customs, reflected in polyandrous marriages, and possibly also in the institution of temple prostitution, which is so important for art history. In several regions of India, but most especially in Malabar amongst the Nayar or Nair caste, matrilocal polyandrous marriages are the custom. This entails that ownership of land and property descends in the female line, and that a woman takes several husbands, who have no rights of ownership, but only rights of access to her, and of support by the female land and home and who return on death to the land of 'The Mothers' (*Mātṛikās*) for rebirth. The sexual imagery to which this situation gives rise obviously centres upon the Goddess, whose person is both the focus of marital desire, and the embodiment of the fertile land. The individual woman thus represents an eternal female principle which is invested with all the appropriate qualities of procreation, fertility and continuity, giver of life, love, and death. As a matter of historical fact the Nayars, for example, have been skilled professional mercenary soldiers, absent for long periods on service, returning to wife and home only at intervals. They have also been devout worshippers of the Goddess to whom sacrifices are made, and who is often represented in their temples and festivals by an extravagantly shaped sword. It is more than likely that in large areas of Southern India the same customs once prevailed. For images of Goddess Dūrgā, associated in one way or another with the buffalo, and often with rites of self-decapitation or hook-swinging, have a wide diffusion in the Tamil-speaking regions. Orthodox, male-orientated Hinduism has, however, been almost completely imposed.

The fact that matrilocal polyandry is also found in Himālayan regions, in the North Eastern Frontier region, amongst some tribal peoples, and among castes which are vestiges of tribes, suggests that this must once have been more widely distributed. The Eastern region of India where the Shakti cult, with its images of a dominant goddess, prevails, may once have followed this custom before the imposition of Brahmin orthodoxy. Many images from the South and from the East, which present the Goddess as the erotic focus of a masculine group, may rest at long range on matrilocal polyandrous habits of thought, though they have been successfully syncretized with Brahmanical mythology. We shall, however, discuss the Goddess in detail in Chapter Four.

Interesting intermediate stages between such polyandry (one wife, many husbands) on the scale towards polygamy (one husband, many wives) can be found in India. One such, which appears in the epic *Mahābhārata,* and is still known in the Himālayan region, is the marriage of one woman with a group of brothers – Draupadī and the Pāṇḍavas. Monogamy, too, has always been normal. But the condition which has always appealed more than any other to the masculine Indian imagination is a splendid polygamy. The hero of one of the most famous love stories of India, Kālidāsa's Shakuntalā, has two wives at home already whilst he conducts his passionate love affair with the pure forest girl. The ideal household, *8* the paramount image of luxury and royal ease, the true heroic ménage of the palace, contains several wives and an indefinite number of concubines, serving maids, female musicians and dancers, all dedicated solely to the master's sensual pleasure. Amongst them the hero moves, a bull amongst his cows. The splendid description

VI Album miniature. Rāja on his terrace enjoys the extreme of sexual pleasure, following the ancient heroic ideal. Kotah state, Rājasthān, *c.* 1870

of Rāvaṇa's ménage, when the monkey king Hanuman visits it secretly by night, which appears in the epic *Rāmāyaṇa*, is worth quoting *in extenso*. It represents the *summum bonum,* the consummation of all Indian desires, the epitome of Indian eroticism.

Hanuman saw innumerable women lying on rugs, dressed in every kind of clothing, with flowers in their hair, who had fallen asleep under the influence of drink, after spending half the night in play. And by their silence that great company, covered with lavish ornaments whose tinkling was stilled, resembled a vast lake full of lotuses where there is no sound of swans or humming of bees. He gazed on the faces of those lovely women whose eyes and mouths were closed, and from them rose a flower-like fragrance. They were like lotuses, their petals closed at evening, waiting for the dawn to open them once more; or like water-lilies which the bees continually visit, intoxicated by love. Rightly the strong and noble monkey compared them to nymphae, for the harem was bright with their radiance like the starry heavens and tranquil autumn night, in the midst of which the colossal Rāvaṇa shone like the brilliant moon encircled by attendant stars. Hanuman said to himself 'Comets that have exhausted their virtue and fallen from the firmament are gathered here.' Indeed the women in their grace, beauty and splendour shone like blazing meteors. Some lay fallen into slumber in the middle of their dancing and feasting, their hair and coronets in disarray, their ornaments scattered by them; other lovely creatures had lost their anklets and the red marks on their foreheads were smudged. Some had let their garlands slip off, some had broken their strings of pearls and unfastened their girdles, their clothes disordered, and looked like unburdened animals. Others, who had lost their earrings, their garlands all torn and crushed, looked like flowering creepers, trodden down by great forest elephants. Here and there the loose pearls lay, glimmering moonbeams, between the women's breasts like sleeping swans. Chains of emeralds and chains of gold were like drakes and Chakravāka birds. The women lay like rivers, their thighs the banks between which played swans, geese and water-birds; like rivers asleep, the rows of golden bells on their girdles the ripples, their faces the lotuses, their amorous desires the crocodiles (*graha* – the seizer, crocodile), their charming bodies the river beds. On their soft limbs the marks of their ornaments sat like bees. The veils of some, that rose and fell as they breathed, fluttered gracefully before their faces like bright rainbows streamers, and earrings tinkled in the softly moving air.

Their breath was subtly perfumed, impregnated with the aroma of the sugar-sweetened wines they had drunk, and caused the sleeping Rāvaṇa deep delight. Some of the girls as they dreamed savoured each other's lips repeatedly, as if they were their master's. Their passions for him aroused drove these lovely sleeping women to lose control of themselves and make love to their companions. Some slept in their rich garments propped on their bracelet-laden arms; some lay across their companions, on their bellies, their breasts, their thighs, their backs; clinging amorously to one another, with arms entwined, the slender waisted women lay in sweetly drunken sleep. The

32

interlaced groups were like garlands of flowers attended by lovesick bees, like interwoven creepers with their clustered blossoms opening to the caress of the spring breeze, or like the intertwined branches of great forest trees full of clouds of swarming bees. So seemed Rāvaṇa's consorts, and as they slept closely entangled it was impossible to tell whose were the bangles, scarves and garlands that encircled their limbs. As Rāvaṇa slept the radiant beauty of his women, like golden lamplight, played upon him. Some were daughters of royal sages, of giants and celestial beings of whom the warlike giant king had taken possession as consorts when he had defeated their relatives. Some had come to him of their own accord from love, and none had been forcibly ravished who had not fallen in love with him for his prowess and vigour, and none had belonged to another save the daughter of Janaka (Sītā) whose heart was set on Rāma. None lacked nobility, beauty, intelligence and grace, and each was the object of Rāvaṇa's desire.

(It was, we know, normal for a man in the epic age to impress into his service as many women as he could from among the wives and daughters of his peers, subjects and defeated enemies.)

Further, so that we might know how the women of such a heroic ménage must be supposed to feel, we can read in the other epic, the *Mahābhārata,* how the wife of a dead hero boasts of his shattered hand: 'This is the hand which slaughtered heroes, gave (to Brahmins) thousands of cows, dealt death to warriors. This is the hand that unfastened women's girdles, pressed swelling breasts, caressed navels, thighs, and secret parts, and opened skirts.' The possession and enjoyment of many beautiful women was the highest aim of the heroic man – that pattern of masculine conduct – his right, and the crowning joy of his life. And, of course, the glowing portrayal of the erotic ménage so stupendously portrayed in the Kāvya-verse of the *Rāmāyaṇa* is itself an image of the state of sexual desire. The goal of Indian eroticism in art was not mere orgasm, but the state of radiant desire itself; it was the presence of the divine afflatus of sex, not its expenditure. And this condition was to be the reward of the hero after death. Times without number it is repeated in the epics that the reward of the hero in heaven is the boundless enjoyment of erotic pleasure with troupes of celestial girls, the Apsarases, who are 39/81 the essence of beauty, and whose amorous desire for the virtuous dead is insatiable. In fact, such pleasures are to be the reward as well for all the other virtues of Indian society – asceticism, alms-giving to Brahmins and so on. Heroes returned from battle may even be entertained in this world by Apsarases who have been called down to earth by noble sage-magicians.

Ideas of beauty

Many important points can be found in the *Rāmāyaṇa* description of Rāvaṇa's harem which have an important bearing upon erotic art. First there is the style of the poetry itself, which is based upon a profuse and continuous invocation of simile and metaphor. Beauties are seen to be beautiful because they suggest other different but related experiences of pleasure and splendour. Faces are like lotuses, jewel-strings are gorgeous water-birds, women lying with parted legs and undulant clothing resemble rivers, amorous women coil like creepers, glorious girls are comets descended from the sky. Indian visual art attempts to create exactly such poetical analogies for its forms. Sculptured or painted forms are never merely descriptive. They convey metaphors. The long eyes of a girl are like silver fishes – which flash swiftly in the dark water – in *shape*. Her breasts are like deep golden cups; her legs like smooth columns or an elephant's trunk. Her fingertips are like pink-pointed lotus petals; her lips are like the sesamum petal. Her buttocks swell like gourds; her eyebrows are like a bow; her gauzy clothes do indeed show the same pattern of folds as ripples on a stream. A man's arms are like plantain-tree trunks, his chest like the face of a cow, his legs like stone pillars, his kneecap shaped like the back of a crab. Sculpture and painting set out expressly to convey such complex analogical experiences by means of the actual *shapes* and *colours* they employ.

8   The canons of masculine beauty are embodied in the hero. He must have thick legs and arms. His body must be plump – indicating abundance of food. His eyes must be wide and long. But of course the canons of masculine eroticism are focused principally upon the feminine image. The male Gandharvas, celestial beings of enormous sexual appetite, are relatively little defined. However, the Apsarases, the divine women of heaven who are the patterns for all earthly women, especially for the courtesans and prostitutes who perform their function upon earth, are the subject of elaborate poetic eulogy, and of innumerable temple sculptures. The Apsaras Rambhā is asked in the *Rāmāyaṇa*:

23   Where are you going, beautiful hips? What pleasure are you seeking for yourself? For whom is the sun now rising under which he will enjoy you? Who will drink his fill of the lotus-perfumed liquor of your mouth, sweet as nectar? To whose breast will those swelling, close-set breasts of yours, like golden goblets, grant their touch? Who will now mount into your broad secret parts, like a great golden wheel adorned with a golden band, and which are the embodiment of heaven?

Another Apsaras, Ūrvashī, goes out when the moon has risen:

24   The broad-hipped girl . . . shining in her soft, curly long hair, wherein she wore many jasmine flowers, the breaker of hearts, went her way. With the moon of her face, and the delightful movement of its brows, the sweetness of the words tripping from her mouth, her charm and soft loveliness, she seemed to be challenging the moon as she walked along. As she went her breasts, scented with heavenly salve, black-nippled, rubbed with heaven's sandalwood and shining with necklaces, were shaken up and down. By the upborne burden of her breasts, and their heaving at every step she was bowed forward, she whose surprisingly beautiful waist was ringed with the three soft creases. Below, spreading like a mountain, with its high, swelling buttocks, shimmered the sanctuary of the temple of the god of love, encircled in dazzling splendour, adorned with the band of her girdle; her faultless seat of modesty, covered with thin muslin tempted with stirrings of the senses even divine

30 An Apsaras unfastening her skirt. On the heaven-bands of the Rājaraṇī temple, Bhuvaneshvara, Orissa. Early 12th century AD

31 (*left*) Pillar from the early railing at the Buddhist shrine of Bodhgaya, Bihar, with an erotic dance scene, probably representing the heavens. 2nd century BC

32 (*below*) Small stone figure of a female attendant. The forms illustrate the use of poetical metaphor as a sensuous enhancement. The garments are executed 'like the ripples on a river'. Sarnāth. 5th century AD

33 (*bottom*) Lotus-rosette, symbol of the creative feminine. Stone relief on the railing of the Buddhist shrine from Barhut. 2nd century BC

34 (*below*) Miniature terracotta plaque representing the goddess of Wealth. Ganges Valley. 3rd century BC

35 (*right*) Terracotta figurine of a dancing girl, her skirt billowing. Patna. 3rd century BC

36 (*bottom*) Ivory panel for the side of a box, with scenes of erotic fantasy. Bhirbum style, Bengal. *c.* 1630. The female vulvas are touched with lac-pink

37 Devadāsī performing a gymnastic sexual act with a pair of soldiers who engage in sword-play at the same time. This scene records a motif for a spectacle. Wooden relief panel from a temple-car. South India. 17th century

38 Terracotta head of a courtesan, representing the old Indian ideal of sexually provocative beauty. Banāras. *c.* 4th century AD

M

39 (*far left*) The kiss. Rock-carving in a cave-temple at Ellora, Deccan. 9th century AD

40 (*left*) A lady and her maid with three men. Rock-carving on a balcony at the Ellora cave-temples. 9th century AD

41 Amorous couple, on the stone pillar of a temple at Aihole, Deccan. This is probably the earliest Hindu temple carving of sexual intercourse. 6th century AD

42 Yaksha pair from Aihole. The horse-
headed female is a familiar Indian night-time
bogey, who carries men off for sexual
purposes. She has a touch-hole at her vulva

43 Goddess figure. Rock-carving in a
cave at Aurangabad, Deccan.
She has a touch-hole at her vulva.
8th century AD

44 Collection of sculpture from collapsed stone temples at Tewar in Central India, showing the essentially sexual quality of temple art. There is a lingam on the right, and a naked Yoginī garlanded with skulls. 11th century AD

45 and 46 Figures carved on a balcony in the rock-cut temples at Ellora, Deccan, illustrating the delights of heaven, or temple-love. 9th century AD

48 Courtesan and soldier carved on a pillar of a temple at Pattadakal, Deccan. 8th century AD

47 Courtesan and soldier. Rock-cut figures at Ellora. 9th century AD

49 Gymnastic intercourse. Rock-cut figures on the Raṅganāyakula temple at Gandikoṭa, Deccan. 9th century AD

50 Inverted intercourse. From a primitive stone temple in Bastar state. c. 13th century AD

51 and 52 Amorous couples on a stone temple at Puri, Orissa. 12th century AD

53 and 54 Apsarases, from the heaven-bands of temples at Badoh, Central India. c. 1000 AD

55 and 56 Sexual intercourse with Apsarases. Stone reliefs from the heaven-bands of the Devī Jagadamba temple at Khajuraho. *c.* 1000 AD

58 An Apsaras. Stone figure from a temple at Khajuraho.
c. 1000 AD

57 Inverted intercourse with an Apsaras. Stone relief from the heaven-bands of the Devi Jagadamba temple at Khajuraho. *c.* 1000 AD

ascetics. Her feet, in which the ankles were deep imbedded, and in which her toes made deep, pink crevices, glittered with small bells, and her insteps were arched like a turtle's back. Her demeanour was made captivating by her having taken heavy drink, by her contented anticipation, by her awoken passion, and by her coquetry . . . even in heaven an eye-catching figure, in the thinnest of bodices that shimmered with misty colours, like the slender sickle moon, as it rides along veiled in cloud.

Drink, of course, enhances a woman's beauty, abolishing her reserve, and giving her amorous desires free play. Jewels are abundant; they are as essential to a *34* woman's beauty as the canonical creases of soft flesh at her waist and neck. Without them she lacks status, glory and opulence. Everything about her person and her clothes suggests unnamed but implicit delights. In the face of such an idea as this, repeatedly conveyed by all the resources of poetry, music, sculpture and painting, down the centuries, we can easily understand how Manu, 'the lawgiver', could write that love springs from the idea of love, sexual excitement springs from the idea, as well as from sound, taste and form, when the mind is absorbed in the awakening of the senses. The idea, as I have said, enhances sensation; jointly they enhance the fact of sex into an experience of love which is uniquely Indian. It is not surprising that India has always held that a man who has not experienced love to the full is incomplete and unfulfilled. He cannot, let it be spoken softly, even become a true sage. And love, of course, is itself enhanced by memories of past pleasures shared – hunting, music, sexual intercourse, and so on.

The cult of pleasure

It was not through the fictive arts alone that this idea of erotic experience was conveyed. Life itself was organized to offer opportunities for practical eroticism as art. The descriptions of beauty and delight conveyed in the epic, imaginative as they may seem, were in fact paralleled in Indian life. The descriptions of the great cities of Northern India, which are given in the epics and in early Buddhist literature, are now being fully corroborated by archaeological research. From the sixth century BC onwards they flourished all over the Northern plains. They had vast and elaborate fortifications, and contained some tens of thousands of inhabitants. India then was not the deforested and often ravaged country it now is. It was perhaps the most naturally beautiful land there has ever been, filled with gardens and flowering trees. Even today, as one stands on the Cyclopean walls of old Rājgir, the landscape is stupendous. So too is the Yamunā at Kaushambī. Man, if the surviving accounts, Indian and Greek, are true, was conspicuously less vile than was usual elsewhere at that time. Laws were strict, but punishment relatively mild.

In those days it was possible for Indian princes to choose their city sites and dwelling places with some freedom, and the conscious enjoyment of life was a normal goal. The laws under which the citizens lived were framed to take account of these natural aims. And the picture of life as it was then lived was idealized and

59 Sexual intercourse with Apsarases. Stone relief from the heaven-bands of the Devī Jagadamba temple at Khajuraho. *c.* 1000 AD

incorporated into the classical epics. As the centuries rolled on society became gradually more rigid, whilst the ambitions of militarists and puritans became more assertive. During the early Middle Ages India became almost completely Brahmanized, with Brahmins coming to dominate and schematically to reinterpret old ways of life and thought according to their caste and theological prepossessions. Nevertheless the old canonical literature, especially the epics, and the drama of the Gupta era (fourth-fifth centuries AD) continued to transmit its flavour of sublimely erotic secular hedonism. This flavour is evident in numerous secular works of art that survive from pre-Gupta days. But since it is a matter of historical fact that the great religious monuments, Buddhist, Jain and Hindu, from the second century BC onward, owed their decoration to artists whose principal occupation was secular art, the religious art has the same flavour.

For the literature tells us that the houses of these Indian cities, both private and public, were filled with painting and carving, every last fragment of which, since it was executed in perishable materials, has disappeared in India's devastating climate. Such houses must once have existed in their millions. We know today only *2/3/122* a few nineteenth-century examples, which still retain something of old traditions, and we illustrate one or two pieces. The religious monuments were executed in stone – since part of their symbolic meaning was *Shāshvatā*, the quality of the eternal. Some of them have partially survived. But so too have a few ivories, for various reasons, and thousands of small terracottas from Ganges valley cities, of *23* which only a tiny fraction has been published. At Begrām in Afghanistan, in a sealed underground chamber, possibly a merchant's storeroom, were found numerous ivories of the first century AD. Nearly all of them represent sweetly *25* flavoured scenes of beautiful girls at their toilet, or lounging at ease. Another similar ivory was found at Pompeii. In Allahābād, in Patna, Banāras and Calcutta *26/35* are preserved thousands of tiny terracotta plaques and figurines representing girls and pleasure parties, music and dancing, and many other attractive subjects including erotic scenes, belonging to the third century BC–fifth century AD. Amongst them are numerous little figures of animals – geese, monkeys, ducks and others. For, of course, all those creatures who feature in poetic descriptions of beauty as the second comparative term of a simile or metaphor, shared in the affectionate appreciation bestowed upon the first term. A fond comparison between a girl's emeralds and a drake with its emerald plumage grants as much glory to the duck as to the necklace.

This generous, erotically-slanted appreciation was fostered in the pleasure gardens with which the cities were surrounded. They were full of flowering trees, *29* ponds and little pavilions. It must indeed be true that the wealthy – lords, landowners and merchants – would derive the greatest benefit from these. But the texts are emphatic that there were beautiful *public* pleasure groves and gardens provided by the rulers, where men and women resorted in the evening to enjoy all the pleasures life had to offer, including love. Literature is full of descriptions of the joyful, riotous noise that filled the air at dusk in the city parks. It was in such surroundings that the Buddha often preached. These pleasure gardens existed probably into the early Middle Ages. But gradually they seem to have come to depend less on 'civic' than on private support.

Inside the cities themselves were large and wealthy communities of courtesans and female musicians – for music and love have always been associated in India, right into modern times. Many works of art illustrate this association, and music *28* in India is still profoundly erotic in character. These courtesans were, of course, *38* the women who gladdened with their presence the public parks. But public quarters were provided inside the cities for the courtesans by local rulers – for they drew from them a substantial part of their income, and the girls usually rated as part of the official establishment. We know from several sources that these houses were lavishly painted with erotic scenes. There is even a description in an old source of one intelligent courtesan, who had her reception hall painted with a variety of different scenes, all evoking different emotions. She used to show them to each male client, and was able, from his reactions to the various scenes, to gauge his character and tastes. As in ancient Greece, the courtesans took great pride in their intelligence, culture and artistic ability – both in the arts of expression and of love. There can be no doubt that they were regarded, and regarded themselves, as the earthly counterparts of the celestial Apsarases, representatives of a divine order. It was in this environment that the material for the great erotic classics of India, the *Kāmasūtra,* the *Kokashāstra* or *Ratīrahasya,* the *Anangaranga,* the *Rahasya Kalolini* and other books was developed and elaborated. In India traditions, once established, persist for millennia unchanged. The city prostitutes of medieval and modern times, whose profession was esteemed, and whose apprenticeship was thorough, have retained their traditional arts and sciences with great fidelity.

Erotic techniques

This is not the place to discuss the *Kāmasūtra* and the other texts in detail. But they do have bearing upon art. These books are systematic encyclopedias of erotic method. Every possible aspect of the love relationship is discussed and analysed. They contain the essential knowledge for making of love a rewarding art. Each text gives a descriptive listing of the human sexual types, based upon the size of organs; the kinds of men and women, their ages, temperaments and seasons; the characteristics of the women of different parts of India; the different parts of the body in which women are sensitive to erotic stimulation at successive stages of the lunar cycle; the range of possible embraces, kisses and love scratches, blows and bites; the postures of sexual intercourse, how they are done and under which conditions they are suitable; various auxiliary methods of satisfaction; how to woo a new bride, a stranger, and so on. They usually conclude with folk-recipes and spells for remedying various defects, and, of course, aphrodisiacs. The most striking and important aspect of all these texts is that they convey a vivid sense of the man's responsibility towards his partner. His is the responsibility. It is up to him alone to see that social conditions are fulfilled. He must act as a paragon of gentleness and consideration. His every thought must be for his partner's pleasure and satisfaction. Although the Indian woman is in society totally subject to masculine control, in love she is entitled to claim from the man every conceivable indulgence. Pleasure and fulfilment are her right, no less if she is courtesan or prostitute, than if she is a wife. It will be noticed how frequently erotic art represents the woman taking the active role in love. In religious imagery the same idea prevails. This is because the nature of woman is conceived as entirely sexual, either maternally or erotically. She is the one who claims the field of eroticism as her own preserve. She it is who must be satisfied, who need think of nothing else but her own pleasure. Once modesty is overcome, like an Apsaras, she eagerly seeks what her body desires. A man's aim in love should always be to promote in her the deepest ecstasy of which she is capable. Much of his own joy will consist of pride in his prowess in this.

The aim of love should be to work out in practice a long, carefully studied series of variations and combinations of the techniques given by the encyclopedias. The art of prose writing does not consist of copying out the dictionary; nor does dancing consist of stringing together all the positions. No more does the art of love consist in merely running through the erotic Shāstras. It demands artistic composers and choreographers. The story about the sage Koka, author of the *Ratīrahasya*, recorded by Burton, illustrates how the book came to be written:

> A woman who was burning with love and could find none to satisfy her inordinate desires, threw off her clothes and swore she would wander the world naked until she met with her match. In this condition she entered the levee hall of the Rāja upon whom Koka Pandit was attending, looked insolently at the crowd of courtiers around her and declared that there was not a man in the room. The king and his company were sore abashed, but the Sage, joining his hands, applied with due humility for royal permission to tame the shrew. He then led her home and worked so persuasively that wellnigh fainting from fatigue and from repeated orgasms she cried for quarter. Thereupon the virile Pandit inserted gold pins into her arms and legs, and, leading her before his Rāja, made her confess her defeat, and solemnly veil herself in his presence. The Rāja was, as might be expected, anxious to learn how the victory was won, and commanded Koka Pandit to tell his tale, and to add much useful knowledge on the subject of coition.

The secret of this story is that the Sage never achieved his victory by committing *himself* to repeated orgasms, but by restraining his own, and playing with sublime and prolonged expertise upon the woman's susceptibilities.

The aesthetic basis

We have seen already that in Indian art the aesthetic and the erotic are virtually synonymous. The poetic descriptions I have quoted from the epics are both aesthetic and erotic masterpieces. There is behind the whole of Indian art a superb aesthetic theory which consummates the ultimate purpose of Indian eroticism. For the aim of the Indian erotic life, as I said in Chapter One, is not merely orgasm, but the experience of enhanced sexual conjunction, that divine afflatus, for its own sake. And this experience is both aesthetic, as well as a legitimate mode of religious release. *But* it can never be reached by anyone who has not a background of vivid, varied and true erotic experience of his own.

86

VII An Apsaras, whose gesture signifies her willing youth. Sandstone, about half life-size. From Khajuraho, Bundelkhand. *c.* 1000 AD

The way the theory works is this. Every experience we have leaves behind in our minds its memory-traces, charged with echoes of the absorbing emotions we experienced at the time. The emotions, and the memory-traces, fall into certain categories. These include the sublime, the wrathful, the terrible, the comic and the disgusting. But chief of them all is the erotic, because, as Abhinavagupta (*c*. AD 1000) wrote, 'the erotic contains the least that repels the mind, and the most that inevitably attracts'. Art works upon our sensibilities not by evoking any of the direct emotions themselves, which would overpower the mind and lead to inappropriate and undesired results; we would not wish to run screaming in panic from the theatre, vomit in the stalls from disgust, or leap onto the stage to ravish the beautiful heroine. Instead, art sets out by all the means at its disposal to evoke all the memory-traces associated with its subject that we possess. We experience not the direct emotion, but a long series of our own emotive memories; our memory-traces are evoked and brought together into a composite conscious image. Thus, the more varied and vivid our own actual experience has been, the more intense will be our aesthetic response to any work of art. We will have more memory-traces ready for it to work upon. The immense ramifications of similie and metaphor in Indian poetry and art all help to reinforce the experience with their own memory-traces. (In the case of music too the memory-traces and associations would in India be mainly erotic.) So, when we come to the erotic temple sculpture and the erotic paintings, the more of our own erotically coloured memories we can carry with us, the more of our own experiences of actual love there are ready to be invoked, of remembered forms, softnesses, caressing movements, pressures, muscular tensions, associated sensuousnesses like birds' feathers, iridescent colours, bees on the skin, the more acute will be our aesthetic experience. This is the way Indian art was made to work. It is an art for experienced adults, not for inexperienced children. Perhaps I should just mention, in conclusion, that many other modes than the erotic are, and can be developed in art.

The 'educative' sets of erotic paintings that I have mentioned in Chapter One were many of them based upon the classical encyclopedias of erotic technique. Some were specifically illustrations of the texts. Others were selections or derivatives. The texts too served as a repertoire of ideas for poets and artists who were to treat erotic themes. And one can find many manuscripts of the epics, or of the loves of Krishna, or temple sculptures, where the artists have used the varied types and postures recorded in the encyclopedias as inspirations for their work. The correspondence was not close, or systematically exhaustive. That was not the point. Indeed there are many erotic devices represented in temple sculpture that have no place in the encyclopedias. And, of course, not all of the conceptions recorded in the encyclopedias were – or could be – represented in erotic art.

VIII Album miniatures. (*Left*) Prince and lady on the riverside. Panjab hills, *c*. 1820.
(*Right*) Brahmin and lady. Kangra style, 19th century

3 Temple Art

Origins

The Hindu temples of India are world famous for the superb erotic sculptures with which many of them are adorned. Most of the best examples were built in the North between the ninth and thirteenth centuries AD, and in the South between the sixth and seventeenth centuries AD. In addition many temples still in worship have one or more immense wooden wheeled chariots – called 'cars' – which are constructed after the pattern of structural temples, with towering, piled-up canopies and spires. These cars are chiefly used to carry the main divine images of the shrine on their festival processions along traditional routes – perhaps for a bathe in a sacred river or lake. Many of their wooden posts and panels are carved with the same sort of erotic scenes as the temples themselves are. It is probable that most temples once had such cars. In the North few cars survive; for there many traditions were obliterated during the twelfth to fifteenth centuries AD by the incursions of Moslem invaders, who usually destroyed all the Hindu art they could. But in Orissa and South India, where old traditions remain still intact, temples still have their cars.

On the fabric of both cars and temples appear sculptures of men and women in various postures of sexual intercourse. They are not by any means always in couples; three or more participants are common. And many of the representations show forms of pleasurable association which are not normal congress, such as *cunnilinctio, coitus per anum* and *fellatio*. The scenes in fact, have a distinctly genre character; the participants are self-absorbed, and do not address themselves directly to the beholder in the manner of the icon. And although the types of women are more or less consistent on each temple, portraying the ideal of feminine beauty current at the particular time and place, the male figures vary considerably. Many are magnificently bearded, and some carry weapons which show them to be 'heroes' in the epic vein.

There can be no doubt that this erotic art was based upon the old erotic legends of the epic period. For the epic poems themselves were held by the Brahmins who preserved them to be of sacred origin, dealing with the exploits of heroes who were regarded as divine incarnations. I have suggested that there was behind the imagery of the epic a secular eroticism which flourished in the open cities of the early period of Indian history. It was paralleled or typified in religious imagery of a heaven of sensuous delight. As time went on, probably during the early Middle Ages when every department of life was being gathered together by Brahmin scholastics, and fitted into the framework of religion, when the *Kāmasūtra* was becoming recognized as holy writ, this erotic imagery was assimilated into the

8/37

40/59/60/96/97/98

58/73/76

48/95

90

whole scheme of Hindu iconography. The fully developed medieval temple was intended to display in its decoration an epitome of Hindu iconography as a whole – including the erotic. But just as the heavenly parallels or types of the earthly courtesans, the Apsarases, were assimilated to the imagery of the temple, so the activities of their earthly counterparts were also taken over as part of the temple's social and magical function.

Devadāsīs

The Devadāsīs (slave-girls of God) who flourished during the Middle Ages and modern times came to fulfil the roles of female courtiers to the temple deity, of temple and public dancers, musicians, and sacred prostitutes. They must have lent an ultimate conviction of truth to the imagery of the Apsarases and heavenly musicians and dancers who figure in vast numbers in all sorts of seductive postures on the temple fabric. In Western India and in Mysore the erotic scenes usually occur as punctuations in a continuous frieze of figures of dancers and musicians. The connexion between dancing and eroticism, which is here canonized, is ancient in many other parts of the world.

However, there is no certain evidence for the existence of the institution of the Devadāsī earlier than the third century BC in India when an inscription was cut in a cave at Rāmgarh to record the love of a young painter for a 'slave-girl of the god'. Elsewhere in the world we know that similar institutions were of considerable antiquity and great respectability. So too it may be in India. But we do have a full knowledge of the cult of the Devadāsī as it existed in recent times from European writers, who were fascinated by it.

Devadāsīs were women and girls attached to the temples as a part of their official 'establishment'. Their duties were to see to the day-to-day running of the shrine, sweeping it and attending to the needs of the image. This they would anoint, dress and garland each day, and adorn it properly for different festivals. And at certain times of day or on special occasions of public need they danced and sang before the image to please the divinity. The documentary evidence is united in describing the dancing and singing as highly licentious. In fact the Devadāsīs served the deity of their temple as Rāvaṇa's women would have served him. In addition these temple dancers served as prostitutes, living in the neighbourhood of the temple, and bound by the terms of their contract to entertain any man who might pay a sum into the temple funds. H. M. Penzer has fully documented the inescapable fact that in ancient and medieval times in India the terms 'dancing girl' and 'prostitute' were synonymous.

Two different oral traditions have been recorded purporting to 'explain' the erotic aspects of medieval temple arts. In Orissa it has been said by Brahmin officiants that the sexual images 'preserve the temple towers from lightning'. How or why no one knows. But the magically prophylactic effect attributed to them associates them with one of the oldest prime symbols for divine potency, the thunderbolt. Marco Polo records (c. 1446) that he was told that the lewd dances of the Malabar dancing girls were designed to stimulate the divinity to have sexual connexion with his goddess. And in this case the sexual references in the art of dancing are supposed to promote the proper union of the double divinity, the cosmic dyad, and so maintain public affairs in a healthy condition. From both these explanations, it is possible to see that sexual art was held to express and stimulate the divine power which maintains the universal order, and which I have pointed out was identical with the sexual afflatus. The activities of the Devadāsīs, including their prostitution, thus played an important part in the temple's social and magical functions. They represent a day-to-day continuation of a spiritual purpose – the spreading abroad throughout society of the divine sexual power. This purpose may also be fulfilled seasonally, at harvest or seed time by great public festivals of the Saturnalia type, such as Holī in India. Only during the last forty years has Holī ceased to be an occasion of general sexual licence, involving public and promiscuous intercourse. Nowadays only the squirting of coloured powder or water serves as the sexual symbol. But many other Indian ceremonies, like the ordinary wedding ceremony, or the Shākta *Chakrapūja* which will be discussed later, emphasize the way in which sexual relations are held to confer something of divinity on the participants. There are, however, other aspects of temple sexuality which can amplify the meaning of the cult.

Although official dancing girls were the chief prostitutes at medieval temples, in some circumstances it was considered an act of piety for a respectable woman, married or single, to prostitute herself at the temple gate either to Brahmins or to casual strangers. The purpose of this was perhaps most commonly to remove the curse of barrenness, but not always. For Indian mythology, in common with much of the world's folklore, has recognized the probability that the God will avail himself of the opportunity to have sexual intercourse with a woman, who is anyway his by right, when it is offered. Brahmins, as priests, and strangers, who may be God in disguise, or at least his representative, are the legitimate partners on such occasions. Also in many parts of India the divinity of the local shrine was supposed to exercise a genuine *droit de seigneur* over local women before they were married. Early Western writers darkly suggest, certainly correctly, that Brahmin officiants at the shrine played the divine role – as we shall see that the nineteenth-century 'Mahārājas' did.

But to return to the official Devadāsīs; the ritual whereby they were adopted into the temple establishment consisted fundamentally of a marriage ceremony, in which the God was the bridegroom, and was impersonated by a sword, upon which a fruit was often impaled, by a tree, or by an image. So the Devadāsī became in effect a wife of the divinity and thus, by normal caste rules, attracted divine status to herself. As consistent intercourse with strangers was a part of her duties as a wife of the god, it is clear that there was some intention that the prostitute's patrons should come by association with her to partake of the nature of the divinity. In this way sexual relations with temple prostitutes, undertaken for pleasure, constituted at the same time a ritual act whereby prostitute and client were augmented in their divine nature, each by their connexion with a representative of the divinity.

If we then consider the temple carvings against this background of custom and belief, we can perhaps see how they serve as emblems of something divine, at the same time as being pictures of enjoyment. They represent the sexual activity of the 'wives of the god', which is a 'type' of the activity of the Apsarases (not bound to any man) whose function is described in the epics and in the story (below) of Nanda's education. The temple offered to living men an experience of the joys of heaven, thus reinforcing its claim to be a complete image of the divine upon earth. But on the magical level, where so much of the temple's symbolism operates, the erotica, like the 'Fescennine' jests of ancient Mediterranean festivals, and the erotic songs and dances of the dancing girls, served to stimulate and increase the world's store of sexual power upon which its well-being depends. In later chapters it will appear how this theory of the meaning of the sexual image applies at the level of personal psychology.

The earliest erotic art

The actual history of the evolution of erotic art in India helps to amplify the meaning of the great erotic temple sculpture. From a very early date, as I have said, there was erotic secular art in India, the clues to which are partly literary, partly in the form of small works like the Ganges valley terracottas and the Begrām and Pompeii ivories, which must once have existed in considerable numbers, and partly in the form of stylistic indications in surviving early works of religious art. The last point, however, is an important one, which I have not yet discussed. It is tied up with a conception of the meaning of temple art as a whole in the Indian context.

In several early or fairly early works of art we have representations of Indian court life. In the reliefs from Buddhist shrines at many sites between the first and third centuries AD we can find scenes that are, as it were, waking, daytime views of the harem of Rāvaṇa, where the prince – usually the Buddha-to-be – sits surrounded by beautiful women and girl-musicians. An interesting feature of the reliefs is that these panels, and others like them, are punctuated by larger figures of amorous couples, images of physical well-being, incorporating ideal sexual types. There are also, amongst the second–fifth century AD Buddhist sculptures from Gandhāran shrines in the Kabul river valley, reliefs showing the self-indulgent life of royal ease led by the Buddha before he abandoned the world to live as an ascetic. Here too beautiful women play their part, and the prince is occasionally shown having sexual relations with them – as any prince should. The style of these images is close to that of the Hellenistic and Roman erotic images of the Mediterranean world. In Ashvaghosha's long epic-like poem on the life of the Buddha there is a famous set-piece description of his sleeping harem, as the Buddha abandons it by night, clearly inspired by the *Rāmāyaṇa* description of Rāvaṇa's harem. Here, though, to accord with Buddhist puritanism, the sleeping women are described not as attractive, but as abandoned and disgusting. On the Sihagiri rock in Ceylon a few late fifth-century AD plaster-paintings survive in a sublimely erotic style which represent Apsarases bringing offerings to the king whose palace crowns the rock – celestials playing courtier. Their style is virtually identical with that of the contemporary Buddhist paintings at the Ajanta caves. We know they are Apsarases because on the smooth wall of the pathway to the top are numerous scratched inscriptions, some going back to the eighth century AD. The wall-scribblers proclaim their love for these heavenly girls in poetical stanzas. They declare that 'the lily-coloured ones', 'the golden deer-eyed beauties', 'bewilder the mind'. The cruel beauty of these celestial beings with fluttering eyes and flowers combed into their hair has turned the hearts of some away from their homely wives, and destroyed their sleep. And one declares that now that he has glimpsed these beautiful girls, death cannot perturb him!

All this goes to indicate that religious shrines were from early times decorated with art of a courtly type, executed by artists whose normal *métier* was the execution of images of the secular paradise, parallel to the literary images of courtly life in the epics. It also suggests, in conjunction with what follows, that the shrine itself, to whomever dedicated, Buddha or Hindu deity, was conceived as a princely court, the role of prince being played by the central holy image. Thus all the sculptured figures which adorn the early Buddhist, Jain and Hindu shrines represent 'courtiers'. It is, in fact, impossible to overrate the fundamental importance of the image of the 'court' in Indian temple art. The women, who are often identified as minor deities on early shrines, and are given great prominence, parallel those wives and daughters of peers, subjects or defeated enemies, whom the princes of the epic age used to impress into their harems. Thus were the little goddesses of the countryside impressed into the 'courts' of the Buddhist shrines at Barhut, Sānchī and Mathurā, and of the Hindu temples of Aihole, Badāmi and Ellora.

The specifically sexual images are an essential ingredient in the whole image of the 'divine court', as we might expect. Among the reliefs on the earliest Buddhist monuments of India (second century BC–first century AD) are representations of a man and woman with their arms around each other (the *dampati*). These figures are not erotic in the full sense of the word. Nevertheless the early idea of the *dampati* as a proper architectural ornament was one of the sources of the medieval erotica. By the second century AD at Mathurā the prototype of the classical type of temple doorway had been developed, which was itself the inspiration for later architectural ideas. Its jambs were ornamented with rows of panels containing *dampati* reliefs. And on the Nahāpāna *vihāra* at Nāsīk in the Deccan, of mid-second century AD date, the same idea is found again. In addition, on the capitals of the great *chaitya* cave at Karle in the Western Deccan, at Bhājā not far away, and on those of the gateways of stupa I at Sānchī, all dating from the first century AD, beautiful embracing couples appear riding pairs of animals. Whilst at Karle, the colossal couples on the façade, immense images of opulent physical well-being, are, like those at Nagārjunakonda, among the greatest works of early Indian art. There has also been found a *dampati* image, out of any context, but of fairly early date, in which two figures stand in the traditional 'donor' attitude, right hand raised. The man is *ūrdhvalinga*, with erect penis, and is usually interpreted as Shiva. So it is clear that even in early times the sexual – if not actually copulating – couple was considered as adding something to the virtue of a building, by reason of its courtly and royal associations, in the same way as all the astrological emblems, minor deities or narratives did. On Kanherī and Karle *chaitya* caves there are a number of reliefs of the first century BC depicting dancing couples – for dancing was one of the most characteristic courtly activities.

There is another early religious relief in which the connexion between sex, *31*
dancing and religion is most clearly expressed. It is on one of the chief pillars of the
oldest railing at Bodhgaya, probably of the late second-first century BC. It shows
a woman dancing whilst a man holds one of her hands and unwinds a draped
shawl from her body. Unlike the other feminine figures on comparable reliefs at
Bodhgaya, she is naked, and in the plastic execution her buttocks are stressed in
conformity with Indian ideals of feminine beauty. The background shows a curtain
between two pillars over which a third person is looking. Rather similar scenes
are also known from Mathurā, and most probably represent the joys of heaven.

Mathurā

At Mathurā, the great ancient spiritual centre of India, which produced during
the early centuries of the Christian era a vast and varied quantity of art, as well as
the usual *dampati* scenes, there were three other developments of particular
interest for us here. They were all direct consequences of the liberation of the
relief style from earlier and stricter canons, and the incorporation of secular
images into monumental art. First: a number of representations of couples in sexual
intercourse have been found. They are generally merely incidental passages in a
continuous narrative, but are the earliest stone-cut instances we know. Second:
there are a number of larger, enigmatic reliefs which represent drinking scenes, and
do not appear on the surface to have any religious connotation. It is tempting to
interpret them as having some connexion with the Tantrik ceremonial we shall
discuss later, but there is no obvious reason to do so. However, it is likely that they
do have a reference to life in the heavens rather than merely on earth, since in the
succeeding Gupta and Chalūkya periods of art a motive was derived from them,
representing a couple of flying Gandharvas – erotic heavenly beings – bearing
cups.

The third and most important of these developments was in the female 'Yakshī' *24*
figures with which the railings of Mathurā's shrines were so liberally adorned.
Earlier monuments, like those at Barhut and Sānchī had figures of women clasping
trees, whose secondary sexual characteristics were well in evidence, carved on the
chief pillars of their railings. At Barhut they are expressly named by inscriptions
as Yakshīs, the local godlings of trees and tanks. But at Mathurā we can trace the
development of this Yakshī type, in association with the female 'donor' type, into
unmistakably seductive damsels who make a lavish display of their primary as well
as their secondary sexual charms. These ladies of Mathurā are made not simply
to clasp their trees, but to posture under balconies, to wash under waterfalls, to
undo their girdles or carry small birds about on their shoulders. They are often
overlooked by the inhabitants of houses in the background who watch them, or
make love on balconies. But again it is clear that they are not intended as ordinary
earthly women, for, in the manner of gods, they are frequently given *vāhanas*
(vehicles) consisting of animals or dwarfish men under their feet.

How to interpret these feminine types, and their association with the sacred
sites of Buddhism and Jainism – those rigorously ascetic religions – has long been

a mystery. It is, of course, clear that they are the direct ancestors of the Apsarases and dancers who display themselves all over the fabric of medieval temples. But I think that the story of the Buddha's conversion of his brother Nanda, as it is recounted by Ashvaghosha, at a time not at all remote from the execution of the sculptures themselves, can offer a further clue as to how they should be interpreted. Nanda was deeply in love with a girl and devoted all his care and thought to pleasing her and making love to her. But the Buddha wished to make him into a monk. So by a trick one day he separated him from his beloved, and carried him up to heaven and there showed him the Apsarases. Of course, they completely eclipsed Nanda's earthly lover by their beauty; he was consumed with a desire to enjoy them, and forgot his old love utterly. The Buddha then took him back to earth and telling him that the attainment of his desires was only a matter of time and religious effort, quickly received him into the Order. After a period of contemplation, however, Nanda came to realize the vanity of his sexual desires, and reached the true religious goal. In this story we can see how the old picture of the heavenly realms conveyed in the epics came to be assimilated into Buddhist religious imagery. But we can also infer that, if this is so, and if the Mathurā females are types of the Apsarases, the shrines with which they were associated, but which have unfortunately perished, must have served, as did the later temples, as courtly images of the heavens, complete with inhabitants. It would not be surprising to find that in this, too, Mathurā was in advance of the rest of India. For we now realize just how important as a creative centre Mathurā was in the three or four centuries before the advent of the Gupta dynasty (mid fourth century AD).

Also, we find exemplified first at Mathurā the plastic versions of the canonical patterns of ideal beauty described in the epics, which were to dominate Indian art for centuries to come. For it is one of the characteristics of Indian aesthetics that divine beings or the heroes of literature and legend were always required to conform in bodily pattern to certain norms, which served to identify them as at once superior and sexually desirable. These norms represent the constant obsession of Indian idealism. They came to be composed according to strictly prescribed canons of proportion, as diagrams of the most desirable qualities grouped within one body, which were repeated and given infinitely varied expression down the centuries. It is interesting to find that the specific sexually attractive attributes such as the narrow waist, the large hips and buttocks, and long eyes in the case of women, or the great round arms, bow-like eyebrows and block-like body in the case of men, are the same in descriptions both of sexual heroes or heroines, and of religious saints. Medieval figurines from South India representing male or female saints, and all the images of divinities like Pārvatī, Shiva-Dakshiṇamūrti, Vishṇu, Lakshmī and Kṛishṇa are expressly designed to appeal to sexual emotions. For Indian religion has always expressed the desirability of its goals in this way.

78

The early Middle Ages

During the Gupta period in the north of India, and especially under the Chalūkya rulers of the Deccan during the fifth to the eighth centuries AD, erotic art was

60 Sexual intercourse with Apsarases. Stone relief from the heaven-bands of the Vishvanātha temple at Khajuraho. c. 1000 AD

The way the theory works is this. Every experience we have leaves behind in our minds its memory-traces, charged with echoes of the absorbing emotions we experienced at the time. The emotions, and the memory-traces, fall into certain categories. These include the sublime, the wrathful, the terrible, the comic and the disgusting. But chief of them all is the erotic, because, as Abhinavagupta (c. AD 1000) wrote, 'the erotic contains the least that repels the mind, and the most that inevitably attracts'. Art works upon our sensibilities not by evoking any of the direct emotions themselves, which would overpower the mind and lead to inappropriate and undesired results; we would not wish to run screaming in panic from the theatre, vomit in the stalls from disgust, or leap onto the stage to ravish the beautiful heroine. Instead, art sets out by all the means at its disposal to evoke all the memory-traces associated with its subject that we possess. We experience not the direct emotion, but a long series of our own emotive memories; our memory-traces are evoked and brought together into a composite conscious image. Thus, the more varied and vivid our own actual experience has been, the more intense will be our aesthetic response to any work of art. We will have more memory-traces ready for it to work upon. The immense ramifications of smilie and metaphor in Indian poetry and art all help to reinforce the experience with their own memory-traces. (In the case of music too the memory-traces and associations would in India be mainly erotic.) So, when we come to the erotic temple sculpture and the erotic paintings, the more of our own erotically coloured memories we can carry with us, the more of our own experiences of actual love there are ready to be invoked, of remembered forms, softnesses, caressing movements, pressures, muscular tensions, associated sensuousnesses like birds' feathers, iridescent colours, bees on the skin, the more acute will be our aesthetic experience. This is the way Indian art was made to work. It is an art for experienced adults, not for inexperienced children. Perhaps I should just mention, in conclusion, that many other modes than the erotic are, and can be developed in art.

The 'educative' sets of erotic paintings that I have mentioned in Chapter One were many of them based upon the classical encyclopedias of erotic technique. Some were specifically illustrations of the texts. Others were selections or deriva-   5
tives. The texts too served as a repertoire of ideas for poets and artists who were to treat erotic themes. And one can find many manuscripts of the epics, or of the loves of Kṛishṇa, or temple sculptures, where the artists have used the varied types and postures recorded in the encyclopedias as inspirations for their work. The correspondence was not close, or systematically exhaustive. That was not the point. Indeed there are many erotic devices represented in temple sculpture that have no place in the encyclopedias. And, of course, not all of the conceptions recorded in the encyclopedias were – or could be – represented in erotic art.

89

VIII Album miniatures. (*Left*) Prince and lady on the riverside. Panjab hills, *c.* 1820.
(*Right*) Brahmin and lady. Kangra style, 19th century

3 Temple Art

Origins

The Hindu temples of India are world famous for the superb erotic sculptures with which many of them are adorned. Most of the best examples were built in the North between the ninth and thirteenth centuries AD, and in the South between the sixth and seventeenth centuries AD. In addition many temples still in worship have one or more immense wooden wheeled chariots – called 'cars' – which are constructed after the pattern of structural temples, with towering, piled-up canopies and spires. These cars are chiefly used to carry the main divine images of the shrine on their festival processions along traditional routes – perhaps for a bathe in a sacred river or lake. Many of their wooden posts and panels are carved with the same sort of erotic scenes as the temples themselves are. It is probable that most temples once had such cars. In the North few cars survive; for there many traditions were obliterated during the twelfth to fifteenth centuries AD by the incursions of Moslem invaders, who usually destroyed all the Hindu art they could. But in Orissa and South India, where old traditions remain still intact, temples still have their cars.

On the fabric of both cars and temples appear sculptures of men and women in various postures of sexual intercourse. They are not by any means always in couples; three or more participants are common. And many of the representations show forms of pleasurable association which are not normal congress, such as *cunnilinctio, coitus per anum* and *fellatio*. The scenes in fact, have a distinctly genre character; the participants are self-absorbed, and do not address themselves directly to the beholder in the manner of the icon. And although the types of women are more or less consistent on each temple, portraying the ideal of feminine beauty current at the particular time and place, the male figures vary considerably. Many are magnificently bearded, and some carry weapons which show them to be 'heroes' in the epic vein.

There can be no doubt that this erotic art was based upon the old erotic legends of the epic period. For the epic poems themselves were held by the Brahmins who preserved them to be of sacred origin, dealing with the exploits of heroes who were regarded as divine incarnations. I have suggested that there was behind the imagery of the epic a secular eroticism which flourished in the open cities of the early period of Indian history. It was paralleled or typified in religious imagery of a heaven of sensuous delight. As time went on, probably during the early Middle Ages when every department of life was being gathered together by Brahmin scholastics, and fitted into the framework of religion, when the *Kāmasūtra* was becoming recognized as holy writ, this erotic imagery was assimilated into the whole scheme of Hindu iconography. The fully developed medieval temple was intended to display in its decoration an epitome of Hindu iconography as a whole – including the erotic. But just as the heavenly parallels or types of the earthly courtesans, the Apsarases, were assimilated to the imagery of the temple, so the activities of their earthly counterparts were also taken over as part of the temple's social and magical function.

Devadāsīs

The Devadāsīs (slave-girls of God) who flourished during the Middle Ages and modern times came to fulfil the roles of female courtiers to the temple deity, of temple and public dancers, musicians, and sacred prostitutes. They must have lent an ultimate conviction of truth to the imagery of the Apsarases and heavenly musicians and dancers who figure in vast numbers in all sorts of seductive postures on the temple fabric. In Western India and in Mysore the erotic scenes usually occur as punctuations in a continuous frieze of figures of dancers and musicians. The connexion between dancing and eroticism, which is here canonized, is ancient in many other parts of the world.

However, there is no certain evidence for the existence of the institution of the Devadāsī earlier than the third century BC in India when an inscription was cut in a cave at Rāmgarh to record the love of a young painter for a 'slave-girl of the god'. Elsewhere in the world we know that similar institutions were of considerable antiquity and great respectability. So too it may be in India. But we do have a full knowledge of the cult of the Devadāsī as it existed in recent times from European writers, who were fascinated by it.

Devadāsīs were women and girls attached to the temples as a part of their official 'establishment'. Their duties were to see to the day-to-day running of the shrine, sweeping it and attending to the needs of the image. This they would anoint, dress and garland each day, and adorn it properly for different festivals. And at certain times of day or on special occasions of public need they danced and sang before the image to please the divinity. The documentary evidence is united in describing the dancing and singing as highly licentious. In fact the Devadāsīs served the deity of their temple as Rāvaṇa's women would have served him. In addition these temple dancers served as prostitutes, living in the neighbourhood of the temple, and bound by the terms of their contract to entertain any man who might pay a sum into the temple funds. H. M. Penzer has fully documented the inescapable fact that in ancient and medieval times in India the terms 'dancing girl' and 'prostitute' were synonymous.

Two different oral traditions have been recorded purporting to 'explain' the erotic aspects of medieval temple arts. In Orissa it has been said by Brahmin officiants that the sexual images 'preserve the temple towers from lightning'. How or why no one knows. But the magically prophylactic effect attributed to them associates them with one of the oldest prime symbols for divine potency, the thunderbolt. Marco Polo records (c. 1446) that he was told that the lewd dances of the Malabar dancing girls were designed to stimulate the divinity to have sexual connexion with his goddess. And in this case the sexual references in the art of dancing are supposed to promote the proper union of the double divinity, the cosmic dyad, and so maintain public affairs in a healthy condition. From both these explanations, it is possible to see that sexual art was held to express and stimulate the divine power which maintains the universal order, and which I have pointed out was identical with the sexual afflatus. The activities of the Devadāsīs, including their prostitution, thus played an important part in the temple's social and magical functions. They represent a day-to-day continuation of a spiritual purpose – the spreading abroad throughout society of the divine sexual power. This purpose may also be fulfilled seasonally, at harvest or seed time by great public festivals of the Saturnalia type, such as Holī in India. Only during the last forty years has Holī ceased to be an occasion of general sexual licence, involving public and promiscuous intercourse. Nowadays only the squirting of coloured powder or water serves as the sexual symbol. But many other Indian ceremonies, like the ordinary wedding ceremony, or the Shākta *Chakrapūja* which will be discussed later, emphasize the way in which sexual relations are held to confer something of divinity on the participants. There are, however, other aspects of temple sexuality which can amplify the meaning of the cult.

Although official dancing girls were the chief prostitutes at medieval temples, in some circumstances it was considered an act of piety for a respectable woman, married or single, to prostitute herself at the temple gate either to Brahmins or to casual strangers. The purpose of this was perhaps most commonly to remove the curse of barrenness, but not always. For Indian mythology, in common with much of the world's folklore, has recognized the probability that the God will avail himself of the opportunity to have sexual intercourse with a woman, who is anyway his by right, when it is offered. Brahmins, as priests, and strangers, who may be God in disguise, or at least his representative, are the legitimate partners on such occasions. Also in many parts of India the divinity of the local shrine was supposed to exercise a genuine *droit de seigneur* over local women before they were married. Early Western writers darkly suggest, certainly correctly, that Brahmin officiants at the shrine played the divine role – as we shall see that the nineteenth-century 'Mahārājas' did.

But to return to the official Devadāsīs; the ritual whereby they were adopted into the temple establishment consisted fundamentally of a marriage ceremony, in which the God was the bridegroom, and was impersonated by a sword, upon which a fruit was often impaled, by a tree, or by an image. So the Devadāsī became in effect a wife of the divinity and thus, by normal caste rules, attracted divine status to herself. As consistent intercourse with strangers was a part of her duties as a wife of the god, it is clear that there was some intention that the prostitute's patrons should come by association with her to partake of the nature of the divinity. In this way sexual relations with temple prostitutes, undertaken for pleasure, constituted at the same time a ritual act whereby prostitute and client were augmented in their divine nature, each by their connexion with a representative of the divinity.

If we then consider the temple carvings against this background of custom and belief, we can perhaps see how they serve as emblems of something divine, at the same time as being pictures of enjoyment. They represent the sexual activity of the 'wives of the god', which is a 'type' of the activity of the Apsarases (not bound to any man) whose function is described in the epics and in the story (below) of Nanda's education. The temple offered to living men an experience of the joys of heaven, thus reinforcing its claim to be a complete image of the divine upon earth. But on the magical level, where so much of the temple's symbolism operates, the erotica, like the 'Fescennine' jests of ancient Mediterranean festivals, and the erotic songs and dances of the dancing girls, served to stimulate and increase the world's store of sexual power upon which its well-being depends. In later chapters it will appear how this theory of the meaning of the sexual image applies at the level of personal psychology.

The earliest erotic art

The actual history of the evolution of erotic art in India helps to amplify the meaning of the great erotic temple sculpture. From a very early date, as I have said, there was erotic secular art in India, the clues to which are partly literary, partly in the form of small works like the Ganges valley terracottas and the Begrām and Pompeii ivories, which must once have existed in considerable numbers, and partly in the form of stylistic indications in surviving early works of religious art. The last point, however, is an important one, which I have not yet discussed. It is tied up with a conception of the meaning of temple art as a whole in the Indian context.

In several early or fairly early works of art we have representations of Indian court life. In the reliefs from Buddhist shrines at many sites between the first and third centuries AD we can find scenes that are, as it were, waking, daytime views of the harem of Rāvaṇa, where the prince – usually the Buddha-to-be – sits surrounded by beautiful women and girl-musicians. An interesting feature of the reliefs is that these panels, and others like them, are punctuated by larger figures of amorous couples, images of physical well-being, incorporating ideal sexual types. There are also, amongst the second–fifth century AD Buddhist sculptures from Gandhāran shrines in the Kabul river valley, reliefs showing the self-indulgent life of royal ease led by the Buddha before he abandoned the world to live as an ascetic. Here too beautiful women play their part, and the prince is occasionally shown having sexual relations with them – as any prince should. The style of these images is close to that of the Hellenistic and Roman erotic images of the Mediterranean world. In Ashvaghosha's long epic-like poem on the life of the Buddha there is a famous set-piece description of his sleeping harem, as the Buddha abandons it by night, clearly inspired by the *Rāmāyaṇa* description of Rāvaṇa's harem. Here, though, to accord with Buddhist puritanism, the sleeping women are described not as attractive, but as abandoned and disgusting. On the Sihagiri rock in Ceylon a few late fifth-century AD plaster-paintings survive in a sublimely erotic style which represent Apsarases bringing offerings to the king whose palace crowns the rock – celestials playing courtier. Their style is virtually identical with that of the contemporary Buddhist paintings at the Ajanta caves. We know they are Apsarases because on the smooth wall of the pathway to the top are numerous scratched inscriptions, some going back to the eighth century AD. The wall-scribblers proclaim their love for these heavenly girls in poetical stanzas. They declare that 'the lily-coloured ones', 'the golden deer-eyed beauties', 'bewilder the mind'. The cruel beauty of these celestial beings with fluttering eyes and flowers combed into their hair has turned the hearts of some away from their homely wives, and destroyed their sleep. And one declares that now that he has glimpsed these beautiful girls, death cannot perturb him!

All this goes to indicate that religious shrines were from early times decorated with art of a courtly type, executed by artists whose normal *métier* was the execution of images of the secular paradise, parallel to the literary images of courtly life in the epics. It also suggests, in conjunction with what follows, that the shrine itself, to whomever dedicated, Buddha or Hindu deity, was conceived as a princely court, the role of prince being played by the central holy image. Thus all the sculptured figures which adorn the early Buddhist, Jain and Hindu shrines represent 'courtiers'. It is, in fact, impossible to overrate the fundamental importance of the image of the 'court' in Indian temple art. The women, who are often identified as minor deities on early shrines, and are given great prominence, parallel those wives and daughters of peers, subjects or defeated enemies, whom the princes of the epic age used to impress into their harems. Thus were the little goddesses of the countryside impressed into the 'courts' of the Buddhist shrines *24* at Barhut, Sānchī and Mathurā, and of the Hindu temples of Aihole, Badāmi and Ellora.

The specifically sexual images are an essential ingredient in the whole image of the 'divine court', as we might expect. Among the reliefs on the earliest Buddhist monuments of India (second century BC–first century AD) are representations of a man and woman with their arms around each other (the *dampati*). These figures are not erotic in the full sense of the word. Nevertheless the early idea of the *dampati* as a proper architectural ornament was one of the sources of the medieval erotica. By the second century AD at Mathurā the prototype of the classical type of temple doorway had been developed, which was itself the inspiration for later architectural ideas. Its jambs were ornamented with rows of panels containing *dampati* reliefs. And on the Nahāpāna *vihāra* at Nāsīk in the Deccan, of mid-second century AD date, the same idea is found again. In addition, on the capitals of the great *chaitya* cave at Karle in the Western Deccan, at Bhājā not far away, and on those of the gateways of stupa I at Sānchī, all dating from the first century AD, beautiful embracing couples appear riding pairs of animals. Whilst at Karle, the colossal couples on the façade, immense images of opulent physical well-being, are, like those at Nāgārjunakoṇḍa, among the greatest works of early Indian art. *17* There has also been found a *dampati* image, out of any context, but of fairly early date, in which two figures stand in the traditional 'donor' attitude, right hand raised. The man is *ūrdhvaliṅga*, with erect penis, and is usually interpreted as Shiva. So it is clear that even in early times the sexual – if not actually copulating – couple was considered as adding something to the virtue of a building, by reason of its courtly and royal associations, in the same way as all the astrological emblems, minor deities or narratives did. On Kanherī and Karle *chaitya* caves there are a number of reliefs of the first century BC depicting dancing couples – for dancing was one of the most characteristic courtly activities.

94

There is another early religious relief in which the connexion between sex, *31* dancing and religion is most clearly expressed. It is on one of the chief pillars of the oldest railing at Bodhgaya, probably of the late second-first century BC. It shows a woman dancing whilst a man holds one of her hands and unwinds a draped shawl from her body. Unlike the other feminine figures on comparable reliefs at Bodhgaya, she is naked, and in the plastic execution her buttocks are stressed in conformity with Indian ideals of feminine beauty. The background shows a curtain between two pillars over which a third person is looking. Rather similar scenes are also known from Mathurā, and most probably represent the joys of heaven.

Mathurā

At Mathurā, the great ancient spiritual centre of India, which produced during the early centuries of the Christian era a vast and varied quantity of art, as well as the usual *dampati* scenes, there were three other developments of particular interest for us here. They were all direct consequences of the liberation of the relief style from earlier and stricter canons, and the incorporation of secular images into monumental art. First: a number of representations of couples in sexual intercourse have been found. They are generally merely incidental passages in a continuous narrative, but are the earliest stone-cut instances we know. Second: there are a number of larger, enigmatic reliefs which represent drinking scenes, and do not appear on the surface to have any religious connotation. It is tempting to interpret them as having some connexion with the Tantrik ceremonial we shall discuss later, but there is no obvious reason to do so. However, it is likely that they do have a reference to life in the heavens rather than merely on earth, since in the succeeding Gupta and Chalūkya periods of art a motive was derived from them, representing a couple of flying Gandharvas – erotic heavenly beings – bearing cups.

The third and most important of these developments was in the female 'Yakshī' *24* figures with which the railings of Mathurā's shrines were so liberally adorned. Earlier monuments, like those at Barhut and Sānchī had figures of women clasping trees, whose secondary sexual characteristics were well in evidence, carved on the chief pillars of their railings. At Barhut they are expressly named by inscriptions as Yakshīs, the local godlings of trees and tanks. But at Mathurā we can trace the development of this Yakshī type, in association with the female 'donor' type, into unmistakably seductive damsels who make a lavish display of their primary as well as their secondary sexual charms. These ladies of Mathurā are made not simply to clasp their trees, but to posture under balconies, to wash under waterfalls, to undo their girdles or carry small birds about on their shoulders. They are often overlooked by the inhabitants of houses in the background who watch them, or make love on balconies. But again it is clear that they are not intended as ordinary earthly women, for, in the manner of gods, they are frequently given *vāhanas* (vehicles) consisting of animals or dwarfish men under their feet.

How to interpret these feminine types, and their association with the sacred sites of Buddhism and Jainism – those rigorously ascetic religions – has long been a mystery. It is, of course, clear that they are the direct ancestors of the Apsarases and dancers who display themselves all over the fabric of medieval temples. But I think that the story of the Buddha's conversion of his brother Nanda, as it is recounted by Ashvaghosha, at a time not at all remote from the execution of the sculptures themselves, can offer a further clue as to how they should be interpreted. Nanda was deeply in love with a girl and devoted all his care and thought to pleasing her and making love to her. But the Buddha wished to make him into a monk. So by a trick one day he separated him from his beloved, and carried him up to heaven and there showed him the Apsarases. Of course, they completely eclipsed Nanda's earthly lover by their beauty; he was consumed with a desire to enjoy them, and forgot his old love utterly. The Buddha then took him back to earth and telling him that the attainment of his desires was only a matter of time and religious effort, quickly received him into the Order. After a period of contemplation, however, Nanda came to realize the vanity of his sexual desires, and reached the true religious goal. In this story we can see how the old picture of the heavenly realms conveyed in the epics came to be assimilated into Buddhist religious imagery. But we can also infer that, if this is so, and if the Mathurā females are types of the Apsarases, the shrines with which they were associated, but which have unfortunately perished, must have served, as did the later temples, as courtly images of the heavens, complete with inhabitants. It would not be surprising to find that in this, too, Mathurā was in advance of the rest of India. For we now realize just how important as a creative centre Mathurā was in the three or four centuries before the advent of the Gupta dynasty (mid fourth century AD).

Also, we find exemplified first at Mathurā the plastic versions of the canonical patterns of ideal beauty described in the epics, which were to dominate Indian art for centuries to come. For it is one of the characteristics of Indian aesthetics that divine beings or the heroes of literature and legend were always required to conform in bodily pattern to certain norms, which served to identify them as at once superior and sexually desirable. These norms represent the constant obsession of Indian idealism. They came to be composed according to strictly prescribed canons of proportion, as diagrams of the most desirable qualities grouped within one body, which were repeated and given infinitely varied expression down the centuries. It is interesting to find that the specific sexually attractive attributes such as the narrow waist, the large hips and buttocks, and long eyes in the case of women, or the great round arms, bow-like eyebrows and block-like body in the case of men, are the same in descriptions both of sexual heroes or heroines, and of *78* religious saints. Medieval figurines from South India representing male or female saints, and all the images of divinities like Pārvatī, Shiva-Dakshiṇamūrti, Vishṇu, Lakshmī and Kṛishṇa are expressly designed to appeal to sexual emotions. For Indian religion has always expressed the desirability of its goals in this way.

The early Middle Ages

During the Gupta period in the north of India, and especially under the Chalūkya rulers of the Deccan during the fifth to the eighth centuries AD, erotic art was

60 Sexual intercourse with Apsarases. Stone relief from the heaven-bands of the Vishvanātha temple at Khajuraho. *c.* 1000 AD

61 Apsaras and partner. Stone relief from the heaven-bands of the Vishvanātha temple, Khajuraho. *c.* 1000 AD

62 (*opposite*) Sexual intercourse with an Apsaras. Stone relief from the heaven-bands of the Chitragupta temple, Khajuraho. *c.* 1000 AD

63 (*opposite*) Sexual intercourse with an Apsaras. Stone relief on the Vishvanātha temple, Khajuraho. *c.* 1000 AD
64 (*right*) Celestial couple. Stone relief from the heaven-bands of the Lakshmana temple at Khajuraho. *c.* 1000 AD

65 Shaven-headed religious man coupling with an Apsaras. Stone relief from the heaven-
bands of the Devī Jagadamba temple, Khajuraho. *c.* 1000 AD

66 Sexual intercourse with an Apsaras. Stone relief from the heaven-bands of the Lakshmaṇa temple at Khajuraho. *c.* 1000 AD

69 (*right*) Naked religious man coupling with an Apsaras.
Stone relief from the heaven-bands of the Lakshmana
temple, Khajuraho. *c.* 1000 AD

67, 68 and 70 (*opposite and below*) Three scenes from friezes
of the ritual orgies of a Kaula sect. Stone reliefs on the
plinth of the Lakshmana temple, Khajuraho. *c.* 1000 AD

71 (*opposite*) Intercourse with an Apsaras. Stone figures from the heaven-bands of the Rājaraṇī temple, Bhuvaneshvara, Orissa. 12th century AD

72 Intercourse with an Apsaras. Stone figures from the heaven-bands of the Rājaraṇī temple, Bhuvaneshvara. 12th century AD

73 *Cunnilinctio*. Stone figures from the heaven-bands of the Rājaraṇī temple, Bhuvaneshvara. 12th century AD

76 (*opposite*) *Penilinctio*. Stone relief on a temple at Khiching. 12th century AD

74 (*left*) Lovers. Stone relief from the base of a temple at Khiching. 12th century AD

75 (*below*) *Cunnilinctio*. Stone relief on a temple at Khiching. 12th century AD

77 (*left*) Naked Yoginī. A stone bracket figure from a temple at Narayanpur, Deccan. 12th century AD. Such a girl would be a heavenly partner in sexual yoga

78 Female naked ascetic performing asceticisms. Although an ascetic her sexual beauty is pronounced. From the pillar of a temple at Vijaynagar, Deccan. 14th century AD

79 The Goddess adored by sages; perhaps Viṣṇu as Mohini. Stone relief on a pillar of a temple at Vellūr, Deccan. 14th century AD

80 Lovers. Stone relief on a pillar of a temple at Vellūr, Deccan. 14th century AD

81 (*above*) Celestial lovers. Stone relief from the heaven-bands of a temple at Khajuraho, Bundelkhand. *c.* 1000 AD

82 (*opposite*) Hero and Apsaras. Stone relief from the Sun-temple at Konārak. Early 13th century AD

84 (*above*) Heroes and Apsarases in sexual enjoyment. Stone relief from the Sun-temple at Konārak

83 (*opposite*) Heroes and Apsarases in sexual enjoyment. Stone relief from the Sun-temple at Konārak. Early 13th century AD

85 Amorous couple: roundel from a spoke of one of the wheels of the sun-chariot. Stone relief from the Sun-temple at Konārak. Early 13th century AD

86 A hero demonstrates the weight of his penis with a balance. Stone relief from the Sun-temple at Konārak

88 (*above*) The kiss. Hero and Apsaras. Stone relief from the Sun-temple at Konārak. Early 13th century AD
87 (*opposite*) Hero and Apsaras. Stone relief from the Sun-temple at Konārak

89 (*left*) Torso of an Apsaras. Stone relief from the Sun-temple at Konārak. Early 13th century AD. The vulva is shown as opening of its own accord, an essential feature of many sculptures of Apsarases

90 (*opposite*) Hero and Apsaras, in inverted intercourse. Stone relief from the Sun-temple at Konārak. Early 13th century AD

91 Hero and Apsaras. Stone relief from the Sun-temple at Konārak. Early 13th century AD

92 Detail of the intercourse of a
hero with two Apsarases,
involving *penilinctio*. Stone relief
from the Sun-temple at
Konārak

93 Detail of caressing hand on the
leg of an Apsaras. Stone relief
from the Sun-temple at Konārak

94 Heroes and Apsarases in sexual enjoyment. Stone relief from the Sun-temple at Konārak. Early 13th century AD

95 Hero and amorous Apsaras. Stone relief from the Sun-temple at Konārak

96, 97 and 98 (*above and opposite*) Terracotta panels from the revetment of Bengal temples, with reliefs of erotic scenes. 17th century AD

99 Stone image of the Buddhist personification of Wisdom. From Orissa. *c.* 1100 AD. Although the subject is an abstract concept, the execution is of an extreme sensuality

further developed. The *dampati* reliefs of the doorways of Gupta shrines became fixed canonical elements in architectural ornament and often became fully erotic. And in the Deccan, first at Aihole then at Badāmi and at Pattadakal, the successive capitals of the Chalūkya rulers, the characteristic medieval idea of the temple as an image of the heavenly realm, with its population of Apsarases, Gandharva couples, and divinities was fully established. Particularly in evidence are the beautifully adorned feminine dancers (Nāyikās), derived from the female types of Mathurā and Amarāvatī, who populate the brackets and friezes of the temples. On a small fifth-century shrine at Aihole however, as one of a set of four couples *41/42* on the façade, occurs the first large-scale representation of the sexual act which survives. Thereafter embracing and copulating couples became a standard part of the decor of all the Chalūkyan temples. In many of them, from Pattadakal for *48* example, the male participant is clearly identified as a hero. The great ninth-century AD Rāshtrakuta temple, the Kailāshanātha at Ellora, which represents the cul- *39/47* mination of the Deccan style of early medieval architecture, is still lavishly orna- mented with sculptured scenes of intimate sexual relations – some fragments, too, in painting. In particular certain balconies of its caves bear continuous series of relief panels of copulating couples, in which the majestic forms of the sexual organs are greatly emphasized. Here and there appear groups of three or four men and two girls engaged in multiple intercourse.

From the ninth century onwards the sexual imagery on Indian temples becomes profuse. For from that epoch the temple itself takes on a special significance. Hindu temples have usually begun their evolution as accretions round some numinous hallows, whose sanctity is immemorial, and where generations of villagers had left their offerings to the deity. It did happen, though, that temples were founded on sites suitable for other reasons – one of them being that a sublime pair of lovers had coupled there! Often the sanctuary of vast and powerful shrines is occupied by a broken anthill or the stump of an ancient tree – the body of the original numen. At various points in its evolution the hallows would have been enclosed in a wall, perhaps given a finely sculptured form as lingam or anthro- pomorphic icon, then enclosed in a constructed cell – the *garbha-griha* or womb- house – with a portico attached. As its fame and wealth grew, elaborate verandahs, ambulatories, halls and aligned pavilions would have been added to it, and in the South successively larger walled enclosures with colossal gateway towers. The exterior walls would be developed with elaborate systems of buttresses, rebates, friezes and sculptured panels. The roofs would be developed into terraced tiers; the spire above the *garbha-griha* with multiple abstract elements of rhythmic character – mouldings, fluting and gadrooning, intaglio patterns – and often in the North into a flight of smaller engaged spires, leading up towards the cul- minating central pinnacle, which was crowned by a flat, gadrooned amalaka fruit.

The temple as symbol

By AD 1000 the symbolic pattern of the temple had fully developed. This rests upon the ancient concept of the cosmic mountain, Mount Meru. It is an image of the whole world. For just as medieval Hindu philosophy was constantly striving to sum up all human knowledge into a systematic whole, so was the temple an effort to summarize the whole mythical basis of religion. The temple's base rests upon earth, the goddess Pṛithivī, the eternal mother of all. The base itself, in contact with the earth, its columns, panels and friezes, are carved with scenes from heroic legends which are supposed to have happened upon earth – usually from the epic. The base supports the floor of the cell and its portico. The outer wall of this level bears bands of relief sculptures which represent the heavens and their inhabitants – deities, Apsarases, Gandharvas and so on. For Mount Meru is conceived as bearing all the regions of the cosmos hung garlanded around itself. The main cell and its approaches on the same level are thus conceived as being identical with the halls of heaven. Above them soar the towering regions beyond represented form. These image the remote reaches of the empyrean, the ultimate realm of the spirit, recalling the vast, silent peaks of the Himālaya that tower white into the depths of the violet sky.

But Hindu temples, although they do often have ornamented interiors, are really conceived as huge, complex, outward-facing sculptures. The wealth of encrusted carving and stucco-work all over their exteriors represents the outward efflorescence of the spiritual power lodged inside the womb-house; the more opulent, the better. The foliage in bands and panels shows that the juice (*rasa*) flows like sap through the fabric; the full, inflated forms of the sculpture show that they are imbued with the divine numen, ripe like fruit to bursting. And if we remember that this divine power is also conceived as the sexual afflatus, we should not be surprised to find that direct sexual imagery is one of its natural products. The court of the deity of the temple, the ultimate numen of the world, is the cosmos itself. The temple car is a kind of temporary travelling temple for the deity, analogous to the travelling palace of the human king, complete with courtiers of every kind, of which history tells us.

The erotic figures

The styles in which the sexual images on the temples are executed are meant to suggest an opulent juicefulness close to the heavenly source of life, as well as conveying all the metaphorical beauties of the actual forms. The subjects of the images are expressions of this same idea. They can best be discussed in three main categories, though, of course, the categories are physically mixed on the actual fabric of the temples. First: the single figures, mainly girls; second: the couples; third: the more complex groups. Finally we shall discuss the greatest of the erotic temples, the 'Black Pagoda' at Konārak, in Orissa.

The single girls on the temples are plainly meant to epitomize the sexually desirable image, to crystallize the goal of male sexual desire. They are, in a sense, 'pin-ups' – but pin-ups of the highest artistic quality. Of course, they are endowed with all the canonical attributes of beauty current at each place and time. Their sexual characteristics provide the whole basis for the formal ideas. They are not simply ideal types, but compendia of stimulating attributes. Nothing about their figures that is not of sexual interest is included in the image. Their smooth, inflated and undulant surfaces invite the stroking hand. They have the long, high-caste Aryan nose 'like a parrot's beak'. Their eyes are long and especially at Khajuraho *54* (*c.* AD 1000) somehow liquid – due to the way the sculptors allow the eyeball to follow the length of the lids, rather than achieve an independent roundness. The *53* draperies are mere enhancements – floating scarves or loose cloths that slip willingly off to reveal the most intimate charms. Breasts, usually, are of an opulent fullness, as they so often are on Indian girls of the true 'goddess' age of sixteen. For in *VII* India eroticism and the maternal image of the full breast are in no way irreconcilable. Navels may be deep-set, spines have a charming channel, necks ringed with creases that reveal the softness of feminine subcutaneous fat. Chignons are large and elaborate; jewels are abundant, for Indians hold that they add greatly to a woman's charm – partly for their own beauty, partly as 'status' symbols, partly for their symbolical value as crystalline glory, but also partly for their plastic qualities. The way in which a necklace embraces a neck, an armlet an arm, making a closed circle around it, always emphasizes the plastic presence of the significant form (in Western art and life garters and stocking-tops may also perform the same office). Jewelry provides too that element of numerical rhythm which the Indian mind finds so entrancing, in the complex drum rhythms of music as in the multiple mouldings of architecture. Finally, the feminine vulva is, by the *64* Apsarases freely offered to view, as a beauty with an expression of its own. The clitoris is often much in evidence, but rarely the labia minora. In Orissa (*c.* AD 1200) for example, the vulva's openness proclaims the eager nature of the Apsaras. *89* Elsewhere, as at Khajuraho, its frontal presentation serves as a mark of desirable youth. But another reason for its being visible is the fact that in India it was always usual for women, especially courtesans, to depilate their pubic region. Special thumb-rings, with small mirrors inset, were used for this purpose.

The postures adopted by the sculptured girls are all those which are best calculated to display the sexual qualities of their figures. Twisted postures with an *57* out-thrust hip, or with lifted breasts, hollowed back and salient behind are very common. So too are charmingly modest postures, with downcast head, but a sideways glance from the lowered eyelids. Often the trees to which the girls cling *77* recall their historical origin in the old images of vegetation goddesses, or the girls who hang like fruit from the wish-granting tree of legend. But it has further implications; Indian folklore holds that a fertile woman can cause a tree to fruit by kicking or embracing it; and a tree was one of the divine 'bridegrooms' of the Devadāsī. But perhaps the most important postures of these girls are those which display that quality I have mentioned which the Indian mind has always considered ideally feminine – the girl's likeness to 'a creeper' (*latā*), both in her softly yielding and twining bodily movements, and in her moral nature, clinging to her man for support as a flowering forest-creeper clings to the great tree.

A few single figures of other kinds need specially mentioning. First there are *96* those engaged in solitary pleasure, masturbating, both men and women. Their faces express delight; they are there simply to make complete the revelation of the essence of sexuality on the temple fabric. If this activity were not represented the image would not be complete. Prurience and guilt do not enter into it. One other image that occurs at Konārak probably goes back to a Hellenistic prototype, *86* for the same rather odd and unexplained subject also occurs in the House of the Vettii at Pompeii. It shows a man weighing his own gigantic phallus on a balance. The whole interest in men with grotesquely gigantic phalloi appears to be characteristic in the first place of Hellenistic Egypt, with its cult of Baubo. In fact India did derive many artistic patterns from Alexandria in the epoch around 10 BC–AD 100. The Pompeiian example probably derives from the same source. In modern Indian folk-art there are similar grotesques.

62/63/88   The second category of erotic temple figures are the couples. These cover a very wide gamut of possibilities. In these groups too the woman's 'creeper' nature is especially evident. There are some extremely beautiful entwined kisses, and, of course, there are numerous representations of various postures of sexual intercourse, particularly those with one of the woman's legs raised. However, because the figures are carved on temple walls, and the normal non-erotic type of temple wall-figure is a standing one in either frontal or profile view, they have certain peculiarities of presentation. For none of these heavenly couples can easily be shown in lying-down positions of intercourse. This has somewhat limited the repertoire of postures, in comparison with the illustrations in manuscripts. Some very odd examples occur at Khajuraho, where a male participant appears to be standing on his head. It has also led to the rather frequent appearance of the postures described in the erotic encyclopedias which are supposed to be carried out standing, for example against a wall or a pillar.

37/45/46   One very striking characteristic of the couples is that the woman is often shown in an acrobatically contorted posture. This, again, was one of the special charms and achievements of the Devadāsīs. Brought up as they were to dancing and other physical arts they had bodies of extreme suppleness. European writers have described the acrobatic achievements of eighteenth- and nineteenth-century Devadāsīs in some detail. Many, for example, were capable of standing, bending over backwards and, with their feet still on the ground, placing their whole forearms on the ground and picking up coins with their lips. There can be no doubt that the ability so to twist, twine and arch during intercourse was an erotic asset highly valued, as an enhancement of the pleasure both of man and woman.

52/79/91   Many of the couples are shown engaged in the preludes to love-making. Sometimes an eager girl is pulling down a soldier who still holds his shield and sword. Sometimes a man is intimately caressing a girl with his hand; and very frequently the girl is engaged in stimulating the man's organ, which is not yet erect. Common too are the oral modes of stimulation, *fellatio* and *cunnilinctio*, often shown as mutual in beautifully elaborated postures. The male organ is often shown on a much enlarged scale, simply as a round-ended cylinder; occasionally the glans is exposed. And at Khajuraho especially it appears sometimes in a thick, bent shape resembling the neck of a swan or goose – an important fact for later symbolism. Occasionally groups of two women occur, sometimes performing *cunnilinctio*.

40   Groups of more than two lovers are common. Many of the arrangements found on medieval temples go back to patterns shown by the very early erotic terracottas of the Ganges valley. Sometimes it is one girl who is embraced by two men; she may be caressed by both of them standing, or she may be in an arched posture having normal intercourse with one, whilst she serves the other by *fellatio*. Sometimes a group includes two men and two girls. As we know that the Devadāsīs

always had at least two maids or apprentices in attendance, it is not surprising that groups of a chief couple with one or two attendant maids are often found, and sometimes a maid is stimulating the man by *fellatio* whilst he embraces the principal girl. Another common form of group is that of one man with several women. Whilst he enjoys intercourse with one woman, he caresses the sexual organs of two others with his hands; sometimes two others are satisfying themselves with his toes. This last combination, of one man with five women, became the canonical image for the extreme of male sexual luxury. It is found again and again in the erotic paintings of later ages. It does, of course, represent virtually the maximum possible degree of sexual sensation, in a polygamous setting. Occasionally there appears one of the combinations recommended in the *Kāmasūtra* – not followed too exactly – whereby the man has intercourse with two women together, delivering alternate strokes to each. *59*

92/94

84

8

Perhaps the most complex single group in the north of India, at Khajuraho, is represented in the form of a long, continuous frieze, on the base of the Lakshmaṇa temple, and is thus identified as an earthly scene. The male participants are shown by their hairstyles to be ascetics. They are engaged both in various acts of intercourse with jewelled girls, and in pounding something in mortars. This last is probably meant to be the Vedic *soma*, the unidentified sacred plant whose juice yielded intoxicating drink, and which has symbolized for some four millennia in India the Dionysiac intoxication of spiritual exaltation. In the rituals of modern times familiar intoxicants have come to take the place of *soma*. There can be no doubt that this scene represents the religious rites of one of the Tantrik sects, such as the Kaulas, whose customs we shall discuss in the next chapter. *65/67/68/69/70*

Konārak

The colossal temple at Konārak, in Orissa, usually called the Black Pagoda, is the most famous site in all India for erotic scupltures. Its walls are encrusted with hundreds of them. It is the greatest temple to love that has ever been built. This temple was abandoned, its vast roofs and spire uncompleted, about AD 1230 and its significance has not yet been explained. However, in the light of what I have written here, it should now be possible to understand it. *82-95*

The temple is dedicated to the sun-god, Surya. In the ancient Vedic hymns there are innumerable references to Surya, the sun personalized; he is regarded as the outward and visible form of the inward spiritual light, which is personalized as Savitar. Very frequent mention is made of the gorgeous celestial chariot in which Surya rides on his daily course across the heavens, with special reference to its wheels, which by their rotation mark out the cycles of time. A feature of the Konārak temple is the set of colossal carved stone wheels, beautifully decorated, with which it is equipped. In fact the huge stone building is conceived both as a temple – the image of heaven, which itself is often called the 'realm of the sun' – and as the celestial chariot of Surya. And since there already was in existence an adequate prototype which combined both the functions of temple and chariot, the temple car, it is natural that the Konārak temple should have been designed *84* virtually as a static, colossal temple car, complete with its heavenly ornaments, and its troops of Apsarases. Many of the references to Surya in other sacred literature, such as the *Suryashataka* of Mayūra, reinforce the image of the glorious chariot. One of the greatest of the Purāṇas, the *Shrimad Devī Bhagavatam,* refers to the strange golden region of the sun and stars, where everything is turned to mirror-like gold, guarded by huge elephants. The Konārak temple has a set of colossal monolithic elephants. But this is not all. Although the descriptions of Surya's chariot are usually fairly general, and limit themselves to epithets denoting its splendour, such as 'jewelled', 'like a heap of rubies', and so on, there is one great description of a celestial chariot, which is specifically a chariot of love. It is virtually certain, but completely unprovable, that this description must have been known to the designers of the Konārak Surya temple, for it appears in the famous *Bhagavata Purāṇa,* which was much read in Orissa. This celestial chariot is not Surya's chariot; but it does represent an extraordinary erotic invention. Once more we may trace its origin to the epics, where chariots full of women and Apsarases are delightfully imagined.

This is the story. One of the great sages of India, Kardama, who had entirely turned away from the world and successfully contained his vital fluid, was begged by his amorous wife Devahuti, to have sexual intercourse with her. (This follows the pattern of the Brahmin's semen-conservation, discussed in Chapter One.) The sage had compassion on his wife, and so by his magical yogic power projected into the heavens a celestial chariot, beautifully jewelled and painted, filled with pavilions and bosomy beds. It was also, interestingly enough, filled with ten thousand beautiful girls. Kardama lifted his wife into this divine chariot and there, dividing himself into nine (a common myth this, in a polygamous society), he passed many years in amorous sport and dalliance with his wife – and presumably also with the ten thousand other girls, or at least some of them. The sage gave his wife only enough of his vital fluid to make her pregnant with daughters. He then departed to lead a totally ascetic life. However, although she was disappointed, she performed penances, and a son was finally born to her. This son was Kapila, the founder of the Sāṃkhya system of philosophy, which is the intellectual basis of the Shākta cult of the Goddess, and of Kaula ritual. Although this story is not strictly relevant to the legend of Surya, its image of a celestial chariot of love probably had a certain independent existence as an autonomous image in literature and legends which have not survived (little has). As such it could have combined with the more general image of Surya's celestial car to give us the Konārak temple of love.

The Temptress

There is one more type of erotic sculpture which is especially common in South Indian temples, and has nothing obviously to do with the legendary heavens. Indian literature is full of scenes where ascetics or forest-dwelling hermits are seduced by beautiful girls. Sometimes these girls are Apsarases; sometimes they are incarnations of a major deity, like Vishnu. These scenes are usually represented in sculpture by a group of figures, amongst which the divinely beautiful woman is far the largest. The ascetics are often represented with erect phalloi, to show their desire. Perhaps the most ancient, and hence most fundamental literary archetype of this scene is contained in the *Kaushitaki Brahmaṇa*; the image it conveys must surely be more fundamental than the various narratives into which it was later incorporated. Here the creative activity of the primal being, Prajāpati (the father of creatures) is described. His desire (*tejas*) produces the five old luminous deities, one of whom is the feminine Dawn, Ushas; amongst the other masculine four is Agni, the fire. Ushas, in the shape of an Apsaras, stands before the others, and their seed flows out at the sight of her. Prajāpati collects their seed in a golden bowl, from which arises the thousand-limbed original creative deity, as yet unnamed and unparticularized. I illustrate a panel from a South Indian temple car where this *20* scene is shown, acted only by Ushas and Agni. The psychological significance of this image is related to material discussed in the next chapter. But it is obviously a mythical expression of Brahmin speculation based on the involuntary emission of semen.

The last group of erotic monumental sculptures I have to mention are the strange land-boundary stones which are found in parts of Southern and Western India. The one illustrated is dated AD 1198. They are carved with a representa- *22* tion of a woman coupling with a male elephant. The significance of this can only be a fertility charm. For in Indian literature the association between elephants and the towering dark clouds of the monsoon rains is constant. Elephants are likened to clouds, clouds to elephants in thousands of metaphors and similes. The woman must be the earth, whom the monsoon, personified in the elephant, is fertilizing. We shall encounter this most fundamental image in other contexts.

4 Tantrism

Yoga and the physical

There is an important strand of thought running through Indian religion which has attracted the fascinated attention of many modern Western and Indian students. This can broadly be described as Tantrik, and involves religious rituals in which sex plays the fundamental part. Tantrism is sex as philosophy, philosophy as sex. There can be no doubt that one of the reasons why people nowadays find it so fascinating is that it somehow legitimizes and makes 'respectable' an interest in sex itself. For all the original texts that deal with it, both in Indian languages and English, are full of dark warnings of the dangers involved, of insistences that none of it must be confused with ordinary, bestial sexuality, and of declarations that the true Tantrik tradition has too often been hideously degraded into mere orgies by crowds of unspeakable low-class folk. Therefore people whose minds are in bondage to the anxieties and rigid taboos of modern religious institutions, Christian or Brahmin, have been enabled in contemplating passively 'Tantrism as literature' to give some rein to the natural opulence of their human libido, whilst paying a kind of lip service to the 'proprieties' of their institutions. And it must never be forgotten that a modern's interest in the Tantra can *never* be the same as the interest in it of the ancient people who evolved the Tantra. For, apart from anything else, one of the ingredients in many tantras is indeed magic of the 'basest' kind. The modern may be fascinated by the picturesque and stimulating aspects of this sex-oriented religion, but he could never conceivably bring himself to perform all the various. rites and yogas it requires. There is, without any doubt, an immensely powerful current of truth running through the Tantra; but it is of an order as yet incompletely clarified, and certainly not yet assimilated through freshly evolved rituals to the needs of modern man. Perhaps a few possibilities may emerge from this chapter. But unavoidably we shall encounter what the honest mind can only call absurdities amongst Tantrik rites and beliefs – absurdities, that is, in the modern context. In the context of medieval India they would be by no means absurd, far more sensible indeed than many Western medieval idiocies.

Perhaps the most important single thing that has to be remembered whilst studying the subject is this. There are many physiological activities of the human body – those especially of the glandular and sympathetic nervous systems – which are outside the control of the conscious will, but which can be effectively governed to some extent by means of evocative mental imagery. Anyone who has had to master a wide variety of difficult physical activities in which unconscious 'natural responses' have continuously to be controlled, including, for example, battle, opera-singing, or certain branches of athletics, will know how important a role

100 Small bronze image of a dancing goddess of initiation, Vajrayāna Buddhist, from Sikkim. *c.* 1500 AD. The sexual aspect of initiation is stressed

102 (*above*) Mandala painting on cloth, representing the six chief divine principles of Vajrayāna
Buddhism, each in union with his female counterpart. Tibet. 19th century
101 (*opposite*) Ritual painting on cloth representing a Knowledge-holding deity of Vajrayāna
Buddhism in union with his female counterpart. Other symbolic figures surround them. Tibet.
18th century

106 (*opposite*) The Goddess as destroyer, worshipped by ascetics who are her victims. Her sexual attributes and beauty are pronounced. Stone relief on an unidentified temple in Northern India. *c.* 1000 AD

103 Bronze figurine, supposedly the female partner of a *Yab-Yum* combination, but actually endowed with male members, by exchange. Tibet. 17th century

105 The Goddess as destroyer, who in her creative aspect draws the lingam of her husband, the 'corpse-Shiva' into her genitals. Folk painting. Orissa. Modern

104 Bronze emblem of the male and female elements of the Divine combined on a Mandala altar. The triangles pointing down are female, up, male. Bengal. 19th century

107 Birth scene. Wooden panel from a temple-car. South India. 17th century

108 The Goddess adored by sages. Carved wooden relief from a temple-car. South India. 17th century

109 (*opposite*) A knowledge-holding deity embracing his female counterpart. Tibetan bronze figurine. 16th century

110 The Goddess in union with her husband, manifesting different aspects of her creative personality, sprung from the streams of blood flowing from the decapitated body of her destructive aspect. This recalls old customs of self-decapitation in her honour. Album painting. Bengal. 19th century

111 The Goddess as Destroyer in union with her husband, the two aspects of Shiva, in the cremation-
ground. Painting of the Bengal School. 20th century

113 Kṛṣṇa and Balarāma enjoying amorous 'water-sports' with the Gopīs. Painting. Rājasthān. 18th century

112 (*opposite*) Kṛṣṇa and Rādhā dance embraced, playing the same flute. Miniature bronze image. Eastern India. *c.* 13th century

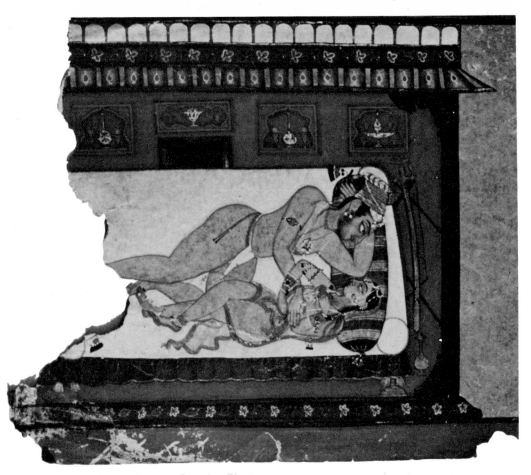

114 The Nāyikā and her husband in bed. Miniature album painting. Basohli state, Panjab hills. Late 17th century

115 Prince and lady. Fragmentary miniature painting, in primitive Rajput style. 18th century

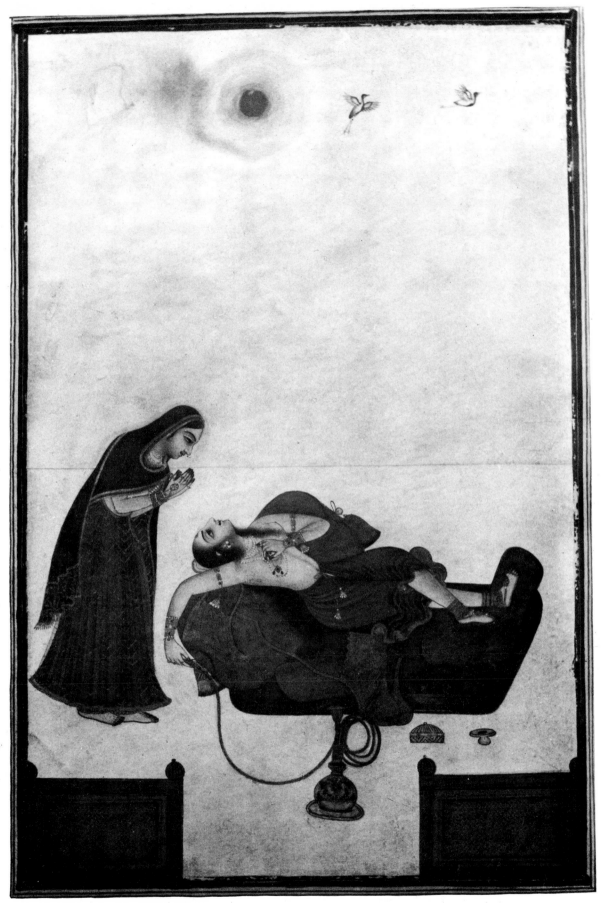

116 Lady languishing for passion, under the blazing sky which symbolizes the state of her own
desire. Album miniature. Bundi, Rājasthān. Late 18th century

117 Prince and lady at home. Miniature album painting from Mewar, Rājasthān. Mid 17th century

118 (*above*) Figure of an elephant compounded out of interwoven couples. Miniature drawing. Rājasthān. 18th century

119 (*above right*) Prince and lady. Miniature album painting from Rājasthān. 18th century

120 Couple in a garden. Provenance unknown. 19th century

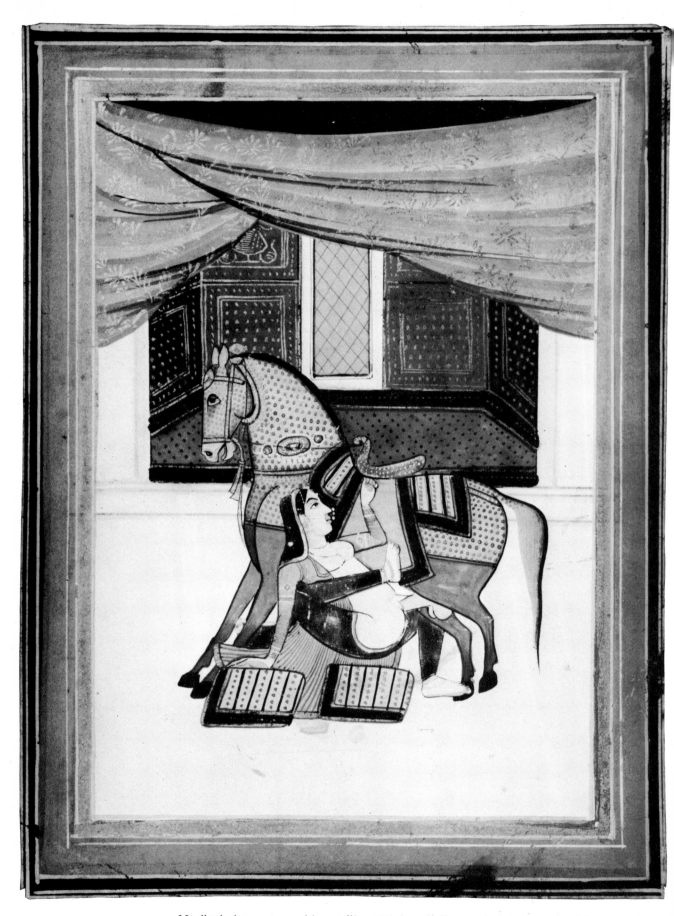

121 Nāyikā in intercourse with a stallion. Miniature album painting. Deccan. 18th century

mental images can play, that are apparently illogical, but are nevertheless effective. The whole of Tantrism is based on this principle.

Once again we have to look for the fundamental idea that lies behind all the rituals we shall discuss. And it is not hard to find. It is an extension of the notion which is by now familiar – that the sexual afflatus is in its nature divine. But for the purposes of Tantrism it must be taken further. The 'afflatus' which Tantrism of all kinds pursues is an exaltation which is at once physiological and cerebral, which has its roots in the most fundamental excitation of the sexual organs, but which is never discharged. It is turned back inward into the roots of the organism, transmitted through the whole nervous system into the brain and there consummated as an unspeakable bliss, which is identified as divine, and is the whole justification of the efforts of the Tantrika. This turning back inward and upward is the key process, often referred to in the texts by the Sanskrit term *parāvṛitti*, which means 'turning back in'. And it will be obvious that Tantrism is in fact a yoga – a yoga for all, one might say; although, of course, within the numerous and varied Tantrik sects there are orders of more or less elevated achievement. The common factor uniting all the Tantrik sects, Buddhist or Hindu, is the pursuit of this absorbing physiological bliss, which is at the same time a state of consciousness. The essential *parāvṛitti* is achieved by means of an elaborate system of imagery, combined with certain physical activities which are described in the chief handbooks of Hatha Yoga.

The tantras themselves, as we now know them, are texts, indeed they are comprehensive textbooks. There are many of them, and each usually includes philosophical speculation, medical and magical recipes, spells, as well as the chief ingredient – ritual, both external and meditative. The meditative ritual is linked with yoga and speculative philosophy. In fact each Tantrik text represents the specific tradition of a particular family of teachers – usually, but not always, Brahmin. These families would in the first place have been local; but exchanges of place, and exchange of traditions between members of different families occurred. There are thus local and sectarian differences between Tantras, but their common elements can easily be disentangled.

The two chief elements are these. First: the assumption that the whole external universe is a mere 'extension' through his body of the consciousness of man. Hence understanding and mastery of the body is synonymous with the mastery of the external universe. This is the basis for the magical claims of Tantrik yogis. As an assumption it has much to recommend it, if it is taken symbolically; for without the brain and organs of man there can be nothing definable as 'universe'. However this argument is not our concern. The second chief element is very much our concern. It is this. That in Tantrism sexual intercourse is practised as a ritual act, and supplies the basic imagery of the religious expression, especially in visual art. Actual sexual intercourse is the basic fact; but at certain stages of religious evolution the intercourse becomes figurative only. Nowadays puritanical and prejudiced opinion is hard at work attempting to obscure the historical truth, and there are plenty of apologists to be found in India and the West who pretend that the sexuality of the Tantra was always only figurative. Some scholars, to their shame, have been guilty of publishing mutilated and expurgated texts, without recording that they have done so. The facts are, however, still clear. It is, perhaps, worth mentioning that these Tantrik customs have something in common with Chinese Taoist practices, as we shall see. Occasionally they are called in Sanskrit *Chināchāra* – 'Chinese customs'. It is doubtful if they can actually be proved to have originated as a whole in China proper.

Fundamental to the ritual intercourse of the Tantrikas is the same old myth that the semen is the actual substance of the divine energy. This semen is to be conserved by the male partner, and it is the semen which is thought to be 'turned back up' to be converted into the radiant energy which ascends into the head. In the Hatha Yoga textbooks there is even one activity, called *Vajroli mūdra,* which a man can learn so as to recover into his body any semen which he discharges during sexual intercourse. One practises it by learning to draw milk up into the urethra. Semen is white, and is called *shukla* – the white. At the same time there is another substance *rakta* – the red – which is supposed to be the female counterpart to the male semen, the essential substance of the female energy. It is probably based on the age-old and universal symbol of the menstrual blood. However the bodies of men and women are supposed to contain both substances, the *shukla* much predominating in the male, the *rakta* in the female. The idea behind many of the ritual acts is to stimulate and set in circulation within one body both elements, and balance them – thus, of course, effectually reconstituting the primal Hermaphrodite of Chapter One.

The purpose of the sexual intercourse ritually performed is to stimulate the sexual and nervous energies of the body. Prolonged actual intercourse does this most efficiently. The male partner has to learn, by practice, to refrain from orgasm, and to prolong his potency. This is anyway something which Oriental men have always felt obliged to do, in order to satisfy the desires of one or many women. The Chinese, also once a polygamous people, do the same. The sage Koka must have had this capacity to a high degree, as I mentioned. However, it does seem, from the inclusion of the *Vajroli mūdra* in the Hatha Yoga books, that total abstention from orgasmic ejaculation was not envisaged. If, as seems likely from certain elements in Hindu Shaktism, and from a passage in the ancient *Bṛihadāraṇyaka Upanishad,* which gives instructions for withdrawal of semen to prevent conception, *Vajroli* is really old, then the idea of totally suppressing male orgasm may well be a foreign intrusion into the age-old Tantrik system, probably Buddhist. *This* may perhaps be a Chinese Taoist element, the *Chināchāra.* Certainly the basic sexuality of Hindu Shaktism, and of many followers of Kṛishṇa, would never have rejected the orgasm altogether. The attempt to banish orgasm from the sexual cults may very well be one more manifestation of puritan anxiety. For the slight lowering of blood-pressure normal after orgasm helps to reinforce the myth that vital energy is actually lost during orgasm (*'post coitum omne animal triste'*!). Here again, it seems, we are up against that fundamental split in the spiritual economy of India that we noticed in Chapter One, between the ideas of those who wish to conserve their energy within themselves, for their personal use, and those who take the wider view of sexual energy, as something genuinely cosmic, which is available to be shared abroad, invoked and reinvoked, and which forges links between man and woman, and men and women. The 'sexual misers' base their practices on the cult of personal aggrandizement through piled up sexual energy converted into *tejas,* and then into *tapas,* power; it is interesting that many of the demons of Hindu mythology were said to be sages, obviously with no moral virtue, who had become immensely powerful simply through the mechanical accumulation of *tapas*. But others, the sexual libertarians, base their beliefs upon the idea that *tejas* is supra-personal, abounding in the cosmos for all to share, so that the experience of sex, complete with orgasm, is the way in which men and women can share in it. The misers look primarily to the inward aspect of the self-as-world (*ātman*), the others look to the outward, Prakṛiti Shakti, the goddess. Generally speaking we may say that the way of the yogīs is the way of the 'misers'. The way of the others is the popular way, the way of the antischolastics, the libertarians, the 'lower classes' even, the way of the Devadāsīs, and of many other sectarian followers of the Goddess. Some of these last have had their cults 'purified' by Brahmin revision and the 'miser' concept has been imposed; but enough survives to show the truth of things. For other regions of the world have produced similar practices. I must point out that here I am interested in getting to the root of the matter, not in repeating the glib, stylized forms of words with which the truth has been overlaid by generations of Brahmin scholastics.

The 'spiritual misers'

It is not possible to say precisely which Yogic sect was actually the first, historically, to develop to the full the spiritual economy of the 'sexual misers'. Certainly we get plenty of evidence for its existence in the Brahmins' literature auxiliary to the Veda, such as the Brahmaṇas – though not in the Veda itself, I fancy. But it was only in the late Middle Ages that this Brahmanical sexual view produced any significant art – and that especially in South India. I have mentioned the legend of Ushas in the last chapter. The first great quantity of art produced by the 'sexual misers', was produced by the Tantrik Buddhists of the Vajrayāna, beginning about AD 600. Vajrayāna means 'way of the *vajra*'. *Vajra* means thunderbolt, diamond, or male organ. The famous Sanskrit formula preserved in Tibet '*Oṃ mani padme Hūṃ*' means *Oṃ* (a spell of cosmic origination) the jewel (diamond = *vajra* = male organ) in the lotus (emblem of the creative feminine organ, like so many flowers) *Hūṃ* (a spell of spiritual impulse). Tantrik Buddhism in a nutshell!

All kinds of speculative interpretations were laid onto that primary image. All the dyads of speculative philosophy and psychological metaphysics came to roost upon it, both Buddhist and later Hindu. Its basic visual representation is the *V* radiant golden couple seated together in sexual intercourse, *mani padme*, the man cross-legged, his arms around the back of the woman who sits facing him, her legs round his waist, her arms holding him. The golden colour of their bodies radiates the *tejas* with which they are filled, their sexual energy aroused, continuously stimulated by intercourse, but 'turned back up' inside of them. The reality behind the image is this. Sometime before AD 600 – probably far earlier – a sect of Buddhist ascetics had begun to flourish. They were probably only adapting older, non-sectarian rituals; they laid claim to magical powers, and these powers were believed actively to benefit the kingdoms where this sect was welcomed and supported. They called themselves Herūkas – male heroes – and Dākinīs – female air-spirits. We have a record, for example, that the Herūkas and Dākinīs were welcomed by a king of the Western Himālayas. Some of their descendants are the Vairagis and Vairagīs of modern India – Hinduized like so many other institutions fostered by the Vajrayāna.

We know something about the customs of the Herūkas and Dākinīs, especially from the *Hevajra Tantra*. Each pair used to spend a year together – and then, at an annual fête somewhere, they would meet together with all the other members of their order in the district, and there they would exchange partners. For, as Buddhists, they were obliged to avoid forming attachments to any person or thing. In one chapter the *Hevajra* gives a list of hand gestures, with their meanings, that the Herūkas and Dākinīs might use to communicate with one another in the presence of the public, to make their private arrangements in pairing off for the following year. The couples would spend the major part of their time during the year in performing yogic postures, cultivating the inner 'powers' of their own bodies, and engage in meditation during prolonged sexual connexion. It is particularly interesting that stories recorded about the great saints of the Tantrik tradition, which have been preserved in Tibet, suggest that the female Dākinīs were very frequently women of great spiritual power, not always but often beautiful, who granted initiations to high spiritual grades to aspiring saints, both by teaching and by sexual connexion with themselves. They are represented often as frequenting the cremation grounds outside villages and towns at night, where ordinary folk would be afraid to go. On occasion they might be the actual wives of great teachers, who transmitted something of the power of the masculine teacher to the pupil when the latter had connexion with them. Potions, containing the teacher's own magical semen, might also be drunk by the pupil – another means of transmitting the substance of radiant spiritual energy. This nuclear fact is expressed in a very wide range of imagery and cult which has survived especially in Bengal and Bihar down to modern times. It explains many features of religious ideas which have hitherto seemed to have little to do with one another, and many of the strange conceptions which have been twined into an abstract, theoretical garland of imagery in later texts. I shall try and explain the different aspects this cult of sexual yoga and initiation presents, in order.

100

Graveyard imagery

IX (right)
111
First: the imagery of the crematorium, the boneyard and various kinds of corpse-ritual. This is of absolutely fundamental importance and appears in countless works of art. For all the great Indian religions, including Vajrayāna Buddhism, teach that spiritual success, the ultimate achievement which triumphs over death and time – we might call it final psychological integration – demands that the person cut himself off from all emotional ties, from all theoretical fantasies, and from all fond attachment to consoling ideas which might bolster up his small personal ego as distinct from the total universe. Many people can chatter happily about doing this, and can speculate freely about 'ultimate principles' and 'release'. But they do not live according to their protestations of belief. Their lives remain

156

IX Miniatures, Kangra style, Panjab hills, *c.* 1800. (*Right*) The dark Goddess tramples the God's inert body in the cremation ground. (*Left*) Kṛishṇa and his queen make love
X (*overleaf left*) Small gilt bronze image from Tibet, 17th-18th centuries. The Buddha whose essence is the *Vajra* in *Yab-Yum*

obstinately fixed in ruts of self-indulgence and self-congratulation. The Herūkas and their descendants believed, quite correctly, that a man's spiritual achievement depends not on what he says or thinks, but on how he lives. And as the central tenet of Buddhism is that attachment is the source of failure and misery, and non-attachment the only hope of salvation, the Herūkas carried this principle to its logical conclusions. For they saw, again correctly, that all 'good religious folk' failed to detach themselves from consoling images of themselves as both respectable and clean. In India they failed to detach themselves from their caste-prejudices. Therefore the Herūkas demanded that their members should succeed in breaking down these last insidious attachments by defiling themselves deliberately, and outraging all respectable conventions. At the same time, they should cut themselves off from the living, and become as the dead, dead to themselves, uniting their bodies (sexually) to the image of death. In India it was only the lowest of the low who could touch a corpse or enter the crematorium. Legend tells us of fastidious high Brahmin initiates who were required by their teachers to drink from an open drain, to copulate with outcaste women, to sit in meditation on – or in – putrefying corpses. Thus only could all the last vestiges of self-congratulation be washed away. India, I have said, was always a land of extremes. And even today it is by no means unheard of for high-caste men or women to earn the violent hatred of their social peers by enlisting in the ranks of the various orders of modern Hindu yogīs who are the spiritual descendants of the Buddhist Herūkas and Dākinīs. There are such orders as the Aghorīs, who are said to live naked and eat corpses, Kāpālikas, who always carry a skull, and the Vairagīs and Vairagīs, who perform ritual copulation with little regard for public opinion. It is certainly true that Hindu orders are as old as the Buddhist, almost certainly older. But they are not so well documented. Certain medieval Hindu temples do bear sculptures of *44/77* naked women, of high sexual interest, who wear garlands of skulls and are called Yoginīs. They may very well represent the Hindu counterpart of the Buddhist Dākinīs. The ritual which all the sects had in common, and which became the nucleus of their cult, was sexual meditation among the corpses.

The meaning of the sexual image

These realities lie behind the immense efflorescence of beautiful visual art connected with the Tantra. Vajrayāna Buddhism evolved a vast iconography of divine *99* principles, which personalized the various categories of Buddhist psychology and metaphysics. This iconography was employed in the visualizations which accompanied the meditative rituals and liturgies which the religious orders performed. It was invented in India, and after the obliteration of Buddhism in India in the twelfth century at the hands of an alliance of Moslem invaders and native Hindus, it was preserved in Tibet and the states of the Indian Himālayas, such as Nepal, Bhutan and Sikkim. Buddhas, who personify the abstract mental elements out of which the universe is compounded, may appear arranged on the petals of a cosmic *102* lotus, each in sexual conjunction with a feminine counterpart, who is seated with spread legs upon his lap, her back presented. Such images may be painted, or cast

161

XI (*preceding page right*) Gilt bronze image from Tibet, 17th-18th centuries. Knowledge-holding deity as *Yab-Yum*, possessed by the 'Great Passion', decked with graveyard imagery
XII Album miniature. The Nāyikā as embodiment of the love of all creatures. Kotah state, Rājasthān, *c.* 1780

in bronze, for example, and have their own symbolic colours. Some of the principles may be shown dancing and copulating at once. Often they have many hands, heads or arms. This is meant to indicate their symbolic multivalency. The copulation itself represents what can only be called their 'potentiation'; it is meant to show that knowledge of them actually consists in the state of active, blissful conjunction. For the notion that a sexual division and conjunction extends through the whole fabric of the universe was present here too. The conjunction must repeat itself in every cosmic image or principle. The axiom 'what a man meditates upon, that he becomes' was applied both directly, and, as it were, in reverse. For a member of the religious orders who sought to lose his narrow self and become identified with the fabric of the cosmos could meditate upon each of the principles, whilst he associated with his female counterpart, and, thus meditating, 'become' the principle, completed by his feminine 'wisdom' or *Tārā*. Each stage of his spiritual advance would be marked by sexual rituals. In all these Buddhist practices orgasm was strictly inhibited, and the ejaculatory fluid was supposed to be converted into the *Bodhichitta* – the 'enlightenment-consciousness' – which was not merely intellectual or mental, but in the fullest way sensory and emotional.

This is the meaning of a certain class of images which has often been misunderstood. These are the so-called 'wrathful' deities so often represented in Tantrik art from India, Nepal and Tibet. Such deities are schematic counterparts to the peaceful Buddhas and their female associates; but they are represented with faces contorted with violent feeling, enveloped in radiant aureoles of flame. They are of two main kinds – the knowledge-holders, who, generally speaking, are human-like, but with many arms, and the true 'wrathful' deities, who have extravagantly bestial attributes like snouts, horns and colossal bellies. Sometimes, when they are shown alone, the males display erect sexual organs, the females large, engorged vulvas. But more usually they are represented dancing, paired in copulation, the males facing towards the spectator, the females backwards. They gaze intently into each other's faces with wild grimaces. The meaning of these figures is not 'anger', but passion in the generic sense. They are possessed by the *mahārāga*, the 'great feeling', i.e. the physiological bliss of enlightenment. They are the visible embodiment of those sexual powers that have been turned-back-up and converted into 'spiritual rocket-fuel'. They are ideal images of the inner nature of the devotee, in the condition of blissful insight into the true nature of one or the other of the cosmic principles – Time, for example, or universal Compassion. They are always associated with 'graveyard emblems' – skull-cups full of steaming blood, flayed human hides, garlands of human heads and hands, thighbone sceptres and so on. These indicate their command over and indifference to the facts of death and corruption. This, supposedly, is what energy, sexual in its origin, can become when it is diverted from its normal end of orgasm and converted into *tapas*, and ultimately *Bodhichitta*. One specially interesting fact is this. Many of the small Nepalese and Tibetan bronze images of the wrathful copulating couples can be dismantled, as they were made in separate parts. In some cases the sexual organs of the male and female partners have been exchanged. They engage, but in the reverse direction. This must represent a complex image of sexual exchange and complementation.

I have indicated the factual basis of this religion, the Vajrayāna, in sexual yoga. But I mentioned also that the sexual imagery did become abstract, and was divorced from the outward physiological realities of sexual intercourse and the bodily practices of sexual yoga. One of the famous Dohas, the religious hymns of the proto-Bengali poet Sarāhapāda, who was a Vajrayāna master, asks 'What need have I of an outer woman?' and refers to the 'inner *Dombī*' with whom he sports night-long in his throat. This, of course, implies that there were those who did use outer women, who were often *Dombīs*, women of the very low, defiling caste of washerwomen. But its main emphasis is on the 'inner woman'. And this concept represents the culmination of the imagery of sexual yoga.

It is based upon the famous 'serpent power', *Kundalinī*, about which there has been mystical lucubration. In fact the image is closely connected with the general theory of old Indian medicine. The human body is held to have a kind of subtle internal structure, a pattern of energies which controls the functioning of the whole organism. This is based upon a central nervous channel which runs up the centre of the spine, called the *Sushumnā*. At successive levels there are centres where the energies of each particular bodily section reside. These are called *chakras* – 'wheels' – and are represented as lotus flowers with different numbers of coloured petals. Different traditions give different numbers of *chakras*. The most generally accepted gives six: that with four petals in the perineum – the base of the pelvis; then one at the genitals with six petals; one at the navel with eight; one at the heart with twelve; one in the throat with sixteen; one behind the forehead – with two petals only. Finally, in the crown of the head, one with a thousand petals. These can be tentatively interpreted as based on autoscopous images of actual spinal ganglia. For the purposes of yoga, however, they must be very clearly 'realized' by the imagination in all their symbolic glory.

At the base of the *Sushumnā*, in the lowest *chakra,* there is supposed to reside a 'force', an 'energy', which is considered as female. Normally, in the ordinary man, this force is supposed to sleep in the lowest *chakra*, its energy being dissipated in ordinary desires and activities. However, the various postures, muscular contractions and breathing exercises of Hatha Yoga are supposed to concentrate the energies of this force, and drive it into the *Sushumnā*. In the late Hindu texts which are our main source for information about this practice this female force is called *Kundalinī*, and is represented as a serpent. The image may indeed be old, in some ways similar to the serpent which so often symbolizes the living spinal marrow or *psychē* of the ancient Greek hero at his tomb. However, in the Vajrayāna rituals it is the femine aspect of this force which is important. It is driven by yoga and meditation to ascend the *Sushumnā*, gradually gaining in power and passion, up through the *chakras*, absorbing the energies of each as it passes, leaving the lower regions of the body cold and inert. The relationship of this 'force' to the spiritualized semen of the male yogin is inwardly sexual. Certainly there is in this subtle physiology a second male–female image involved – the 'sun' and 'moon' of the right and left sides, channels through which the vital breath normally circulates but is brought to balance. It seems probable that in Vajrayāna the female force, the *Kundalinī*, was brought up to the throat *chakra*, there to encounter the spiritualized masculine essence of the yogin's own body in an imaginary, blissful sexual relationship. The last stage of enlightenment would raise this internal couple into the thousand petalled lotus in the crown of the head. When Buddhism was expelled from India this yoga survived; the roles of male essence and feminine power were attributed to Shiva and his wife Pārvatī, personifications of two ancient philosophical concepts, the Purūsha and Prakṛiti. This we shall discuss later on.

The enigmatic image which sums up the erotic secret which Buddhist Tantrism handed on to later Hinduism is contained in a story in one Tantra. The sage Vashishtha, as a reward for his devotion to the Goddess, is granted a visit to the Buddha – here interpreted as one of the incarnations of the Hindu deity Vishṇu. He enters the great country of China, and there sees the Buddha, his eyes drooping and reddened with wine, surrounded by beautiful girls in gorgeous clothes; they are in a state of amorous ecstasy, and the Buddha and his naked followers continuously enjoy them. Vashishtha is deeply perplexed by this for he has been brought up in a strictly puritan tradition. It is explained to him that his own ideas are of an inferior and undeveloped character. The highest rites are those he now witnesses, with wine and sexual intercourse, and meat-eating. What Vashishtha is *65/67/68/69/70* being shown is the doctrine of the Kaulas, whom we have encountered before in a relief on the Lakshmaṇa temple at Khajuraho. Their doctrines and practices supply the link between the cult of the Vajrayāṇa, and the Shākta rituals revolving around the image of the Goddess, which has played an important role in the history of the religion of North-Eastern India since about AD 1100.

The Great Goddess

107 The basis of this religion and its art is this: the entire world consists of the body of the Goddess. She is the creative power whose activity is at work endlessly producing forms, weaving them out of the tissue of her own body. Within her womb is the fertilizing seed of the remote masculine deity. This seed is by itself uncreative. For the male deity, so far as the world is concerned, is passive, absent, corpse-like. The means of knowing this Goddess are at once philosophical and erotic. And thus to know her is to understand the meaning of the process which Western theology has hidden under the blanket term 'creation'.

There must be an element of psychological conditioning, due to the family and social customs under which children are brought up, behind the extravagant adoration accorded to the Mother Goddess in India today. But I should not like here to attempt any glib analysis of what it might be, though I must agree that there is an abyss of psychotic fear behind the adoration. The fact is that many *106* millions of Indians have, during the centuries, felt themselves overwhelmed by an emotion, including both sexual dread and infantile attachment, directed towards the image of the Goddess. This image was the personal focus of both feeling and metaphysics. The metaphysics was not of that kind familiar in the Western world, which attempts to remove the world from man, and present it as an abstract (i.e. dead, crystalline) categorical truth. This notion of 'Truth' is in fact an interesting psychotic product of Western culture – itself symbolic. The Indian idea of metaphysical truth in question here is very different. It is one which, it is said, makes even the random talk of a man who knows it 'full of the sweet nectar of poetry', so that 'numerous women with large, deer-eyes, impatient for his love, pursue him'.

The Indian word for the adoration with which the Goddess – like other deities – was regarded is *Bhakti*. This is often translated as 'devotion'. But that pallid English word by no means conveys the kind of feeling an Indian offers to his personal deity. I have mentioned how sexually attractive the Indian images of *108* deities are. And when it is the Goddess who is adored the sexual element is most vivid.

The Tantrik Goddess is called by Hindus Shakti. This comes from the root √*shak*, to be able. The name means, roughly, power. There are many Shaktis, but they all reduce in the Hindu mind to the one maternal Shakti, the Goddess, who represents the power that weaves the Universe. And since the Universe is a product of the self, as we have seen, then the Goddess Shakti works from and through the self of man. She is internal and external at once. Certainly this Indian Goddess must represent an image of the whole vast realm of the unconscious mind, with its analogical structures, which are the matrix of intelligible forms; and, as Western psychology acknowledges, a preliminary regressive attachment of the libido to the maternal image of the unconscious is a prerequisite for ultimate psychic success. Shakti is said to be 'always united in inverted posture (i.e. herself *111* on top) with the God Shiva who represents the *Saguna-brahman*' – that is, the existential ground endowed with qualities or attributes. This couple rests upon the more remote ground of existence which is *Nirguna-brahman* – that is, the Brahman which is beyond qualities or attributes, and so is without qualities. In this posture, seated upright with the seminal lingam of Shiva embedded in her yoni, 'she becomes passionate, and being herself active . . . enhances her own bliss with waves of natural pleasure'. Such is 'creation'.

This image occurs very frequently in the art of Eastern India, right down to modern times. The Goddess, beautiful and terrible at once, straddles the body of one Shiva, who is shown as alive, moving, with the colours of the living. He represents the Brahman *with* qualities. Beneath him lies another Shiva, shown as dead, inert, with the greenish tint of the corpse. He represents the Brahman without qualities. This scene is usually shown taking place in the cremation ground, which we know to be the place of the dissolution of the self. It is also called the yoni of the Goddess. For it is here that all apparent realities are destroyed – to be born once more.

Once again we can look behind the image to the realities of religious cult. For when Vajrayāna Buddhism vanished from Eastern India in the thirteenth century AD Hindu cults which shared many of its practices, and some of its iconography, were in full flower. Devotees of the Hindu Goddess haunted the cremation grounds, and there performed long acts of ritual sexual intercourse, during which they identified themselves with Shiva and Shakti, the transcendent couple, with the help of spells recited to the rosary. They too performed the *mūdras* of Hatha Yoga, the *Kuṇḍalinī* rites, and *parāvṛitti*. At the same time they cultivated an intense feeling of erotic adoration towards the divinity personified by their partners.

They accepted that such activity was able to identify them with the deity of their own sex. There are known sets of illustrations to major Tantrik texts in which the loves of Shiva and Shakti, in many of the canonical postures, are illustrated as an incentive to the ritual intercourses of the followers of this religion. For the cult did not require that the sexual relationship should be grey, pious and unrewarding. In fact its religious purpose could only be fulfilled if it was fully experienced as true erotic bliss.

For this reason the divine anthropomorphic images of this cult must express the canonical ideals of sexual beauty. Shiva is always divinely handsome, as a man. The Goddess is also divinely beautiful, a woman about sixteen years old. She 'shines like the lotus', as the *Devī Bhagavatam* says, 'her loins challenge the moon, her thighs surpass the plantain tree, her breasts are like bel-fruits'. She is calm, sweet-smiling, passionate towards her husband, and she walks with the heavy grace of the elephant. With her husband she continually enjoys endless amorous delight. Often, in the art, this Goddess is represented as a normal, beautiful woman. But often, especially in Bengal, she is shown as Kālī, the black-bodied destructive goddess, garlanded with human heads and hands, whose womb is Time, who has a lolling red tongue, an angry face, and projecting fangs. But she is *also* beautiful, sexually desirable and sexually aroused. The psychosexual response of the beholder to such an image is most complex and interesting. For this Goddess is worshipped with rituals of bloodshed. Goats, buffaloes, pigeons and men should be offered to her, decapitated with a characteristic, heavy, curved sword before her image in the shrine. The texts point out that these creatures are surrogates for the offerer's own self and its baser passions. And, incidentally, as creatures they are supposed to go straight to post-mortem bliss.

Behind the image are yet more significant facts. It is the custom amongst followers of the Goddess to worship, as images of her, young virgins of great bodily beauty who have certain special attributes. Fundamentally, all women are paradigms of her, but the most evocative for ritual purposes are these virgins. It is also true that amongst certain sects of the Shāktas it was the custom on certain occasions for a specially endowed woman – who was not a virgin – to assume the role of the Goddess by means of invocations and prayers, and then to receive the worship of a group of male devotees, during which she would take each one in sexual intercourse. In other rituals of the same type, the *Chakrapūjas* or circular-rites, male and female couples – who may or may not be husband and wife – worship the representative of the Goddess, take a eucharist of wine, fish, meat, and cereals, which has been dedicated to the Goddess. They then perform ritual sexual intercourse, often exchanging partners around the circle, to confirm the supra-personal nature of the rite. These rituals have been reported by Indian and European writers alike with shuddering horror, and often with pious dishonesty. Even the greatest of their apologists, Sir John Woodroffe (Arthur Avalon), has taken care heavily to stress the purely religious, non-orgiastic nature of the rites. Many of the source-texts go to great pains to point out that such rituals are dangerous if performed by people who are not highly enough developed to perform them properly. But at the same time it is important to remember once again that such rituals are not effective if they are not blissful. Indians love and live by rituals. They do not think of them as grey and restrictive, but as a means of self-fulfilment.

So there is no reason to suppose that such *Chakrapūjas* were anything but pleasing in the highest possible degree to the participants, as well as deeply satisfying in a psychological and religious sense. There would have been no need for so many theological warnings against 'orgies' perpetrated by low-class religious folk, had not such 'orgies' taken place. For popular religion in India has often made a feature of sexual orgies, which would seem scandalous to the eyes of 'sexual misers' but were in fact quite authentic religious expressions in their own right.

Sex as philosophy

In order to explain the more schematic works of art that have originated from this Shākta environment we shall have to look again at the philosophical conceptions with which the idea of the Goddess is invested. This is a very interesting thing to do, as it raises questions which are too seldom raised about all philosophy, as to the extent to which philosophical ideas are not, and never can be, 'eternal verities', all embracing and absolutely true, but are actually psychological symbols charged with libido, having a direct relationship with the psychic structure of the individuals who hold them. In fact the association of a philosophical outlook with the highly erotic imagery of the Goddess in Indian thought must represent a psychological phenomenon of the very first importance.

A passage in the huge *Devī Bhagavatam Purāṇa* illustrates the idea beautifully. The creator god Brahmā tells the story of how he, with other male deities, visited the Goddess to see her. At first they were not sure whether perhaps She was not one of the Apsarases, so beautiful She was, seated on Her cot, in red clothes, jewelled and radiant-faced. As the gods approached Her they were themselves turned into beautiful women, and realized that She was surrounded by millions of other women, all forms and manifestations of Herself. As She smiled at them affectionately the deities suddenly saw in Her pink toe nails a vision of the entire Universe, with its continual waves of movement and change, its cosmoses, oceans and mountains. They stayed there for a hundred years, welcomed as companions by all the attendant women, but happily enchanted by their charms. Vishṇu, who was one of the gods, composed a hymn in honour of the Goddess, in which he praises Her as the great efficient, material cause of all change, manifestation and destruction. For the whole Universe rests upon Her, rises out of Her and melts away into Her. From Her are crystallized the original elements and qualities which construct the apparent world. She is both mother and grave. And what is more, the gods themselves are merely constructs out of Her maternal substance, which is both consciousness and potential joy. This, in Western terms which must be depersonalized, is tantamount to recognizing that the world is fabricated from the maternal substance of the organism, which is both the instrument and product of its own complex but non-material inherent formal principles. One passage of Vishṇu's hymn is specially enlightening. 'Now' he says:

> I realize that only you are the ancient eternal Prakṛiti (Nature, or Form-and-change); from staying with you I see that it is *you* who mercifully teach the

knowledge of the Brahman to the ancient Purūsha . . . and only thus can he realize his eternal nature. Otherwise he will always remain under the delusion that he is the Lord, the Purūsha without beginning, the good and universal soul, and so he falls into all the (ruinous) forms of egoism . . . It is you, mother, who have put out from yourself the representation of all the visible worlds for the spiritual benefit of living creatures, playing all the parts . . . in the theatrical play.

He also refers to the Sāṅkhya system of philosophy as being the key to this vision of truth.

Now the source book of the Sāṅkhya philosophy is the *Sāṅkhyakārikā* of Īshvara-krishna, and in this book is enshrined a philosophical image which serves as a key to much of the erotic art devoted to the Goddess. The basis of Sāṅkhya is briefly this. The 'world', as an experienced fact, can be seen as a combination of two principles, both of which are eternal. One, Purūsha, is the pure, unqualified self. The other is Prakṛiti, Nature, who by means of a great mesh of expanding and interacting principles, ensnares each Purūsha in a delusory universe of reality. Release, the final spiritual goal, consists according to classical Sāṅkhya in the total withdrawal of the Purūsha from any engagement with Prakṛiti into his pure self-hood. This Prakṛiti, however, serves selflessly to nourish the spirit just as milk does the calf. And in the end, like a dancer who has shown herself, and satisfied her audience, understood for what she is, her role finished, she withdraws from view, leaving the spirit in the solitary splendour of release. The classical Sāṅkhya is thus one of those 'spiritual miser' religions of Brahmanical type. However it was the
104 Sāṅkhya system that was taken over by the sexual religion of the Shiva-Shakti cult, Shiva being identified with Purūsha, and the Goddess with Prakṛiti. The relationship between the two principles was thus completely revised and reinterpreted in the light of the image of the primal loving couple. The creative and revelatory role of Prakṛiti, Nature, was exalted with warm affection, and whilst the eternal nature of the two principles was preserved, their mutual engagement was also recognized as eternal, according to the ancient images of the Upanishads. Prakṛiti thus became a warm and vital personalized conception, which is nearer to Schelling's early idea of Nature than to the dead matter of other post-Aristotelian philosophy in the West.

Now the process by which the divine female Prakṛiti was supposed to evolve the material world was clearly mapped out in Sāṅkhya philosophy. The various stages of the process demanded the evolution of successive principles, which were often personalized as feminine deities. Art frequently shows these feminine deities arranged in a schematic fashion, to illustrate the process of creation. Three of the principles especially are very often shown. They are the three *guṇas,* the qualities according to which all matter and events develop. They are symbolized by colours, black, red and white, and are: the principle of inert passive weight and darkness, called *tamas*; the principle of blazing motion, violence and passion, called *rajas*; and the principle of radiant tranquillity, balance and harmony, called *sattva*. One
110 of our illustrations, which is typical of many, shows how these principles of existence are personified as goddesses emanating from the original Prakṛiti, who crouches in sexual union with her impassive Purūsha, whilst from her spring the

three goddesses, coloured like the *guṇas*. The dark one, Tamas, also wears the aspect of Kālī, the goddess of destroying Time.

The body of the Goddess is thus the centre of an intense erotic interest, and the deep roots of the Universe in the structural formulations of the human mind share in this interest. All women, but especially the avowed representatives of the Goddess, such as the Devīs of the *Chakrapūja*, the Shaktis of the devotees, and the heirs of the temple prostitutes, served as paradigms to this philosophical vision of Nature. Reality – not merely the reality of everyday categories, but the reality of unconscious perceptions, patterns and structures – benefits. For it attracts to itself the libido of its followers, amongst whom are numbered the devotees of many modern orders, such as the Nātha Siddhas, the followers of the Dharma cult, as well as all the orthodox Shākta congregations. The religion of the Goddess is thus one of the powerful forces in Indian culture which acts in dialectical opposition to the principle of 'spiritual miserliness'. It has been an essential counterpoise to that deadly schematicism and self-absorbed solipsism which has been one of the constant bugbears of Indian spirituality, devaluing the panorama of Nature, and inculcating a false idea of 'enlightenment' that lacks both a vision of the whole and bliss. It could well serve as a basis for the development of a worldly technology of a purely Indian kind. For, as Ortega y Gasset has observed, without affect there is no interest. And interest in the operation of the Goddess is what India most lacks today.

VIII (*right*)

5 The Legacy of Krishna

Krishna

Perhaps the most fertile of all the Indian erotic traditions, producing an immense quantity of art, has been the literary and religious cult of Krishna. Its great strength has always been its all-embracing eroticism, its cult of personal emotion, and its enlistment of all the arts in its cause. There survive at the present day an enormous number of works of erotic art, chiefly miniature paintings, which owe their origin in one way or another to Krishna. Amongst the Rājasthān and Panjab miniature album pictures, which are now very well known, there are literally thousands of beautiful examples. And it seems likely that almost every series of pictures devoted to the life of Krishna originally included erotic pictures where the story called for them.

The cult of Krishna is based entirely upon love. As we know it today, and as medieval India first became aware of it, it was incorporated in a few important literary works which had been composed in the learned Brahmin vein. But research has enabled us to trace the history of the cult to its origins. For it seems that Krishna was originally the deity of a small group of aboriginal people who, like other similar deities, was forced upon the attention of Brahmin priest-scholars by his immense popularity. The Brahmins of the early Middle Ages were obliged to find a place for him in their theological system, and with their usual syncretic skill, they brought him into it, as they did the Buddha, by identifying him as one of the incarnations of the major deity, Vishnu. This adaptation gave great impetus to the whole cult, and added a deep metaphysical dimension to a religion which was in its origins innocent of any intellectual pretensions. It also introduced adaptations which brought the whole story into line with religious and social orthodoxy.

We can decipher the basic pattern of the Krishna cult from the actual stories told about him in his literature, using comparative methods. For amongst aboriginal (*adivāsī*) peoples of modern India, and in other parts of the world, similar cults and legends survive. It is probable that the literature of Krishna originated in groups of songs which were sung about a hero of the Ābhīra people who lived near what is now Brindaban on the banks of the River Yamunā during the first millennium BC. They were a nomadic, cattle-herding people, and their hero was a cowherd. He was a champion warrior, who rescued his people and their cows from all kinds of demons. But above all he was a champion lover. For his main festival seems to have been a springtime dance-festival, when the men and women performed together a circular dance, singing highly licentious songs, and coupling freely in the forest. The springtime festival survives today as Holī, which is gradually being turned into a fairly boisterous carnival-procession, whose only vestige of sexual licence, as I have mentioned, is the squirting of coloured powder and water, which symbolize the spreading abroad of sexual energy. But not so very long ago in towns of Northern India Holī was still the occasion of wild, orgiastic licence, when crowds surged through the streets carrying sexual emblems, chanting highly erotic songs, with bodies of women offering to groups of men sexual challenges which were freely taken up in the name of Kṛishṇa. Thus was the divine vitality of sex spread abroad and freely shared by the populace.

As time went on, and particularly when the early songs and ballads came into the hands of Brahmin scholars, who incorporated them into their encyclopedias of legend, the Purāṇas, the Kṛishṇa legends crystallized into a more or less coherent biography. This process was taking place during the first few centuries of the Christian era. But even as it went on, the cult's popularity increased vastly, and all sorts of additions were made. By about AD 1100 the legend was virtually complete.

This legend as we now have it contains many accretions. Parts of it, especially those recording the god's victories over various 'demons' or older deities, clearly reflect something of the historical progress of the cult. Kṛishṇa himself is essentially a folk hero of great charm, a doer of good, friend of his followers, enemy to their enemies. But around him there is gathered the aura of divinity in the Indian sense, with all its various emotional overtones. It is indeed said that the followers of Kṛishṇa can love him as a child, wife, mother, husband or heroic companion at their own choice. But they must love him. Their love can be of the fullest, most frankly sexual kind. And it will be to them the purest delight. As can be seen in all the paintings, Kṛishṇa's natural habitat is the landscape of spring, where love prevails, all is joy, and Kṛishṇa himself ensures that nothing disturbs the enchantment of the world. For love converts all actual landscape into the heavenly region, a celestial parallel to Brindaban.

He was born the son of Vasudeva and Devakī. His half-brother, Balarāma, who was born to another of Vasudeva's wives, is also recognized in Brahmin tradition as a divine incarnation of the great serpent Ananta, symbol of the negative ground of Eternity, on whom Vishṇu sleeps, out beyond time and the manifest world. The king at Mathurā, Kaṃsa, a horrible tyrant, had been warned by a voice from heaven that his death would come by a child of Vasudeva's wife, Devakī. He therefore conducted a hideous inquisition and massacred Devakī's children one by one. But by devious means the divine child, the seventh, was saved from death at Kaṃsa's hands, and was handed over to the care of Yashodhā, wife of the cowherd Nanda among the lowly Ābhīras on the other side of the River Yamunā, at Brindaban. There Kṛishṇa grew up in peace and safety. (This must be one of the incidents manufactured later to give Kṛishṇa an ancestry acceptable to Brahmin caste-theory.) Today Brindaban is one of the most sacred spots in India, full of temples and crowded with devotees, many of them ascetics who have come to end their lives where Kṛishṇa lived out his.

During his childhood Kṛishṇa performed many prodigies of valour and strength. As a baby he kicked to pieces a heavy cart under which his mother had laid him out of the sun and on which a demon had settled; he dragged over two trees under which two Yakshas had been imprisoned by a spell. He killed a donkey-demon, a bull-demon, a crane-demon, and banished the many headed serpent-demon, Kālīya, whose presence was polluting the waters of the holy Yamunā. He

171

worsted the ancient Brahmin ruler of Heaven, Indra, the Indian equivalent of the classical Zeus, by holding up on one finger the mountain Govardhana to shelter his people and cows from the stupendous rainstorm with which Indra intended to destroy them. The earliest known work of art devoted to Kṛishṇa, a sculptured icon in the pink sandstone of Mathurā (c. AD 350) shows this last aspect of Kṛishṇa, *Govardhanadhara*; it is a triumphant snub to orthodoxy. On the same icon, his aspect as god of the increase of cattle – itself significant in India – is indicated by the small figure of a bull covering a cow.

When he had attained young manhood, Kṛishṇa performed his ultimate task of heroism. Going to a festival where king Kaṃsa was watching wrestling in a compound, Kṛishṇa and Balarāma, two slightly built and handsome youths, first of all defeated Kaṃsa's mountainous professional wrestlers. Then, to crown the exhibition, Kṛishṇa leapt on to Kaṃsa's royal balcony and flung the tyrant down to his death.

This is the heroic side of Kṛishṇa, incarnate god. It is the side which was most represented in the temple carvings of the early Middle Ages. Then, a little later, the other charming side came into prominence, and there gathered that great wave of popular emotion which culminated about AD 1500 in the lives of the great saints Chaitanya and Vallabha, who acquired an immense following.

This other side stresses episodes of charming naughtiness in Kṛishṇa's childhood when, for example, he steals butter from his mother's churn for himself and his friends. Then, as he grows up he becomes as a youth so divinely beautiful, such a transcendent musician on his flute, that all the married women and girls of the Ābhīras – the Gopīs or cowgirls – cannot help falling in love with him. They watch for him whenever he goes out, or comes home at sunset, driving his father's cattle at the 'hour of cowdust'. He plays tricks on them. He makes them pay toll of their milk and butter. One day, while the Gopīs are all bathing together in the Yamunā naked, he steals their clothes and climbs a tree. When they discover his theft he teases them for their modesty and forces them to come up out of the water to him, to raise their hands and uncover their secret parts before he will let them have back their clothes. Finally he courts, wins and copulates frequently and gloriously with all of them. They experience all the possible varieties of longing, anticipation, delight, jealousy and relief.

The culmination of his prolonged love affair with the village girls is the occasion of the 'round dance', at the springtime festival – commemorated today at Holī. One day he is playing his flute. Gradually the fascination of his music gathers around him the women of Brindaban. He leads them into the forest, then suddenly vanishes. In passionate despair they run through the dense undergrowth, tearing their bare feet on thorns, their bodies and their clothes on briars, wailing and calling for him. Suddenly he reappears, and they are content. They gather in a circle round him and to the music of his flute they dance the round dance. During it, each one of them is sure that Kṛishṇa is dancing, and finally making love, with her alone. But this magical self-multiplication is not the only such magic Kṛishṇa employed. Later legends relate, obviously to combat a logistic complication, that while the girls were with Kṛishṇa, by his powers he projected into her own home an image of each of them who was married, so that her husband believed she was in fact there. This sexual dance is supposed to really be eternal. Thus scope is

112

172

XIII Album miniature. Kṛishṇa and Rādhā make love in the flowering forest. Kangṛa style, Panjab hills, c. 1780

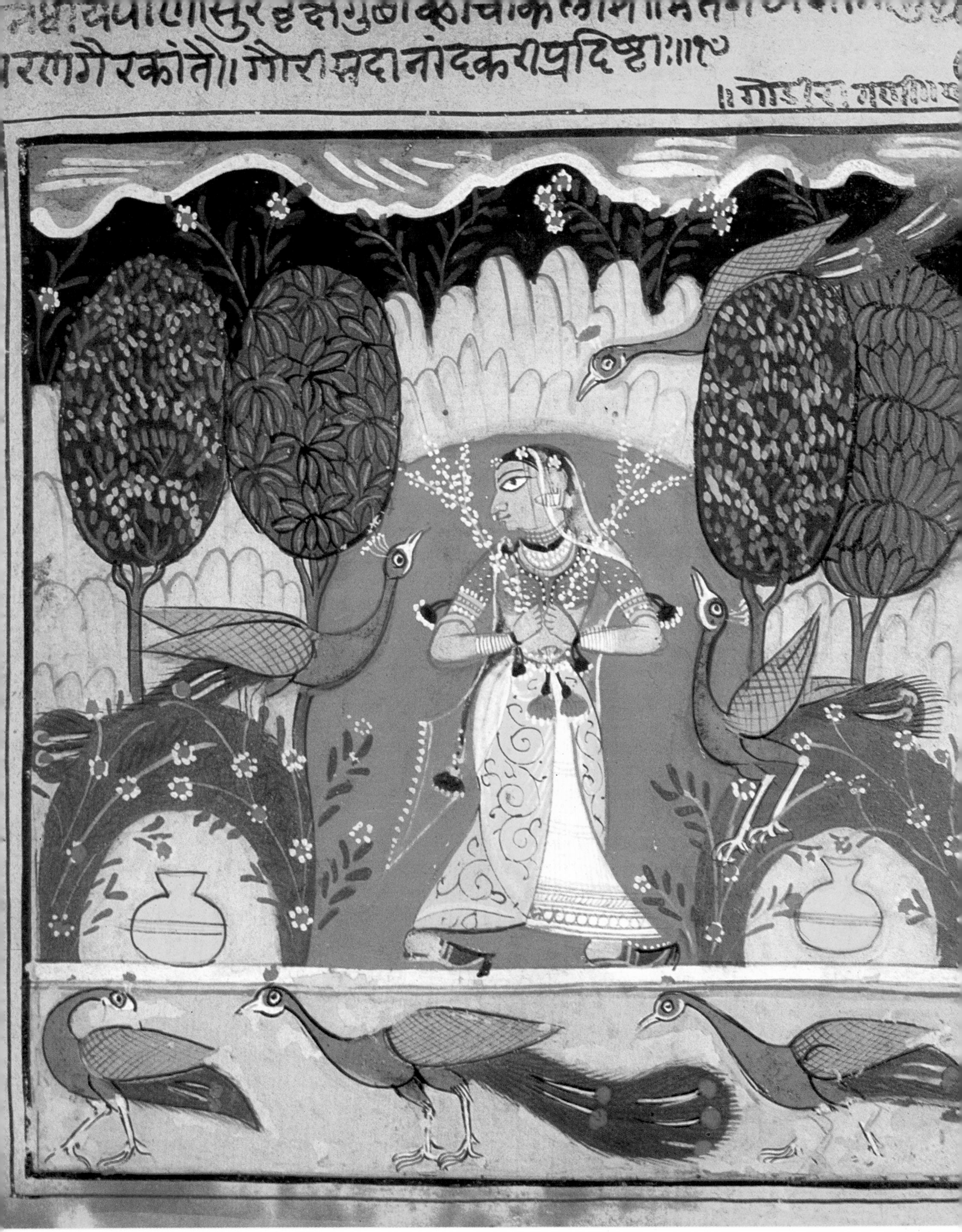
गौरी सदानंदकरी प्रदिष्टा॥

offered for endless artistic variations. For example it may be depicted as 'water *113* sports' during which (according to the *Brahmavaivarta Purāṇa*) Kṛishṇa employs all the canonical postures of sexual intercourse with all the Gopīs.

An interesting extension to the Kṛishṇa legend, in later times forming the second part of his life story, but which is obviously a parallel development of a rather less socially scandalous character, represents Kṛishṇa as abandoning his humble village girls after Kaṃsa's death, and becoming king himself. Enthroned, he marries sixteen thousand one hundred wives, as an Eastern monarch may, and satisfies each of them by the exercise of this same self-multiplying power. His 'death' was a willed one.

The allegory of love

In fact it was the scandalous episodes in Brindaban with the Gopīs that occupied *XIII* the imagination of Indian poets and theologians. From the time of the great *Gīta Govinda* by the poet Jayadeva (later twelfth century AD), in most of the vernacular languages of India, an enormous quantity of violently amorous love-poetry was produced which dealt with all the possible minutiae of physical passion, with desertion, despair, hope, anticipation, all imaginable enjoyments and delights; with toilet, clothing, disordered dress; with lingering glances, legs heavy with passion, small pink-palmed wandering hands, kisses like bees plunging into the perfumed clouds of black hair. In most of this poetry one of the Gopīs above all is represented as the chief love of Kṛishṇa; Rādhā, the wife of cowherd Āyana-ghosha. She is the heroine of far the greatest number of poems and paintings and her great beauty and passion are the subject of innumerable rhapsodies:

> With her jewels abundant her limbs she adorns and spreads out her bed
> Imagining you on her fluttering couch of leaves,
> And so to indulge, in a hundred ways, in the sport of love
> She is fully resolved, arranging her bed with every adornment;
> Not another night may that beautiful girl endure without you.
> Why so much apathy, Kṛishṇa, beside the fig tree?
> O brother, why not go to the pasture of eyes, the abode of bliss?

One point that anyone looking at Kṛishṇa paintings will notice is that the God is shown as having a dark-blue complexion. The most probable explanation is that 'Kṛishṇa', which means 'the dark one', was a name this god was given in Hindu society by reason of his lowly origin among the Ābhīras. Generally speaking, lightness of skin colour is accepted as a natural concomitant of high caste, darkness with low. But Kṛishṇa appears in these paintings not simply as dark, but as blue. The blue must contain a reference to his spiritual prototype, Vishṇu, whose incarnation he is, and whose most subtle and pervading presence supplies the ground of being for all that exists. Vishṇu's symbolic colour is blue, the colour of the empty sky. The supreme image of the Vajrayāna, Vajradhāra, was also blue of body, embraced by a white female.

Once Kṛishṇa was recognized by the Brahmins as incarnate God, his legend was

XIV Album miniature. Excited and lonely girl in the forest is courted by amorous peacocks. The picture is full of erotically symbolic forms, without being overtly erotic. Central India, late 16th century

not regarded as a saucy tale. It came to be seen as an allegory of the relationship of humanity to God, and the passion of sexual love the art depicts, like the love imagery employed by the great European mystics, referred to a transcendent relationship, for which there was no other possible expression. In India the attitude of *Bhakti* demands the highest emotions of which man is capable. But since these are rarely achieved, and since language is made in the market place, the resources of language offer only the imagery of physical love for the mystic's use.

India is a land where age-long tradition regards the things that compose the world as intrinsically devoid of reality, as real only by virtue of a transcendental power perpetually at play presenting them. Form is apparent; only the transcendent Real is real. The principle of form is part only of the Real. Since, to the followers of Krishna, the ultimate Real personified in the God Vishnu made himself apparent in a contingent form as Krishna, this contingent form provides, as it were, a pathway or an opening into the transcendent Real. Earnest, self-abandoning devotion, an attachment that rejects as the Gopīs did all considerations of shame, comfort and social decency, can lead the human soul out of everyday humanity into the transcendent by the same path or opening as God entered the everyday world, in the guise of Krishna. Among the followers of Krishna there arose many curious forms of ritual, many of them owing much to the Tantrik traditions we discussed in the last chapter.

In India, that land of extremes, every possible implication of the Krishna story was ultimately realized in life, usually by a religious order founded by a revered saint. One branch of the male following of Chaitanya, for example, pursues the concept that 'all souls are feminine to God' to its last implications. They dress as women, live as women even to the extent of observing a few days retirement each month. They are still to be seen in India (Ramakrishna is perhaps the most famous instance). And they do not, as a European might expect, dress as pious women, but as gay and flighty girls, in pretty saris and jingling bracelets, with elaborate hairdos; they trip about together giggling and blushing – acting out, in fact, the role of Gopīs to the full. Other orders, often called Vairagis and Vairagīs, travel about in couples, performing sexual yoga and living in a permanent condition of violent erotic emotion. They thus play the roles of Krishna and Rādhā in real life. A famous example of this was the great Bengali Brahmin poet Chandīdās, whose partner was Rāmī – a beautiful girl of the extremely low washer-caste, whom to the scandal of the orthodox, he adored as Rādhā. Amongst the religious laity it was common for the rites of love to be performed with an immense emphasis upon the stimulation of intense erotic emotion in order to approach more closely to the love of the divine dyad. *Rasamandalas,* circles for performing love rituals, were formed and during the centuries from about 1500 on there was a great deal of polemic about the respective virtues of the kinds of social relationship between the partners to such erotic religious unions. Should they be married, or should they each be married to another party? The first relationship, where the woman was a man's *svakīyā* – i.e. his own – was held not to produce so satisfactory a state of exaltation as where the woman was *parakīyā* – someone else's. For this latter case was the same as the case of Krishna himself, whose sexual partners were the wives of others; and in fact, to outrage normal social custom by a *parakīyā* relationship was held to set up a closer bond between the partners, and required an unreserved commitment of each to each 'in the world's despite'. Among these Vaishnavas girls particularly skilled in love were highly esteemed.

Another cult was that of the so-called Mahārājas. They were the object of extreme reverence by followers of the sage Vallabhāchārya. They were supposed to be hereditary representatives on earth of Kṛishṇa, and as such were required to have sexual intercourse with the women of their congregations on certain occasions – in particular with unfortunate Hindu widows and with girls who were to be married. It is, of course, certain that in doing this they were merely continuing a traditional practice which was normal in many parts of India during the Middle Ages. But in the nineteenth century one Mahārāja was the object of a famous prurient prosecution in Bombay, at which much evidence of the 'depravity' of the Mahārājas was produced. Incidentally it was obvious even from the prosecution's own witnesses that the custom was the cause of great happiness to many women. Amongst this evidence was the allegation that the saints used paintings of the loves of Kṛishṇa and the Gopīs as an 'aid to the seduction' of the women. This casts an interesting light on the whole matter of the art. For very many of the illustrated manuscripts of the Kṛishṇa literature from many parts of India – for example Rājasthān and Orissa – contain sets of what I have called 'educative postures' at appropriate points. It is very likely that the joint study of a manuscript of one of these great classics of erotic religion was one of the ways in which the everyday fact of sexuality was converted into a paradigm of the cosmic dyad. And the qualities of the paintings were expressly meant to be erotically stimulating. The *4* superb curvilinear style of the Orissan palmleaf and paper manuscripts of the sixteenth to nineteenth centuries offers deeply sensuous diagrams of erotic sensibility.

Kṛishṇa and the arts

In fact all the arts were invoked to aid the cult of Kṛishṇa. Today in Bengal the Bauls, solitary ecstatic mendicants, are known as some of the most inspired musicians in India, who sing their songs in praise of the loves of Kṛishṇa as they wander from village to village. Indeed all the followers of Kṛishṇa make special use of that ancient Indian conception of aesthetic emotion as a genuine way of religious 'release'. They cultivate music, dancing and visual art especially for the purpose of arousing spiritual exaltation – always with a deeply erotic flavour.

The great poet and Kṛishṇa-worshipper Chaitanya developed the technique of the religious *kirtan*, where the worshippers meet in large groups, and, singing Kṛishṇa songs, work themselves into a state of ecstasy. This is, of course, a special type of music with an obviously religious intent. But normal Indian music has a special connexion with Rajput miniature paintings, and with the cult of Kṛishṇa to which they are so intimately related. To understand this, something must be said about the basis of Indian music.

Modern Western tonal music is based on three forms of scale, the major, and the melodic and harmonic minor scales. This limited group of scale forms has become fixed in pattern owing to the Western development of chords, chordal progressions and the concept of key. Older, medieval Western music was often based on the 'modes' of classical antiquity, which can roughly be described as sequences employing the same seven notes of our familiar major scale, in the same order, but starting each on a different degree, and so displaying a different pattern of relationship between the fundamental note and all the others. Each one of these modes was held to have a special realm of feeling of its own. Still earlier, in plainsong and in many folk-melodies, the basis was pentatonic; again the fundamental note of the series used could be any one of the five.

Indian music since the late Middle Ages, being purely melodic and intrinsically monodic, has employed all these Western scale forms, both ancient and modern, as well as many others besides. Some, for example, incorporate even a third between some steps in the series, and quarter tones between others, and most have different patterns in ascent and descent. To each of them are natural certain specific patterns of notes (called *tanas*). Thus each has its special emotional flavour, and is used at appropriate seasons and times of day, with appropriate words if the music is to be sung. These scales or modes are called *ragas*.

Love, laughter, compassion, heroism, anger, fear, disgust, wonder and peace are the nine moods of dramatic art. Similar emotional qualities are given to each of the *ragas* by the emphasis placed on certain of its intervals: 'For laughter and love the fourth and fifth are used; in the heroic mood, in anger and wonder, the tonic, fifth and second. For compassion the minor seventh and minor third; in disgust and fear the sixth; in peace the fourth.' Even the qualities of individual notes of the scale are sometimes indicated. 'The tonic is bright like lotus petals, the second tawny or like a parrot. The minor third is golden and the fourth like jasmine. The fifth is Kṛishṇa – the dark one – and attracts; the sixth is yellow and the minor seventh is many-hued.'

The scales are amplified, and their special qualities enhanced by the use of various patterns of chromatic passing-notes at given places in the scale as the musical line moves upwards or downwards. Since much of the best Indian music is played extempore, and composer and executant are the same person, the scale supplies the fundamental material for the musical structure, and the musician's task is to bring out and display as many of its inherent possibilities as he can. Rhythm supplies the basis in terms of time. Therefore the Ragas, each and every one of them, have been the subject of a great deal of profound meditation, musical and theoretical, and their special emotional qualities have become highly evolved.

Following the deep-rooted Indian habit of personalizing its abstract concepts, and of systematizing knowledge, the Ragas have been identified with men and women of appropriate types, and grouped together. The seven-, eight- or nine-note Ragas have been grouped, according to their basic pattern, under the leadership of one or other of the five- note Ragas. These latter, the pentatonic Ragas are called the male Ragas and the others are called female Ragas, the Rāginīs. During the medieval centuries a number of poets composed series of poems, called 'Rāga-mālas', 'garlands of *ragas*', describing situations that aptly present the characteristic flavours of the different Ragas and Rāginīs. These poems are deeply influenced by the eroticism of the Kṛishṇa cult, and often represent legends associated with Kṛishṇa. Very, very many of the Rajput miniatures illustrate particular examples of these Ragas and Rāginīs, with the related poem written either on the front or back of the picture. These miniatures were usually executed in sets, and were immensely popular. For they are intended to set out the whole range of amorous passion.

One of the springtime Rāginī poems, for example, declares, 'My heart dreams of the firm breasted Hindola with broad hips, who wears bright coloured clothes; with the flower of the lotus she worships lord Kṛishṇa who sits on a swing hung among the twisted roots of a banyan tree. She hears the notes of his flute, her heart full of love, her beautiful limbs adorned with jewels.' The sad Rāginī of the rainy season is 'pale and weak, her voice like the Kokil singing; some cadence of the song reminds her of her lord'. Clasping her *vīṇa*, Mallāvikā 'cries out in misery, anguished at heart with the pain of youth'. Āsāvarī, 'with shining dark skin, adorned with peacock feathers and a necklace of rare, splendid pearls, on the mountain top drags forth the snake from the sandal trees and wears it as a girdle'. The Bangal Rāginī 'Tortured by separation takes on the aspect of an ascetic (to compel by her *tapas* her lover to return to her). She fills her jar with Ganges water, and wears clothes of birchbark.' But Lalitā the happy mistress 'resplendently beautiful lies exhausted with love on her bed at dawn'. The lordly Srī Raga 'sits in a beautiful mansion while a girl waves a fly whisk over him. Contemplating the Raga's splendour the bridegroom gains perfect concentration of mind.'

The variety of emotional suggestion achieved by the *raga* system was paralleled in painting by the use of specific colours and specific colour combinations to create specific emotional atmospheres. And painting was meant to be stimulating to emotions in exactly the same way as music. Unfortunately no written theory on this topic is available. But it is most likely that the method was a product of the fertile seventeenth century when both music and art underwent a splendid transformation, through contact with the sophisticated courtly arts of the Islamic world, imported under the Mogul emperors.

Miniature painting

Islamic painting introduced into India the album-miniature as an artistic type probably during the sixteenth century. At the same time, at the Moslem courts of the Deccan and the North a sophisticated technology of pigments was imported, making available not only a wider range of colours than India had hitherto known, but a new conception of the grouping of colours for differentiated emotional effects. There seems, however, to have been little of erotic interest in earlier Indian Islamic art and during the seventeenth century. For the chief original and hitherto unfamiliar purpose inspiring Moslem painting was historical documentation. There may have been occasional examples of erotic miniatures included in manuscripts of the great classical love stories of Persia, say, about Khasrw and Chirin, where it was necessary to illustrate the happy consummation of the love affair. But in Mogul painting, for example, the instances of erotica are linked with historical record. Such are the pictures painted under the emperor Akbar illustrating the sacking of cities, where the capture and raping of the city's women are represented – appreciatively, for that was the nature of Islam in India. During the eighteenth century Islamic pictures came more and more under the spell of native Indian subject matter, as more and more artists began to leave the courts and compete for custom in the bazaars of the great cities. Images of pure sensual luxury came gradually to predominate over truly erotic themes.

It was during the later seventeenth and the early eighteenth centuries that the greatest movements in Kṛishṇa painting took place at the courts of the Rajput princes – especially in Mewar, Malwa, Bundi, Kotah, Jaipur, Kishangarh, Basohli, Guler, Garhwal and Kangra. At these courts numberless series of Rāgamālas, and illuminations to Kṛishṇa literature were produced in a variety of beautiful styles. These benefited greatly from the technical developments of sixteenth- and seventeenth-century Moslem painting. In many Kṛishṇa series, and in many of the Rāgamāla series I have seen, are representations of sexual intercourse included as a normal and necessary part of the sequence. For example, where Rādhā and Kṛishṇa make love hidden in the forest; or where the *Rasamandala* or love-sports are taking place. Sometimes Kṛishṇa and his queen Rukminī make love in the palace, so deeply absorbed in one another that they do not notice that it is on fire. But apart from the representations of sexual intercourse, all these Rajput *XIII* styles are informed with a deep erotic feeling. The sensuous suavity of their lines echoes the movements of the caressing hand. The colours excite violent emotions. The burnished surfaces of paint suggest the smoothness of skin, silk and feathers. The canonical beauty of the protagonists – the long-lashed charming, deeply curved eyes of Kṛishṇa and the girls, their henna-dyed palms, foot-soles and fingertips, their sensuous lips, their jewels, all confirm the erotic impression, as do the deep feelings of love they express by face and gesture.

XIV There is, however, more. These pictures are full of sexual symbolism. There are, of course, the flowering sprays and amorous birds, which would be the normal stage properties suggesting youth and desire. There are symbolic animals, like the small horned deer who approach the lovesick girl in the forest. But there are also purely pictorial sexual symbols, such as the open vases, the spouted pots, the sinuous-necked bulbous-headed birds, and the trunks of trees which plunge up into the clutch of their own foliage. The meanings of all these have been revealed in their modern reinterpretation by artists like Avinash Chandra. The very ways in which the forms are drawn, especially in the more primitive-seeming examples, are infused with eroticism, and especially with direct references to the sexual organs and their engagement. To understand these calls for that same habit of reading analogies between forms – analogies of shape – as inspires the whole Indian theory of aesthetics I discussed in Chapter Two.

In fact an enormous variety of subject matter with an erotic significance was evolved by the Rajput schools of art. As the poetry of the Kṛishṇa cult, and its visual art, was intimately concerned with the minutiae of amorous emotion and its expression, the gestures, glances, gait and mien of amorous girls are delineated in affectionate detail. The great fourteenth-century Kṛishṇa poet Vidyāpati wrote:

> The sun rose
> On the lakeshore.
> The wind was cool as dew.
> I was tired from lovemaking;
> O friend, my night of spring

Was spoilt by sleep.
Cruel it was of Kṛishṇa
To go, without a word.
If only he had spoken
I would have embraced him
Like waves rolling
On a stony shore.
The more I dwell
On all my passionate thoughts
Unspeakable sadness
Drains my lonely love.

Of Rādhā he wrote:

Each day the breasts of Rādhā swelled.
Her hips grew shapely, her waist more slender.
Love's secrets stole into her eyes.
Startled, her childhood slipped away.
Her plum-like breasts grew large,
Harder and tauter, aching for love.
Kṛishṇa soon saw her as she bathed
Her filmy dress still clinging to her breasts.
Her tangled tresses falling on her heart,
A golden icon brushed by plumes of yak-tail.

Says Vidyāpati:

O wonder of women,
Only a handsome man can long for her!

The painters pursued these same highly charged subjects, such as the first meeting of the lover's eyes, the nursing of secret passion, jealousy, and the bitterness of unfulfilled desire.

A great poet of the sixteenth century, Keshava Dās, developed the conception of the Nāyikās. These were types of girls of different personalities, characters and moods. His great work, the *Rasikapriya* was often illustrated, and so the different Nāyikās were given pictorial expression, and patterns were set up which were followed by the various schools and ateliers of painters. The eight basic types – which have many subdivisions and varieties – are: the loyally loved, whose lover is subject to her will; she who is yearning for an absent or tardy lover or husband; she who is aroused, her bed made, waiting on it or at the door for her lover; she 116 who is angry, rebuffing her lover, but who repents too late; she whose lover has spent the night with another woman, and who reproaches him; she whose lover is away, and is not expected; she whose lover has failed to keep their assignation, and who has spent the night, waiting alone; the bold girl who goes out after her lover. Three further types were later added: the girl who anticipates separation, 114 knowing her lover is to go on a long journey at dawn; she who has had news of her lover's return from a long journey; she whose lover has just come back from a long absence, and at once seeks her out. Upon this set of fundamental themes a virtually endless series of variations could be developed.

V
117   The Nāyikās thus became the heroines of seventeenth- and eighteenth-century Rajput painting. And there can be no doubt that the mantle of the Apsarases fell upon them. Where poets and artists of the heroic and golden ages had occupied themselves primarily and without psychological discrimination with the passionate and unpersonalized beauties of heaven, those of later centuries were able to descry the light of divinity in the demeanour of earthly girls possessed by love. This particular spiritual achievement – for achievement it is even though it never extended to individual compassion – was made possible by the evolution of the cult of Kṛishṇa, with its explicit mutual assimilation of divine and human love through the process of incarnation. At the same time, it is also clear that the Nāyikās had become, as individual types, paradigms of the original Nāyikā, Rādhā, who came to be seen as transcendent. The older religion to which the Apsarases belonged had not envisaged a condensed, central divinized image of the woman in love, such as Rādhā was. It is thus not surprising that the Nāyikā, based upon Rādhā, turned into the personification of love, just as Aphrodite did in the ancient Greek world. This is the meaning of one of the most interesting of the colour plates

XII   reproduced in this book. Here Nāyikās, paradigms of the one Nāyikā, and all of the same type, are shown in sexual intercourse with many different male animals, whilst around them couples of other animals copulate. Two of the Nāyikās are also embraced onto a double-ended dildo – a common instrument in the polygamous societies of the East. There must, too, be an element of fertility magic, as it was represented in the boundary stones, but here recollected as an aesthetic element. For in the painting one Nāyikā is shown coupling with a male elephant. It may also be that the different male animals symbolize human masculine types. But at bottom the image signifies that it is the Goddess of Love who is both the goal and inspiration of every desire. Love, in the human sense, is universal amongst creatures, and their Goddess is our Rādhā. Most interesting of all, this is surely an inversion of the maxim of orthodox Brahminical (and Western) mysticism I have already quoted that 'all souls are feminine to God'. It must mean that 'all creatures are masculine to the Goddess'. Males in love truly pursue a deity. From her all forms spring. Perhaps, too, she represents the cosmic force of Love, somewhat as it was conceived by Empedocles of Acragas in the fifth century BC.

This idea has been explored further in works of art where the Nāyikā is shown in sexual relations with many types of men, women and animals – dogs, bulls, monkeys, bears. For to her no possible kind of sexual relationship is alien, and every encounter is an erotic one. There are illuminated manuscripts where all the possibilities are explored, and old legends are revived. One painting illustrated

121   here has ancient ritual overtones. For the Nāyikā who couples with the stallion recalls the old Vedic rituals centred on the horse-sacrifice. This sacrifice could only be performed by a king whose power was such that his chosen stallion had wandered freely for a year without anyone daring to capture him. It was thus an emblem of the solar power of the king. At a certain point in the sacrifice his queen lay coupled with the horse. The horse in our picture is obviously a symbol for the masculine libido, and as such can function as a highly illuminating symbol even today.

One very common type of erotic painting explores this possibility still further – though more ingenuity than aesthetic exaltation is involved. During the eighteenth

XV Oil-painting. Triptych, by Avinash Chandra, 1963

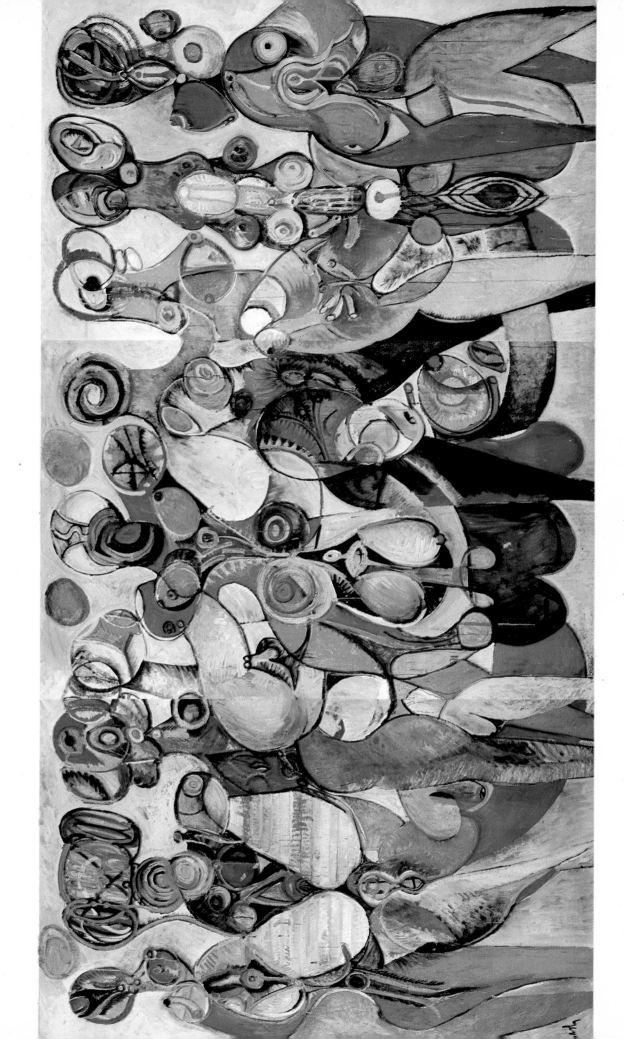

century a kind of puzzle-picture became popular, which survived into modern *118* times. It illustrates animals or swings or temples that are made up of human or animal figures twined together. It was inevitable that the Indian imagination should envisage the twining as erotic. I illustrate the earliest I have been able to discover, the forepart of an elephant.

Followers of the divine example

I have mentioned that men and women used to attempt to live out the legend of Kṛishṇa and Rādhā in their own lives. We know of one most remarkable instance where a royal couple, both considerable religious-erotic poets, lived the Kṛishṇa-Rādhā life and were served by a court-painter of genius, Nihal Chand, who matched their poetry with his pictures. This was at the small Rajput court of Kishangarh in the middle decades of the eighteenth century. The Raja, Savant Singh, whose poetical name was Nāgarī Dās, had a prolonged, passionate love affair with a zenana-girl, a poetess called Banī Thanī. Together they performed their devotions, worshipping the liṅgam, hymning Kṛishṇa and Rādhā in passionate verses. Nihal Chand painted for them some of the most expansive and most sublime miniature paintings as images of delight ever produced. Human figures and landscapes alike are exhibited in the sweet sensuous lines and brilliantly combined colours of love; the paradise of Brindaban blossoms under its sunset skies full of golden cockles of cloud, its flowering trees filled with birds, its celestial river Yamunā bearing gently its little orange-lacquered boats – that paradise for which Nāgarī Dās expressed his longing:

> Seeing the idiot world around me, I long for Brindaban
> > and the Yamunā's sweet waters;
> But life is slipping by. How deeply I yearn for Brindaban;
> > how afraid am I that life is slipping by!

I have seen no Kishangarh pictures that depict the lovers in sexual intercourse. But they must have been painted. Such a deep-dyed erotic art can never have lacked its culminating images.

This phenomenon, however, explains the basis for further developments in Rājasthān and Panjab painting, in which the mantle of Kṛishṇa and Rādhā descends *I/III* upon the human prince and his lady (or ladies) authenticating the image of courtly love. Sometimes the erotic couples in these paintings are identified as other heroes and heroines of romantic legend, such as Baz Bahādur and Rupmati. But more usually they are simply indefinite royal and heroic lovers. For we must allow for the recrudescence and reinterpretation in Rajput miniature style of far older images of the heroic ménage, and the erotic enjoyment of the epic hero as described in Chapter Two. He now wears the clothes of the Post-Mogul Mahārāja, and even his mutton-chop whiskers. He appears many times in that old Indian ideal erotic *VI* situation, having intercourse with five ladies at once – with penis, both hands and feet. He rides a horse or elephant whilst having intercourse with one of his ladies – their pleasure increased, no doubt, by the jolting and swaying of the animal's gait.

XVI Watercolour paintings. (*Above*) The blind man's wife entertains a lover while her husband milks the cow, and (*below*) prince amongst his ladies, Patna style, late 19th century

115/119

IV/VIII (left)

120

Virtually every conceivable sexual variation is portrayed. There are series of pictures illustrating schematically all the erotic delights available to a man, by varied posture, clothed or naked, in settings of palace, garden, desert or country-side, in water, with one or several women. Homosexual congress scarcely features at all in these series; though congress with female monkeys does. More interesting still are those series which illustrate with the same schematic variety the pleasures available to a woman. These do include many homosexual varieties of pleasure, especially the use of skilfully conceived implements.

Along these lines fantasy has been pursued to its extremes. A number of superb Nepalese manuscripts exist (as well as Rajput) of a text called *Rahasya Kaloḷini* – 'the courtesan's secrets'. In these the same kind of images are deployed as in some of the original illustrations to de Sade's works – without, needless to say, the Sadism, which India does not know. But elaborate combinations are assembled that involve several interlinked couples, including aboriginal people. Much emphasis is laid upon the sexual juices. One superlative large manuscript of this is in the National Museum, New Delhi. It is a matter for great regret that know-ledge has been obstructed by the fact that illustrations of this work, as of many others officially requested from the same source, were not supplied. For the style is superb. Its heavy and strongly schematic contouring, emphasized with red edge-bands indicating receding side-surfaces, recalls wood-carving. It represents an artistic phenomenon unparalleled anywhere in the world. Sexual anxiety has here been splendidly overcome.

Recent art

There remains one final category of recent paintings to be considered. These are genre works, some of 'Rajput' type, in which no trace of the religious-erotic tradition is to be found, nor any purely educative purpose. They are documentary pictures, perhaps vestigially in the Mogul sense, and present some of the facts of sexual life in India as a matter of record. In this they are on the way to doing some-thing both unusual and important in Indian art. For, generally speaking, Indian art has rarely concerned itself with the life of ordinary people, and never achieved any sense of the individual and personal. For example, certain pictures show the proper fate of the adulterer, sword-slain by the returning husband who has caught him *in flagrante* with the wife. Acrobats demonstrate their ability to copulate balanced on the top of a pole – a feat witnessed in fact by many Europeans. A priest, complete with rosary, couples with a courtesan. Europeans making love wearing nothing but their enormous eighteenth-century wigs were obviously a highly amusing subject to Indians just as they were to the Japanese.

126

Perhaps the most interesting group of these genre paintings is that concerned with village life. A few of the Rajput type can be found, probably dating to the middle of the nineteenth century. One, for example, in the National Museum, New Delhi (again refused for illustration) shows a loose village woman receiving a crowd of excited village men in the shade of a tree by a roadside. The Patna school of watercolour painters, who worked under the influence of British watercolour painting, developed other erotic genre themes taken from village life. For example, the wife of a blind man is seduced at her husband's side while he milks his cow; the landowner or moneylender exercises rights over the attractive wife of a peasant client; a village woman fetching water from the well catches one of her fellow-wives on the same errand in the bushes with a lover. There can be no doubt that this tradition of painting continued well into the present century, and may still continue.

XVI (above)
XVI (below)

It only remains to mention that in India, as in many Western countries, erotic toys have been produced for the diversion of wealthy patrons. There are playing cards, toilet boxes and mechanized pictures cut out of – very beautifully – painted sheet metal that make sexual movements by clockwork, boxes with built-in clockwork erotic figures, betel-cutters worked into the form of men and women whose sexual organs engage. These are all part of the setting of luxury which the wealthy were able to establish for themselves during the British period. Certain men even went so far as to have life-size statues of naked female attendants, carved and painted, set up in their bedrooms. In this they were no doubt continuing the tradition of Indian kings of the past who were waited upon by images of Apsarases. Two such figures are illustrated. They are, in fact, good sculptures in a little-known style – a combination of traditional Indian and European ways of thought.

36/123
127

122

Recent art in India has concerned itself very much with erotic themes. Indeed the atmosphere of modern art in India is of an overwhelming erotically-tinged sweetness. The Bengali Tagore family-school, amongst whose alumni have been so many distinguished heads of major Indian art-schools, has left its indelible imprint upon modern painting. Its chief characteristic was a kind of disembodied image of the beautiful, based upon the idea of love without benefit of the body, eroticism without actuality; a sentimental fantasy, in fact. Those modern Indian painters and sculptors who have chosen to stay in India have mostly fallen victim to this cult of the saccharine, unable to escape the demands of their society for an art of innocuous dream without responsibility to any idea of truth. Younger artists are attempting to find an idiom of their own, not so much by reviving old styles or assimilating modern Western styles, as by pursuing the logic of their native language of form and hectic colour: some are succeeding; but much sculpture is of an egg-like smoothness of finish, recalling clichés of physical perfection that have been worked out by other artists.

On the other hand two artists who have chosen to live in Britain have succeeded in forging strong styles, completely Indian and aggressively erotic. One, F. N. Souza, who comes from Goa, paints dark and guilt-ridden Byzantine space-fiction, to which vagrant and arbitrary eroticism contributes its meed. Amongst his images are some which are direct transcriptions of photographs of Indian erotic temple art.

The most important Indian artist of the erotic is Avinash Chandra. His large canvases are entirely composed of fragmentary graphic images of the world interpreted as details of male and female sexual organs, as breasts, buttocks and thighs, woven together into a tissue of sinuous lines often recalling art nouveau design. The lines are glossed with hot colours of hectic brilliance, symbolic of violent feeling. Some of his work is reminiscent of the magical designs of certain

XV

Bengali villages, where symbols for longed-for possessions – jewels, carriages, children – are laid out in coloured powders as petitions to the deity. None of Chandra's canvases add up to representations of a single erotic motive. So therefore we must accept them as images of unparticularized sexual feeling. They thus express beautifully the problem of the educated Indian spirit in the modern world – glorious libido with nowhere to go.

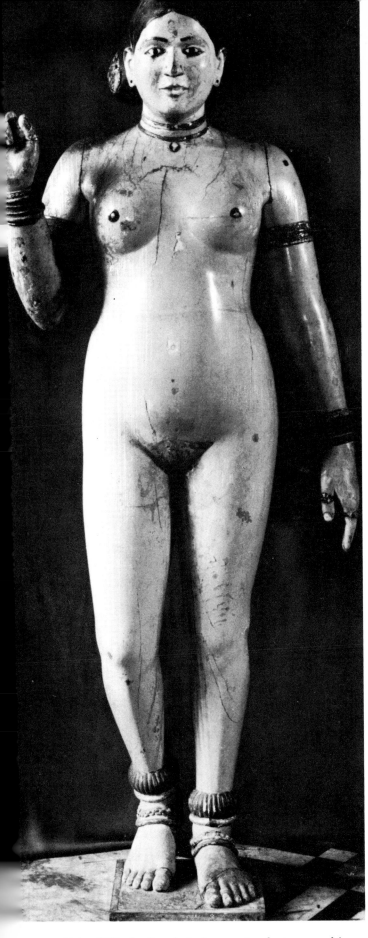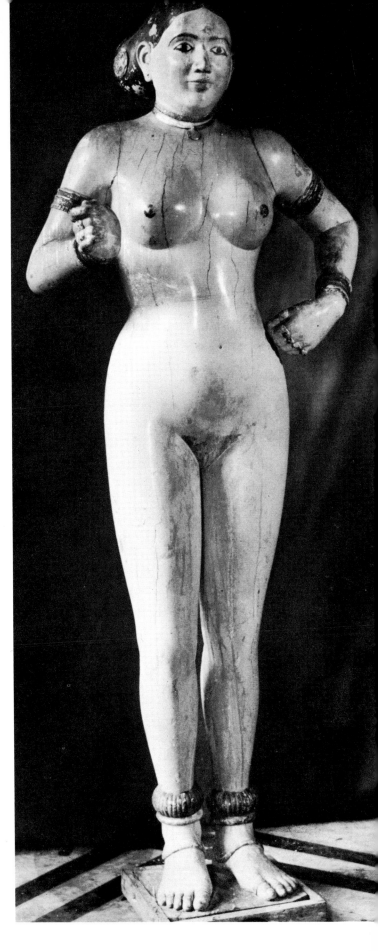

122 Pair of life size female bedroom attendants, carved in
wood and painted. Eastern India. 19th century

123 Small ivory panel with a pair of lovers. South India, or Ceylon. 18th century

124 (*right*) Small figure of lac-painted wood, with a mobile penis and testicles of cloth-balls. Used by mendicants to insult those who refuse them alms. Eastern India. Modern

125 (*above*) Story-teller's illustrative picture, representing a priapic demon. Bengal. Modern

126 (*right*) A European following the Indian style of eroticism. Album miniature painting. Ganges Valley. Early 19th century

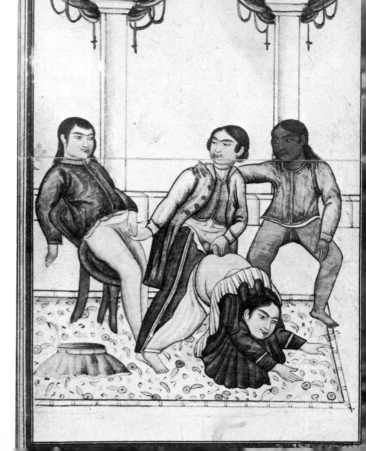

127 Erotic playing cards, painted with a series of postures in lacquer; green and yellow on red. Modern, from Orissa

ISLAM

128 Fragment of an Islamic erotic manual, from the Fayum,
Egypt. 11th century AD

129 Illustration to the Maqamat of Al Hariri. Abu Zaid
exposes his member ironically. Baghdad manuscript.
13th century AD

130 Illustration to a 13th-century Persian manuscript illustrating the coupling of a man with a she-goat

131 Illustration to a 13th-century Persian manuscript illustrating the sexual intercourse of goats and sheep

132 Wall painting in the house of a merchant at Julfa, Isfahan, representing a pair of clothed lovers

133 Khasruw and Chirin toying with each other after their marriage. Persian.
Early 16th century

134 Illustration to a Persian manuscript of the loves of Khasruw and Chirin. 17th century

135 Illustration to a Persian manuscript of poems. 1665

136 A Persian beauty. Album leaf miniature in the style of Riza 'Abbasi. 16th century

137 (*opposite top left*) Youth holding a phallic symbol. A page from a Persian manuscript.
16th century
138 (*opposite top right*) A pair of young lovers in intercourse. Persian album leaf miniature.
17th century
139 (*opposite bottom*) A pair of lovers. Album leaf miniature in the style of Riza 'Abbasi.
16th century

زیاده شود فصل کن اعمال المشتری پاره پلود

بشتابد روز پنج شنبه و قمر ناظر بود بمشتری از قوس از جوت

وعمل باید که در ساعت اول بود تا ساعت دوم و بر آنجا صورت

سروی ساز دکه بر کرسی نشسته و جامه بر و پوشیده وه در دست

او قصدی و زیر نه پره این حروف بنویسد بدین صفت ب پس

ع ال آنکه این مص را بر خاتمی ترکیب کند از برنج و زیر مص چیزی از

کاخوریه و روز شنبه در انگشت کند پیش از آن که آفتاب بر

آید از خاصیت او آنست که هر که آن در انگشت دارد روزها

او مستجاب بود و میان مردم محبوب باشد لجنه زد که رو اکین

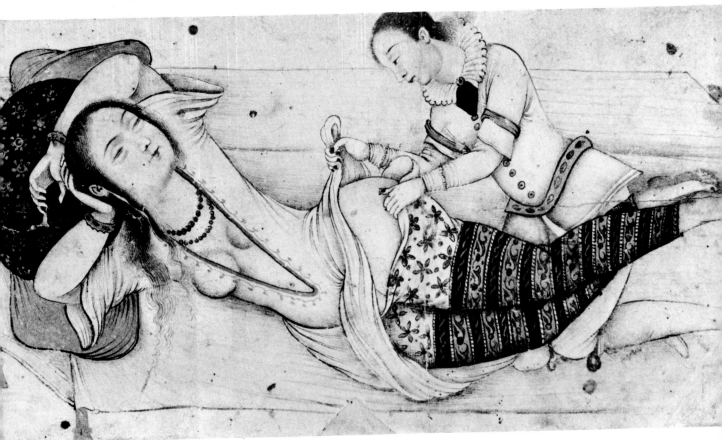

140 (*opposite*) Pair of lovers in intercourse. Persian album leaf miniature, executed in red outline. 17th century

142 (*right*) Miniature drawing in the style of Riza 'Abbasi, representing an old man making a suggestive gesture to a youth. The foliage calligraphy is charged with erotic symbolism. Persian. 16th century

143 (*right*) Miniature drawings in the style of Riza 'Abbasi; mounted as an album leaf. An old man making approaches to a beautiful youth. 16th century

141 (*opposite*) Youth in European clothes undressing a recumbent beauty. Persian album leaf miniature. 17th century

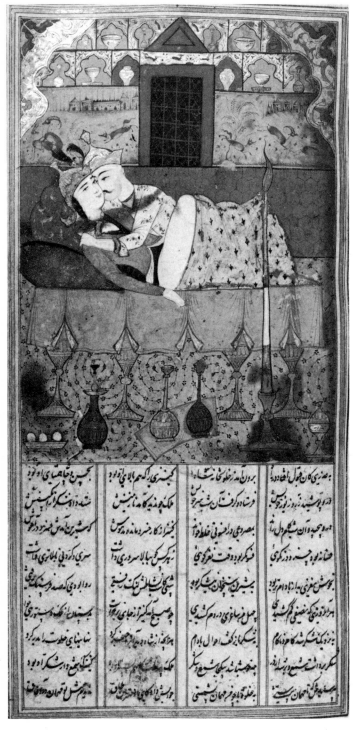

144 Illustration to a Persian manuscript of the loves of
Khasruw and Chirin. 1665

145 Illustration to a Persian erotic manuscript. Kashmir.
17th century

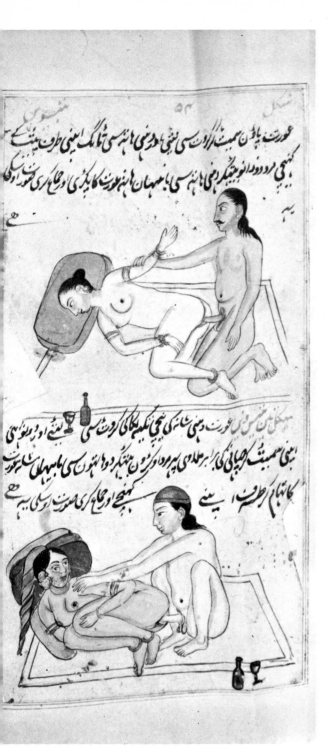

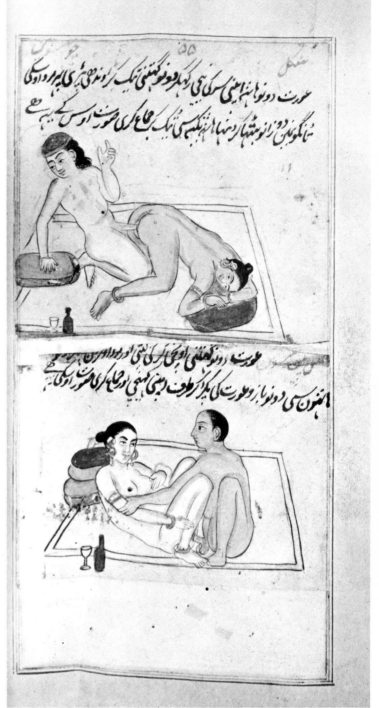

146 and 147 Illustrations to an Islamic erotic posture-manual. Kashmir. 19th century

ISLAM

6 The Arab Inheritance

Early fragments

The possibility of erotic art having flourished, or even existed, in the Islamic world has always been regarded by scholars with doubt and incredulity. For the severity and strictness of Islamic social mores would seem to preclude totally the idea that any art form which may have encouraged licentious behaviour could ever have gained any foothold in those parts of the Near East under the sway of Islam.

Even assuming that some form of erotic art had existed it seemed improbable that much of it could have escaped the destructive fingers of time. But disbelief in its existence is so deeprooted that at least one leading orientalist denies that purely erotic elements could ever have had any place in the visual arts of Islamic society. This belief is all the more extraordinary, as Islamic literature contains vast quantities of the most sophisticated erotic writing. In fact it seems that Puritan obscurantism has been particularly successful in expunging the visual artistic vestiges of ancient Islamic *joie de vivre*. However, despite the heavy hand which time has laid on Arab and Persian painting, despite the inherent dislike of many Moslems for any kind of representational art, and the inaccessibility of much of what is left, it is possible to assert that erotic elements were present, and have, in fact, played a quite substantial part in Islamic art throughout the whole of its existence.

The examples of erotic art remaining today are very few, and can in no way be compared to the wealth of material available to the student of Indian or Japanese erotic art. Therefore what follows must necessarily be only a sketch, the barest suggestion of what must once have been. The whole pattern of eroticism in Islamic visual art must be studied though the few dozen or so examples which enable us to examine some of the mores which they reflect, and to suggest something of the line of development taken by erotic elements in Arab and Persian painting, in medieval and modern times.

The earliest painting which could be termed 'erotic' is in fact well known, for it is at the same time one of the earliest existing examples of Islamic pictorial art. It consists of a wall painting found on the wall of a hunting lodge at Qusayr' Amrah in Syria, which is reputed to have been built by one of the Ummayad Khalīfs Walīd in the eighth century.

Although the wall paintings – or rather the fragments which remain – are not erotic in the sense that they depict scenes of sexual activity, they appear to be erotic in implication, showing plump half-naked dancing girls.

These women, it has been plausibly suggested, represented the Arab ideal of beauty, so often defined and eulogized by poets and writers, 'She must be plump

148 Persian book-cover, of painted leather. 19th century

and lusty . . . with bust and belly large . . .' We learn however from Arnold's *Painting in Islam*, that wall painting was often of a far more drastic nature. Paintings were frequently employed to cover the walls of pleasure houses, pavilions and particularly private and public baths. He relates how the eleventh-century conqueror Maḥmūd of Ghazna discovered that his son had a pavilion decorated from wall to ceiling with paintings taken from an erotic manual. In the same work he gives an account of a bath belonging to the thirteenth-century ruler of Baghdad Sharāf Ad-dīn Hārūn which contained an inner compartment decorated with scenes of sexual intercourse.

There are many references in the writings of Moslem and European authors to the use of erotic images as part of the decoration of baths. The ninth-century Spanish Moslem Ibn Ḥāzm for instance in his treatise on romantic love makes an interesting reference to 'Those pictures (of women) they paint on the walls of the public baths', no doubt of the type referred to above. It appears that erotic illustration became a widespread and important characteristic of bath decoration from the eighth century onwards, being no doubt one of the many traits taken over by the Moslems from the Greeks, Persians and other conquered races.

Although such practices were occasionally attacked by religious dignitaries, an extremely interesting defence (also quoted by Arnold) is put forward by a fourteenth-century physician:

> The wise men of old who invented the bath . . . with their keen insight and penetrating wisdom, recognized that a man loses considerable part of his strength when he goes into the bath; they made every effort to devise a means of finding a remedy as speedily as possible; so they decorated the bath with beautiful pictures in bright cheerful colours. These they divided into three kinds, since they knew that there are three vital principles in the body, the animal, the spiritual and the natural. Accordingly they painted pictures of each kind, so as to strengthen each one of these potentialities . . . for spiritual power, pictures of love and of reflection on the lover and his beloved, and pictures of their mutual recriminations and reproaches, and of their embracing one another etc. . . .

In short the contemplation of pictures of a sexual nature could have a certain therapeutic value, replacing energy lost by languishing in a hot bath. Despite this, many of the subjects employed in the decoration were of a purely licentious character, in keeping with some of the activities which went on there.

The number of baths in any medieval Moslem city must have been enormous and therefore it seems possible that the decoration of these places was carried out by a special class of artisans. Though there is no evidence to prove it, there may well have been a guild of decorators, whose repertoire included such erotic scenes. There is in the keeping of the British Museum a large sheet of paper from Fatimid Egypt on which is drawn the figure of a near-naked dancing girl. It has been suggested by the late D. S. Rice that this is a preparatory sketch or cartoon for a wall painting. If the attribution is correct then it could possibly have come from the hand of an artisan engaged in bath or pavilion decoration.

Although nothing remains – with the exception of Qusayr' Amrah – of erotic wall decoration there are enough literary references for us to know that it occurred on a wide scale. There are in Isfahan in Persia certain houses belonging to Armenian merchants dating from the sixteenth century. Many of these houses are decorated with wall paintings. Some exhibit scenes which are of a mildly erotic *132* nature showing lovers caressing, and are interesting in that they give some slight indication as to what large-scale erotic decorations must have been like.

Though bath decoration seems to be the commonest use to which erotic painting was put, this is by no means the only sphere in which it existed. There were at least two other media in which illustrations of a sexual nature were employed. The first and most important is the employment of erotic miniatures in manuscript illumination. The manuscripts which contained erotic material were of three types. First the erotic manual, where illustrations were used to illustrate the various *146* methods of sexual intercourse; second, poems and romances, where miniatures may illustrate part of a text in which a seduction or the consummation of a lovers' union is described. Third, scientific and pseudo-scientific works. In zoological, natural history and other works of a legendary character, there are often scenes depicting copulation between animals, but very occasionally there may be a scene that is erotic in nature, for example showing bestiality.

The second type of erotic material is produced purely for its own sake. Many pictures were made illustrating various aspects of sexuality, including homosexual intercourse. Many objects of daily use, such as trays, boxes and vessels – even embroidered slippers – had sexual illustrations applied to them.

The erotic manual – that is to say the work dealing with the mechanics of sexual technique and necessary details of coital posture – seems to have been very popular among the Arabs and Persians, down to the end of the last century. Numerous works, and the titles of many more, have come down to us today; the best known of course being *The Perfumed Garden* of Sheikh Nifzāwī. There are many others, mentioned by Burton in his *Arabian Nights,* including the *Rujū' ash sheikh i la ṣabani figūwwat-il-bāh* (Book of age rejuvenescence in the power of concupiscence) – which can still be purchased today from under the counter in Damascus, and the *Kitāb al-īdāh fi' ilm an-nikāk,* the latter accredited to historian and theologian Jallāl ad-dīn As-suyūtī.

The typical Islamic erotic manual is a potpourri of psychology, poetry, historical anecdotes, natural curiosities and old wives' tales. The influence of the great classics of Indian eroticism is very apparent throughout; some are in fact Islamicized translations of the *Kāmasūtra, Anangaranga,* etc. Though whether the Indian works are the direct inspiration of the Islamic is another matter.

These works were sometimes illustrated. Though the majority of Arabic copies in existence today are without pictures, we have evidence that illuminations were employed. A fragment of manuscript from the Fayum, Egypt, dated to the eleventh *128* century, is in the National Library in Vienna. This papyrus fragment contains an ink-drawing of a couple copulating and purports to come from just such an erotic manual as those mentioned above. This battered fragment is so far as we know the only surviving example from the medieval Arab world, our only other examples coming from the licentious period of Persian history in the nineteenth century.

Without denying the obvious debt of the sexual treatise to India, it would seem that the origin of these works lies rather in the Middle-Eastern tradition of medicine than in the boudoir. It is known that many medieval medical works contained sections on the various aspects of sexual intercourse. Ar-Rāzi's great compendium of medicine contained chapters on sex and hygiene, while that same physician devoted himself to works on aphrodisiacs. And the inclusion of such material in the work of a physician with the repute of Ar-Rāzi gives an indication of the Islamic attitude to sex.

Despite the severity with which Islam punished adultery – 'For a woman not virgin who fornicates with a man not virgin, a hundred stripes and stoning', is the penalty mentioned by Ibn Hāzm quoting a reliable *hadīth* (saying of Mohammed) – and the apparent inferior position of women in Moslem society, the approach of Islam to the sexual act is fundamentally liberal, with an understanding for human needs.

Moslem attitudes

Sex in the Islamic world was not looked on as it was in medieval Christianity – an inherent evil in the nature of man. On the contrary the sexual act is accepted as a natural and necessary part of human activity. It is only the illicit extramarital intercourse which is condemned, not because it is inherently 'sinful' but because it is potentially disruptive to the structure of the Islamic community. Thus although erotic manuals produced in many parts of the Islamic world during the last century may have been more or less pornographic in inspiration, the earlier type of manual would have met the approval of any religious dignitary; for its avowed purpose was by bringing about a harmonious relationship between a man and his wife, with consequent individual happiness, to ensure the stability of the home. Note the comment of the Wazīr (Vizier) to Nifzāwī on an earlier erotic work of the Sheikh 'I swear by God that it is necessary to know this book ... it is only the shameless bore and the enemy of all science who will not read it or will make fun of it.' In addition we have the fact that even religious scholastics themselves composed such works. As-suyūtī for example is accredited with the authorship of the short erotic essay mentioned above. It is also worth pointing out that many of the greatest saints of Islam were both married and esteemed as practitioners of the erotic arts.

This attitude manifests itself in the literature of the Arabs and Persians and similarly in the illustrations which that literature contains. One of the earliest and most interesting examples occurs in the *Māqāmāt* of Al Harīrī (*c.* AD 1110). The twentieth chapter of this great work of Arab scholarship and erudition contains a scene wherein the hero Abū Zaid speaks the funeral oration of a valiant knight, beginning by praising his strength:

> His rigorous onset straightest places oped
> And easy passage through all narrows groped
> He ne'er encountered foe in single fight.
> But came from tilt with spear in blood stained bright.

and then his chivalry:

XVII Illustrated page of the poems of Sa'adi. Persian, 17th century

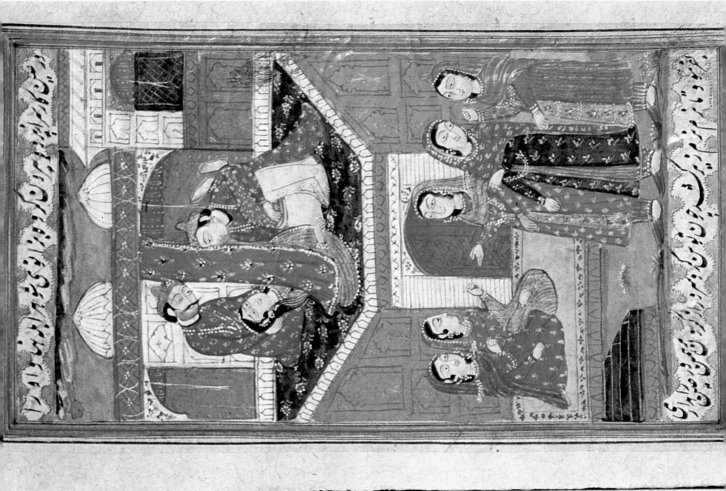

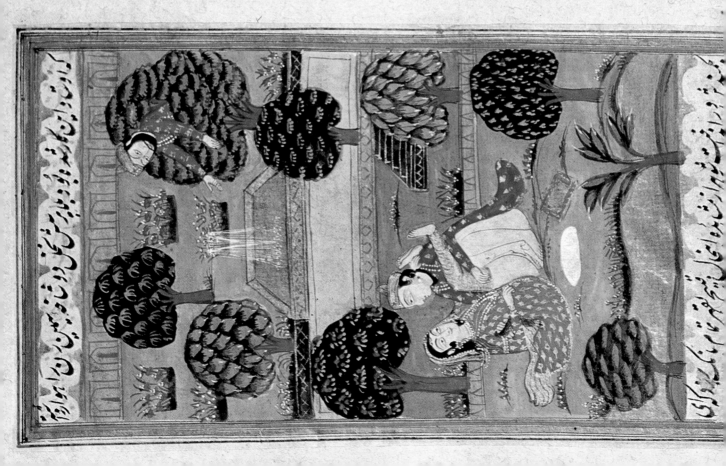

Dealing to the fair young girl delirious joy
And no less welcome is the blooming boy.

Finally after lamenting the declining years of the champion, and being awarded an ample bounty by the listeners to the oration, Abū Zaid leaves. One of the listeners follows him hoping to learn the identity of the knight. With a laugh Abū Zaid raises his shirt to expose his own withered member – the brave knight is none other than his own penis. With this knowledge the poem takes on a totally different complexion.

The *Māqāmāt* was one of the earliest manuscripts to be illustrated, and several thirteenth-century copies show the scene described. A miniature in a manuscript   *129* from thirteenth-century Baghdad depicts Abū Zaid standing exposing his naked genitals before the questioner, while the latter raises his hand to indicate shock and surprise.

The significance of this poem, and of the accompanying illustration is that the manuscript in which they appear is the very height of orthodox literary respectability. A work in fact read by the gravest and most worshipful men, and which became second only to the Qūrān itself in popular esteem.

Thus Harīrī could treat the subject of sexual prowess with perfect ease. Moreover although this book was copied many times, and was used in the most conservative religious institutions, there is no record of these verses ever having been deleted. This is almost certainly attributable to the ability of the Arabs to treat love as simply another passion, and to regard sex as a natural part of the divine design.

This is even more true in the *Arabian Nights*. This huge work, composed over a long period of time during the Middle Ages, is a treasure-house of Islamic manners and behaviour, in all their various aspects. In the *Arabian Nights* sex is very much on the surface, not submerged as in many contemporary Western medieval works, and is treated as a natural part of human behaviour, neither ignored nor appearing as a disproportionate obsession with the writers of the *Nights*. Unfortunately we know of no early illustrated copies of the *Nights*. This may be because the work was only put into its final form when the great days of Arab painting, of the twelfth to fourteenth centuries, were long past, though their existence is not completely out of the question. The John Rylands Library in Manchester, for instance, possesses an illustrated copy from eighteenth-century Egypt, and two late nineteenth-century volumes with illustrations are in the author's possession. The latter however have no openly erotic illustrations, and the illustrations in the former are of little artistic merit.

Illuminated manuscripts

There are other poems, romances and general works of literature from the Arab   *134/145* world and Persia, which do contain erotic illustrations. There is for example a   *XVII* fourteenth-century copy of the *Kalīla wa Dimnā* – a book of fables, originally Indian but translated into Arabic in the ninth century AD – in the Bodleian Library,

211

XVIII Two illuminated pages from a book of stories. Kashmir, late 18th century

Oxford, which contains a scene showing a couple partially covered by a blanket engaged in intercourse while other figures look on. The presence of watching figures seems to be a feature of erotic miniatures, for in a miniature in a copy of the *Kullīyat* of Sa'adī at Edinburgh we see a man and woman copulating in a palace or pavilion while at the same time the scene is watched by four women half concealed behind curtains.

Similarly in a copy of the Five Poems (*Khamsēh*) of the Persian poet Nizāmī in the Bibliothèque Nationale, Paris, there is a miniature showing two figures making love in a luxuriant garden. Present in the garden also are three other figures, all female. Two sit talking while a third watches the lovers from behind a tree. The presence of additional figures in these miniatures, although in many cases it may be demanded by the plot, suggests that there was nothing so shocking or surprising about the sexual act that it had to be hidden.

XVIII   It was, perhaps, in the Moslem regions of India that the Islamic erotic story-text reached its most complete development. During the late eighteenth and the nineteenth century Kashmir in particular became a major centre for the production of both illustrated and unillustrated manuscripts of Moslem classics. These manuscripts, which were certainly exported to Persia and other parts of the Moslem *135/144*   world, were of many different grades. Some of the illustrated examples are finely written, beautifully illuminated with miniatures and decorative borders, as well as beautifully bound. Many of the series of illuminations to the Persian classic tales contain erotic pictures at appropriate points where, for example, the happy union of Khasruw and Chirin is to be portrayed. Collections of genre and humorous tales also include erotic pictures as a natural part of their subject matter. So too do the medical works and erotic posture-books. The style of these works is often somewhat Indianized and there can be little doubt that the Indian interest in erotic art helped to stimulate the production of Islamic work in the same vein. But there are many examples of Kashmir work which must rate as first-class works of Persian inspiration.

Our knowledge of the symbolic use of gesture and natural objects to increase the emotional content of Persian erotic paintings is very limited, though there is *137*   no doubt that it existed, if only on a small scale. In the same way that Arab and Persian poetry abounds with erotic metaphors, painting may have alluded to sexual *142*   matters by the apparently innocent introduction of certain symbolic plants, animals and objects. This, of course, is more familiar in Indian and Chinese art, where seemingly simple landscapes can be highly charged with erotic motifs.

136/139   This idea occurs in many Persian love scenes with the presence of fruit and wine – one the standard poetic symbol for pleasure, the other for the Dionysiac energy expended in sexual fertilization. However, in the scene to which we have referred above, in the *Khamsēh* of Nizāmī, the natural surroundings reiterate the essential erotic element of the scene. This is particularly true of the way in which a tree on the extreme left seems to embrace a poplar or cypress tree lying behind it – more evidence that sexual relations are a natural part of the Grand Design. It further appears in the phallic-looking wine flasks clutched by serving women and in the long-spouted wine flagon standing on a dish. The fact that all shrubs and flowers are in bloom must have some reference to what is being enacted amongst them.

However as in later centuries pictures became more or less straightforward representations of sexual intercourse, the accompanying symbolism grew appreciably less, until ultimately it disappeared altogether, even from those scenes which were produced as independent works of art, unrelated to the text of manuscripts.

Romantic idealism

While we recognize that there is a fundamentally different attitude to the sexual act between Christianity and Islam we must acknowledge the existence of an 'anti-natural' trend in medieval Islam which runs counter to the above attitude and creates a certain dualism. This is the ideal of romantic love, unrequited and unfulfilled.

The literature of the Arabs and Persians contains many stories of tortured love affairs between love-sick youths and unobtainable damsels; some, like the story of Majnūn and Leila are very famous, while others have faded into obscurity, being known only through solitary copies which have survived in libraries in Europe or Istanbul. It is to this type of stylized courtly love that the medieval Spanish writer Ibn Hāzm devoted his famous book *The Ring of the Dove*. According to Ibn Hāzm's conception the contemplation of the beloved by the lover, and his approach to her, are all-important, while physical union – save in so far as they experience each other's presence – is nothing.

In defining the various types of love he puts at the head of his list the love which exists between people who love each other 'in God', and at the bottom he puts 'passionate' love. This latter, however, he refers to later in such a way as to make us realize that 'passionate' love is no less than that melancholia and derangement which we know from the medieval love epics of Europe. To Ibn Hāzm a mere sexual passion was the very antithesis of the pure and delicate feeling to which he was alluding. His work contains several anecdotes illustrating the most commendable and praiseworthy actions of lovers in resisting – often under great duress – the carnal pleasures urged upon them by their beloveds, and the author's desire to exile the carnal side of human relationships is taken to extreme, as we see in the following statements: 'The finest quality that a man can display in love is continence: to abstain from all sin and indecency', and more drastically: 'Without doubt, absolute purity can be secured if a man were to be castrated, and thus have no desire for women and no organ to assist him traffic with them'!

This romantic or Platonic conception of love existed side by side with what we have termed the natural concept of love, throughout the Middle Ages.

During this time the possibility of contact between couples who were not married became in theory increasingly difficult, at first due to the fact that girls were strictly guarded before marriage by their paternal relatives, and afterwards by the seclusion of the harem, which was to make outside contact well-nigh impossible. Extramarital liaisons could only take place if one or both parties were prepared to risk severe punishment, especially where the woman was of high social class. However, the picturesque tales included in many collections – the *Nights* is one – make it obvious that life, especially city life among those of lesser social status, often eluded the prescriptions of orthodox morality, and that punishment for sexual misdemeanours was by no means always severe. It is also important to remember that the female slaves of the household, in addition to the canonical four wives, were available to the master of the house.

Now although many of the romantic poems and tales are centred on such liaisons it is important to remember that the social condition which made such liaisons necessary, the seclusion of women, was not by itself responsible for bringing the Islamic version of romantic love into existence in Islamic society. For, although romantic liaisons were indeed sexual, it was of the essence of the Islamic concept of romantic love that the sexual act itself was eschewed. This concept as we know it in medieval times is in fact only a step away from that mystical form of love cultivated by the order of Sufis which aims at union with the Divine. Thus though certain social circumstances may have fostered and nurtured the romantic concept, they themselves could not be directly responsible for its initiation.

There is little doubt that the romantic attitude appeared in the Islamic world as a result of contacts with the Christian heritage of Greek Platonic philosophy. The ideas of Plato – which were known to Ibn Hāzm – and Christian customs centred on the denial of the flesh very probably gave rise to the romantic concept in Islam; the harem system, and inaccessibility of women gave it its particular colour; while the poets and writers enshrined it in Islamic literature. In the same way that the natural and humanistic attitude to sexual activity has its pictorial art, so too does the romantic.

The best known of the many poems and stories treating love in a romantic way is the legend of Majnūn and Leila; this is the tortured tale of a youth who is prevented from having any contact with his beloved, goes mad and wanders, a wasted lunatic, in the desert. This work was a great favourite among Persian painters, and was illustrated many times between the sixteenth and nineteenth centuries, but without any erotic élan.

In addition to the most famous works in this genre there were others which were not so well known. For instance, the only example of an illustrated manuscript which it is possible to attribute to Islamic Spain is a romance of this nature, entitled *Bayād and Riyād*, in the Vatican Library. One of the miniatures contained in the work shows the hero swooning after receiving a letter from his beloved (reproduced by Ettinghausen in *Arab Painting*, Skira 1961). Some of the manuscript fragments from Fustāt in Egypt seem to have dealt with similar subjects. Several, analysed by the late D. S. Rice, are from a romance similar to those previously described, among them a miniature showing a tree growing from the graves of two lovers, who having been separated in life were now united in death.

Objets de luxe

In addition to manuscript illustrations, erotic scenes were employed on utilitarian objects, and also produced as independent pictures. From the earliest times the theme of two lovers was popular in Persian art. Although our knowledge of pre-Islamic Sāsānīd art is confined almost entirely to metal work, it seems that the motif of lovers was commonly employed alongside those of the enthroned ruler, and Bahram gur killing the gazelle. Some of the finest pieces of early Islamic pottery – like the twelfth- and thirteenth-century *minai* ware from Rayy and Kashān – are decorated with scenes of lovers. Many of these scenes on the *minai* ware are however of an idyllic character, showing a youth and girl seated in a verdant garden. None of the known examples of these love scenes seems to be of a fully erotic character. Whether they indicate a potentially erotic situation or whether they should be treated as examples of romantic love is not clear, though the latter seems possible; 'union – the proximity of lover and beloved – is most blessed,' says Ibn Hāzm.

As far as is known there are no erotic scenes surviving on utilitarian objects before the sixteenth and seventeenth centuries. However, The Institute for Sex Research (Bloomington, USA) possesses some ivory plaques from this period depicting couples copulating, which may have been employed in the decoration of caskets or toilet boxes.

It was in the nineteenth century that the decoration of everyday objects with erotic scenes came into its own. During this period many artifacts – wall tiles for example – were decorated with scenes of sexual congress. Such decorated objects, along with the independent erotic pictures, do not belong in either of the two major categories we have discussed so far. Obviously they are not of the 'romantic', or Platonic type, since the sexual act is involved. At the same time, since they are not immediately associated with some written work which reflects the acceptance of sex merely as part of the 'Divine Plan', neither is it possible to consider them examples of the 'natural' concept. Of course, if pictures from a scientific or medical work showing coital postures are extracted and shown independently, dissociated from any text, then the attitude of the observer towards them will at once change; no matter how scientific the original text, once separated the illustrations will become the focus of a uniquely sexual interest. It seems most likely that the original patterns for the independent pieces were such 'scientific' illustrations, detached from their context.

148

Independent pictures

At least as early as the sixteenth century independent erotic pictures were produced for aristocratic patrons, which claimed the same independent aesthetic status as the love-poems of the poets; and these are the most interesting erotic paintings that Islam has left us. Among them is the group of paintings and drawings which are attributed to and in the style of the renowned sixteenth-century master Rizā 'Abbāsi, whose calligraphic perfection and allusive subtlety were widely admired.

These pictures belong roughly to two types. One is straightforwardly sexual and the other which does not exhibit the sexual act taking place, is allusive and suggestive.

We know several examples of the former type, two of which are in the collection of M. Roger Peyrefitte. One shows a woman lying on her back, her arms above her head, her dress around her waist. The man, also naked from the waist down,

138/140

kneels above about to couple with her. The second shows a man and woman engaged in intercourse; the woman kneels, while the man entered her from behind, grasping her around the waist. Apart from the usual appearance of fruit and a wine decanter, the pictures have no background; nothing to distract the eye from the essential features.

139 The second type is represented by examples previously in the Sarre collection, Berlin. These pictures which are particularly interesting show women on the knees of seated men. The pairs are wrapped in embrace; each woman's arms are above her toying with the head of the youth, his arms are in turn entwined around her body; in one he is stroking her face, in both he is fondling her naked stomach. Each girl is portrayed provokingly. Her body which has been slightly elongated curves downwards, with gently swelling belly, large buttocks and substantial thighs. These parts of the body, the focus of erotic interest, are free of any decoration, while the simple dress is stretched tightly over them. Again, the smooth rotundity of the belly and thighs is emphasized by the fact that they are outlined by heavily exaggerated folds running parallel to the natural curves of the body.

It is interesting that the two previous scenes, though openly sexual, are far less exciting than these two. The two earlier scenes are coldly dispassionate; the artist has been almost 'scientific' in his approach, simply and straightforwardly recording for us the action, without comment. On the other hand the pictures showing the caressing couples pulsate with suggestion. The erotic movement of the figure of the woman whose buttocks, belly and thighs are emphasized with sweeping and caressing curves is suggested by the calligraphic inflection of the lines of which it is composed. Her smooth, moonlike face follows the constant canon of Islamic beauty. At the same time the painter is here using the classical psychological device of casting our interest forward in time, by implying what is to come. It may be that what is implied can be far more sensuously arousing than what is actually depicted. Certainly the expectations which are vividly evoked by this scene, culminate in the flower held above her head by one woman, the calligraphic efflorescence of which is almost certainly meant to symbolize an ejaculation.

It is possible, but not demonstrable, that such erotic pictures as these may have had a religious significance, symbolizing, as in Indian art, the union of the soul with the Deity, or the congress of the pious with the heavenly Houris, the Islamic counterparts to the Indian Apsarases. It is known for example that the religious mystics, the Sufis, often used love poems to generate the state of ecstasy necessary for the mystical union. The great fourteenth-century poet Hāfiz refers to the perfume of the genital organs of the Houris as an image of divine intoxication. Quite possibly highly suggestive pictures of lovers could have served the same purpose, particularly in Persia, where some form of religious art existed.

136/141 There was in many parts of the Islamic world, particularly Persia, an immense upsurge of interest in eroticism during the eighteenth and nineteenth centuries. This prompted the production of a large number of independent erotic pictures, although these popular scenes were of far inferior quality to the earlier pieces, made for aristocratic patrons, from which they originated. We do therefore have enough evidence to show that an erotic art did exist in the Islamic world, and that works of erotic art were produced according to traditions in their own right, not merely to satisfy the whims of a few particular patrons or artists. We can indeed go further and assert that there were elements in Islamic culture which, if they cannot be said to have encouraged all forms of erotic art, at least allowed them to exist.

Deviations

In addition to the pictures depicting natural sexual relations between men and women, there are others which illustrate sexual deviations and peculiarities. The deviations especially common in Turkey, the Arab world, and Persia were several and various. However, three stand out above all others: male and female homosexuality and bestiality. All were so common as to rank as normal activities. Homosexuality in particular is still a basic fact of Islamic eroticism.

We have two kinds of sources available for knowledge of homosexuality in old Islam. First, there is the testimony of Arab and Persian literature, and second the reports of Western travellers who visited the Near East in the eighteenth and nineteenth centuries. In many collections of stories it appears as the cause of bitter complaint by wives, neglected by their husbands in favour of boys. There are to be found in Islamic literature detailed arguments in favour of heterosexual love, offered so as to wean husbands away from homo-eroticism. Homosexuality appears on several occasions in the *Arabian Nights* and though it is not treated extensively there is evidence enough that it was a widely practised custom. According to Burton homosexuality in the *Nights* is of three categories: 'The first is the funny form; the second is the grimmest and most earnest phase of the perversion, for instance the debauching of youths, whilst in the third form it is wisely and learnedly discussed, to be severely blamed.' Burton's work and the categorical assertions of Soninni show unequivocally that homosexuality, especially male, was prevalent in all walks of society, particularly in the nineteenth century. We know, for example, of a certain governor of Bushire in Persia who used to invite passing seamen to his palace, and drug and assault them, and of groups of ruffians who used to wait in the caravansereis and at night pounce upon and rape the unsuspecting traveller.

The European travellers in the Near East paint an unattractive picture of the absorption of Islamic peoples in sensuality, homosexual debauchery and licentiousness. Chaudin tells of boy-brothels in Persia, Burton recounts the carnal pleasures of the Turkish bath, Soninni reports how the Egyptian after having 'glutted his favourite and criminal inclination' – unnatural relations – would retire to his 'harem' and burn incense 'in honour of nature'. It is quite certain that the custom was generally regarded as in no way improper or wrong. Homosexuality in the Near East, as in Ancient Greece, acquired a prestige that went far beyond simple toleration. It was regarded by many with veneration as a hallowed custom. The same fervent approbation of the love of boys that was heard in classical times, the same adulation for the beauty of the blossoming youth, we hear again in the poems of Abū Nowās and the odes of Hāfiz. Even the highly orthodox Ibn Hāzm finds nothing odd in discussing the love that may exist between members of the male sex: in fact he seems to make little difference between the relationship which exists between man and man and man and woman. Yet again Sheikh Nifzāwī, who was motivated by the highest of ideals, did not find it strange to include in his book a chapter dealing with homosexuality.

143   One of the group of sixteenth-century Persian drawings mentioned earlier shows a youth approached by an old man; the bare-faced page looks coyly over his shoulder at the greybeard who follows him. The debauchment of youths was as Burton says one of the grimmest aspects of the vice. Youths were in fact in much demand, and were often reared and groomed like prize cattle, often castrated, and 142   then sold or given as gifts to rich officials. Similarly a scene in the Metropolitan Museum, New York, shows an elderly man with a lecherous smile on his face making a suggestive gesture to a youth; he grasps his index finger in such a way as to suggest the penis inserted in the anus – one of many ways in which a procurer of boys would make known his desires.

Familiar arguments are reproduced in favour of the love of youths; the superiority of man, the uncleanness of woman. In addition the Qūrān is invoked: the laws of inheritance and the appointment of blood money favour the man rather than the woman, thus attesting his superiority. Similarly reason exalts the active above the passive.

These arguments were widely accepted and the great number of pictures from Persia depicting delicate and elegantly dressed youths with effeminate features and tumbling curls, were in many cases no doubt portraits of court darlings painted for the owners of such beliefs as those described above.

However, the much exalted love of youths was often held up by its opponents as a cause of weakness in Near Eastern society just as it was in the Roman and Greek. 'For,' said its opponents, 'if the masculinity of a man is what makes him better than a woman, then that masculinity is shamed by baby boys, middle aged men and old men, as well as youths. The pederast, if it is superior masculinity that he loves, should love it in greybeards as much as in boys.'

There were basically two types of homosexuality prevalent in the Islamic world: the first may be termed that of 'necessity' and the second that of 'choice'.

The former is the practice of unnatural relations brought about by the strict segregation of the sexes. The Moslem youth on reaching puberty found no natural outlet for his sexual desires – women and girls being strictly secluded – and was forced to turn to other modes near at hand, for sexual gratification, the chief such outlet being homosexuality, which thus became simply a substitute for heterosexual intercourse. Islam recognized that, if its women were secluded, the sexual urges of the unmarried must be provided for by social custom. Until very recently no social stigma attached to the active partner in a homo-erotic relationship. Any disapprobation there might be was reserved wholly for the passive catamite, who plays the feminine role. The appearance in literature and history of characters who are exclusively homosexual is very rare. Abū Nowās, for example, we are told 'wrote hymns to sodomy, but was more passionate for woman than a baboon'.

The second type of homosexuality is that which is indulged in through choice, in preference to normal sexual relations. This is the 'delight of the Egyptians' spoken of by Soninni, which continued after marriage, and which according to Burton led the Persian women to break out of the harems during the 1856 campaign and to flood the encampments of the British army – such was the extent of their husbands' sodomy.

This latter type is characterized by diverse variations, one of which we have represented in pictorial form. A nineteenth-century album painting in the collection of M. Roger Peyrefitte depicts three youths about to couple with each other. The one in the middle is engaging in anal intercourse with another kneeling before him, while his own posterior is about to be entered by a third youth seated on a chair behind him. Just such activities are reported by the travellers who visited the Near East in the last century, where it is mentioned that a group of persons would even form an unbroken chain, each one connecting with the one in front of him.

And what was the attitude of the Moslem religion towards homosexuality? Here there is some dispute. Burton for instance claims that Islam specifically forbids homosexuality quoting Qūrān 4:20: 'And if two (men) among you commit the crime then punish them both.' At the same time he remarks that the Qūrānic references to Lot and the destruction of the Sodomites are given more as evidences of God's power than as condemnation of pederasty.

A modern commentator, however, doubts the validity of Burton's quotation, and with the help of Moslem scholarship has shown that Burton's evidence is misquoted and in fact refers to the punishment of women who have committed indecencies (G. Algrove's *Love in the East*).

The same author suggests that homosexuality was not legislated against due to the fact that it was not considered to violate any property right; in committing adultery a crime against *property* occurred, and in fornicating with an unmarried woman someone's potential property rights were being violated.

However there may be other reasons – less subtle than the above – to explain the absence of any condemnation of homo-erotic practices. Homosexuality may not have been legislated against in the Qūrān for the reason that it was not seen as a problem. The incidence of homosexuality among the nomads of the desert is generally admitted to be low – Glubb and Thesiger deny its existence almost totally, and there is no reason to suppose that the situation was different in Mohammed's day. The Islamic code of law deals with most aspects of social life in detail, and it seems inconceivable that had homosexuality presented serious problems, it would have escaped legislation condemning it.

However in the century after the prophet's death Islam spread to both East and West, absorbing the remnants of classical Hellenic civilization, and of the Sāsānid Empire. It thus came to embrace peoples amongst whom the practice of homosexuality existed on a very much more extensive scale. With its condemnation of fornication and adultery and its favouring of the segregation of the sexes, Islam tended to increase rather than lessen the incidence of homosexuality amongst these peoples.

The same social conditions which allowed homosexuality to flourish also gave rise to certain other practices, among them bestiality and lesbianism. Bestiality is mentioned several times in the *Arabian Nights* though the instances referred to there usually describe the infidelity of women with apes and baboons, the more fantastic side of animal-human sexual relations and of which there are no known representations in Arab or Persian painting.

219

In reality male bestiality was far more common than female: according to Soninni people could be seen openly consorting with animals in the quieter streets of Rosetta when he visited it in 1779. At least one representation of male bestiality is known. This has been preserved in a manuscript housed in the Ambrosian Library, Milan, and is a fourteenth-century Mameluke copy of the *Zoology* of Al-Jāhiz which was a pseudo-scientific work on natural history. One of the anecdotes mentioned in this book tells how a man came upon his slave having sexual relations with a she-goat. This anecdote like many others in the work is illustrated and actually depicts the slave copulating with the goat, to the mortification of his master who stands nearby in a doorway.

The 'harems' were also naturally hotbeds of lesbianism; amongst large numbers of women kept in strict seclusion without male companionship, it was inevitable that the practice should be well-nigh universal. However, so far as is known although there are references to lesbianism in the *Arabian Nights* there are no pictorial representations in Arab or Persian painting, so we can do no more here than mention its existence.

Though the evidence is meagre, we can quite categorically state that there was indeed such a thing as erotic art in existence in the Islamic world, that the erotic elements in Islamic painting seem to have been continually present from earliest times, and that were examples more readily accessible we should probably find that erotic work formed a major part of medieval Arab and Persian painting, just as it did of poetry.

CHINA

7 The Pervasive Image

Public and private attitudes

China has been governed for many centuries according to a Confucian code of ethics, which adopts a stringently hostile attitude towards the open discussion of sex and love. Repeated attempts have been made at censorship, especially in more recent times, and there have been frequent official drives for 'moral rigour', during which erotic books and works of art have been burned, and sects with a particular interest in erotic practices have been suppressed. The present Communist drive is just such another. But this rigour is merely a matter of law and conformity, which requires that one should not waste one's time talking or ruminating about things which are intrinsically private. There has never been any deep or real feeling that sex and its manifestations are wrong; no religious puritanism cultivating a sense of guilt in connexion with sex has led to the repression of sexual instincts as in Christianity or even Brahmanism. In fact precisely the opposite has been the case. The Chinese have always regarded sex and love as being so normal and so much an essential part of life that they tend to believe celibacy to be both wrong and dangerous, and celibates – especially females – to be suspicious characters who are probably under the influence of evil spirits. Even during periods of Confucian public silence on the matter, private sexual facilities have remained unaffected, and it was possible easily to obtain sexual gratification or the auxiliary implements so much used to assist sexual enjoyment. It is probable that still today, under the mantle of poker-faced public silence, private arrangements flourish, and books and pictures are treasured by families. However, more than anything the Chinese have always guarded their privacy with the greatest care. So it is particularly difficult to obtain material for a book like this.

No erotic art has been preserved from aucient times. More has survived from later eras – the late Ming and Ch'ing dynasties. But it seems that, as might be expected, there have always been various levels or grades of erotic art. Amongst the most highly educated, eroticism has been closely linked with deep philosophical notions, and art, like poetry, has nourished itself on a rich symbolism of poetic analogies, literary allusions, and symbolic suggestions. More than anything the educated Chinese have enjoyed arts which offer them complex multivalent symbolism, awakening numerous echoes of meaning among the valleys of their minds. Such people, learned in old texts and philosophical speculation, have accepted and integrated the sexuality and sensuality of the body into their religion. There has been no conflict or divorce between 'two sides of man'. Man is one with himself and the world.

For the educated, and for the less educated, there was produced in vast quantities erotic art which was intended as an aid and stimulus to sexual life of every kind. There was, of course, frivolous pornography as well, which may have been persecuted by officialdom – but for its frivolity, not for its sexuality. Frivolity, to the Chinese, had a special significance in this context, as we shall see. But in China it seems to have been relatively rare, so far as we are permitted to know, that openly erotic art achieved the same dignity and psychological *sérieux* that it achieved in India. The tendency of high Chinese culture was for eroticism to be subtilized, philosophized, made oblique and allusive. Mere pictures of men and women making love, in so far as they were factual, were held to be of little aesthetic interest, though they may have been useful as aids to the stimulation of desire and informative as to the possible modes of intercourse. In this, of course, the Chinese were led astray by aesthetic snobbery, and a failure of imagination – as the Japanese ukiyo-e demonstrates triumphantly. However, the subtle art of eroticism made for the educated was bound to influence the humbler sorts to some extent. For both kinds shared a common substratum of ideas, and only rarely did the erotic painters and the illustrators of erotic books set their sights high. When they did, though, they were often brilliantly successful.

I shall begin by discussing the superior form of allusive and philosophical art, since it led the cultural field. Western collections contain many examples of it which usually pass unrecognized. Most people will be surprised at what emerges here. Some may even refuse to admit the sexual elements into their minds. In this they will be quite un-Chinese, and the loss will be theirs alone. In this day and age, when psychology has prepared us to understand the workings of symbolic expression both in dreams and everyday life, we must be prepared to see in the self-consciously allusive art of China more than immediately meets the eye.

Here again we must try to discern the underlying imagery behind the manifestations of erotic art. Our main source will be the mass of literary material which is broadly called Taoist, and has been explored by Henri Maspéro and R. H. van Gulik. For throughout their history the Chinese at home have been Taoist, however Confucian in public. And we shall not be wrong if we follow Maspéro in assuming that behind the exaggerated theories and systematic speculations of the historical Taoists, who had special sectarian interests, there lies a far older substratum of ideas and unconscious assumptions which supplied the basis for medicine as well as mysticism, and for sexual imagery as well as for medical theory. It implies a cosmology too. For it was characteristic of Chinese thought to feel a deep association between the individual man and cosmic processes he could never hope intellectually to fathom.

The official Confucianism which conditioned erotic expression in China is at bottom a cult of what the Chinese regard as mere good sense. Such Confucianism is both less and more than the teaching of Confucius – which is hardly relevant at all to our subject. The idea underlying official Confuciansism, which made it inimical to overt eroticism, is the analogy between the duty-structure of the state and that of the family. The state, represented by the Emperor and his centralized civil service, was supposed to stand in the same relationship to its subjects as the paterfamilias to his children, grandchildren and other dependants. The 'filial piety' required in the family was both the pattern and training ground for civil submission and obedience. The preservation of the state depended upon the preservation of the family customs which gave it its meaning. In the family the son's first, overwhelming responsibility was through his father to his fore-fathers, who had established the family's power and status, and of whom his father was the living representative. In civil life the subject's first and overwhelming responsibility was through his officials to the Emperor, the Son of Heaven. Love of wife, children, courtesans or concubines might amount merely to the improper distraction of a man's mind from his primary duty to father and Emperor. Chinese literature is full of moral tales which illustrate supreme examples of filial piety, when a man sacrifices self and loved ones alike for the mere convenience or comfort of his father, mother or emperor. This Confucian code was officially adopted as state doctrine during the Han dynasty, after 125 BC. It was a political contrivance, an intellectual method for bringing discipline to the divided and violent population of an expanding empire. And it was only consolidated when the main bases of Chinese culture had already been laid down. This culture was far older than the Han, far richer and more varied than Confucianism, and included all those elements of metaphysics, medicine and art which the Confucian cult was designed to control, and of which it was bound officially to take no cognizance. These elements therefore came to be expressed in highly abstract, obscure locutions. The Emperor himself had sacred duties which can only be explained in terms of a mythology far older than Han, inexplicable by Confucianism as anything but 'ancient customs'.

The Emperor claimed the title 'The Son of Heaven' from very ancient times. Rain-making, and other affairs in which the relationship between heaven and earth was involved, were his responsibility. The rulers of ancient China were thus much concerned with the sky, the stars, and the apparent movement of the heavens with which earthly seasons and weather were closely linked. They scanned the heavens – or ordered them scanned by their professional deputies – to read 'the signs', and so forestall disasters and seize favourable moments. The processes of celestial change were held to influence human affairs; and this influence extended into all aspects of life and society. The mythical image into which the changing heavens were combined, sometime in the late first millennium BC, was the celestial dragon, circling endlessly through the sky, his body patterned with stars, the incarnation of Te – power. To analyse the heavens and reckon out the year an instrument of jade, a combination of the objects later called pi and tsung, was used, the pi's edge serrated with lugs to focus on the constellations, its face scribed with a horizon line. By about 300 BC the pi had developed into a perforated disc of jade, which was often marked with little raised spirals to indicate the stars, and often it was carved into the form of a dragon with its head meeting its tail. This pi disc was the emblem of Heaven, which was the transcendent region whence came the ruler's authority, imaged as a celestial dragon. Pis were used in later times as the emblems of imperial authority delegated to the district magistrate, and were hung on a silken cord at the magistrate's gate. These talismans were made of jade, that stone so precious to the Chinese, invested with so much mysterious significance – mysterious because it is at bottom sexual. For jade, which occurs naturally in the form of nodular boulders, was interpreted mythically as the congealed semen of the celestial dragon, deposited in the earth. And all jade in China has belonged as of right to the ruler since time immemorial. Strictly speaking only he was entitled to dispose of it to his relatives and representatives – mandarins, magistrates and generals. The forms into which it was carved indicate the role its recipient was meant to play. The general's tally, for example, could be a tiger's face. Jade thus came to be regarded as the embodiment of the power of the celestial dragon, valuable not only for its hardness or rarity, but for its profound symbolic significance. This is the reason too for the common Chinese habit of wearing jade jewelry or of fondling a piece of jade. The latter is not a mere sensuous pleasure but a symbolic contact with the seminal source of celestial vitality.

Yang and Yin

149/150 The same mythology also explains the ubiquity of the dragon, violent, gnarled, whiskered and horned, on Chinese works of art, especially those of the Ming and later dynasties. Robes of emperors, their families and their ministers are embroidered with the dragon, imperial porcelain is painted with dragons, lacquer ware and belt buckles are ornamented with them. And although this type of dragon is cosmic with the generalized significance of universal power, the Te of the Tao, it is also masculine in a subtle way. For there is, as well, a counterpoise, a feminine 157 cosmic component. This may be represented by a female dragon (sometimes wrongly called a baby-dragon) which may carry in its mouth a ling-chih fungus. It is softer, less gnarled and violent than the male and has a decided tail. It adorns countless pots, jades and bibelots, and often 'encounters' the male dragon in one way or another, as we shall see.

At bottom, this feminine component is the spirit of the earth, which is fertilized by heaven. The intercourse of the two is manifested in the rain, the essential juice of heaven, meeting the clouds, which are the essence of earth. The meeting of clouds and rain is the universal Chinese literary image for sexual intercourse. The heavenly male dragon drinks, so folklore says, in the form of the rainbow from the waters of the earth to replenish his own celestial vitality. Like the celestial power the image of the feminine earth underwent transmutation and abstraction into a generic force. The basic text where we find the two forces most completely abstracted and jointly adapted to interpret every possible event in the world is the ancient book of oracles known as the *I Ching*, or *Book of Changes* – familiar to and deeply appreciated by Confucius. Precisely how old this text is, how corrupt and hence how truly intelligible, is the subject of heated discussion among Sinologists. It may well be that its fundamental ideas go back into the second millennium BC. What is certain is that, rightly understood or not, it was much studied, admired and imitated during the whole of Chinese history. Its fundamental idea is that all the changes which take place in any sphere can be interpreted as combinations of the activity of two forces. These are, broadly, male and female, and are represented in the oracular code by the male unbroken line ——, and by the female broken line – –. Questions addressed to the oracles are answered, through numbers reached by chance, either by a complex selection and counting of yarrow stalks, or the throwing of counters. These numbers designate either a male or female line. The lines accumulate, from the bottom up, into two trigrams, one above the other. The accumulation of lines into the trigrams and the consequent hexagrams represents symbolically the auguries for the future. The text of the *I Ching* elucidates these. The assumption is that human events and cosmic movements follow the same laws of change, which can be 'read' by means of the oracle. Each of the trigrams is associated with the change-pattern of one of the seasons: the epitome of masculinity is represented by three unbroken lines, ☰ ch'ien, the creative, or heaven – the dragon, in fact. The epitome of femininity is the trigram of three broken lines, ☷ the receptive, the earth, the dark. Each hexagram contains four trigrams, with the movement of change passing upward. Thus the whole cosmos is woven out of patterns of interaction between the two forces. In Taoism these forces are called by the famous terms Yang and Yin, and the divine Tao itself is the continuous process of their interaction. Yang is bright and masculine, sunlit and vigorous. Yin is dark and feminine, shadowy, abysmal. Most important of all for us, men are by nature full of Yang, women of Yin. The sexual intercourse of men and women thus represents an encounter on the human scale between a pair of cosmic forces. As the *I Ching* says, 'The sexual union of man and woman gives life to all things.' This is the basic idea behind the whole of Chinese eroticism, serious or flippant, sensuous or scatological. It was only forgotten perhaps in the last, degenerate days of the Ch'ing dynasty.

Each of these forces can be represented by a virtually endless series of symbols. Their combination and recombination down the centuries in one context or another has been the great intellectual, metaphysical, and sublimely physical game of educated Chinese. In due course we shall look at some of these symbols and their combination into works of art. Taoism, Buddhism and Confucianism each in their own way availed themselves of this ancient imagery, for different purposes and with different meanings.

One thing we must try to realize in our imagination, if we are to understand the meaning of Chinese art at all, is the ingrained feeling that all Chinese have of the correspondence between outer phenomena and inner experiences and sensations. It would not be too much to say that the Chinese regard the inner and outer worlds of experience as having identical systems of physiology. The whole aim of Chinese medicine and mysticism alike was to keep the two systems working in congruence, attuned one to the other. The earth breathes and man should learn to attune his breathing to that of the earth. The seasons change and man can actually assimilate the spirits of the seasons. The organs of his body perform in sympathy with celestial organs. He can balance in himself the Yang and Yin as they are balanced in the outside world. He changes his clothes and his habits strictly in accordance with the motions of Tao. If he gets into doubt or difficulty he consults the oracles to find out the current patterns of change to which he has to conform. Above all he nourishes in himself a vivid awareness of the principles of Yang and Yin; he feels within his body, as a matter of direct sensation, the interplay of the forces which generate the whole world of phenomena. He never claimed, as Hindu sages did, a massive *control* over the cosmos by virtue of his attuning himself to the Tao, but he did claim sympathy with it and tranquillity, and if not true immortality at least long life. The hero of Chinese thought and art is not the incarnate omnipotent deity, nor the strenuous athlete, nor the divinely beautiful charmer of souls. He is the gnarled ancient who, like the rocks and trees, has lived out time in harmony with the weather, the seasons, and celestial changes. He is everyone's ideal pattern. And sexual relations play a major part in the achievement of this ideal. Every Chinese would like to become an immortal, hsien. And even if one cannot go all the way, one can go part of the way at least, to grow vigorously, gracefully and peacefully old. We must recognize in the typical figure of Chinese art, the aged contemplative sage, extensive sexual implications. And we must never forget that Chinese imagery comes to us bowdlerized not only by European scholars of puritan habit but by generations of Chinese Confucians who expurgated their own texts and suppressed artistic imagery. Fortunately, enough information remains, and enough enlightened research has been done for us to discover the truth. It may seem strange that the image of age should also be the image of sexual achievement, but such is indeed the case.

Sexual practices

The facts of Chinese sexual custom and belief are these. China's was a polygamous society. It was usual for all men of any substance to marry several wives. One reason for this was to ensure a progeny of healthy, surviving sons to continue the family. In addition a man might take into his household a number of concubines. It would be impossible for a common man to satisfy the sexual desires of so many women without destroying himself. Moreover, for the good of his family it was held to be essential that he inject into such progeny as were born the maximum of vital power. Sexual intercourse and erotic feeling were believed to stimulate the vital force of Yang in men and Yin in women. It was essential that such stimulation should be carried out harmoniously and completely. But if orgasm occurred this vital force was expended in the form of bodily effluents, which would be absorbed by the other party, to his or her great benefit. Intercourse without orgasm was supposed to produce a strong enhancement of the Yang in men, of the Yin in women. Thus it was the custom in China's polygamous households for the ideal master to have sexual relations with as many of its humbler feminine inmates as he could, including maidservants, without himself experiencing orgasm. He then had intercourse with the wife who was intended to bear the next of his children in a condition of massively enhanced Yang. This was to ensure fertilization and strong offspring.

The sexual intercourses without himself experiencing orgasm that the master carried out with his concubines and maids were even more beneficial to him if his female partners themselves experienced orgasms, which would release the Yin effluent. This would be absorbed through his penis by the master, and add substance to his own 'cosmic personality'. His ability thus sexually to satisfy his women at the same time made his household a happy one, and produced peace within the walls of his home. This last was a very serious matter; for in Chinese society a man whose household was in a state of upheaval and bickering was highly suspect. His official position or his business reputation would even be jeopardized.

The issue of 'cosmic personality' (a convenient term I have coined) became more and more important according as a person's religious ambitions increased. The full

226

XIX Porcelain vase, enamelled with a design of a peach, metaphor for the female genitals. Ch'ing dynasty, c. 1720

logical implications of the Yang-Yin theory were drawn in the cult of Taoism, which survived centuries of rivalry, persecution and official muzzling. Taoism, in fact, is not merely a specious invention, involving admittedly odd practices. It is a logical extension of ideas implicit in Chinese customs from the most ancient times. The dietary regulations are perhaps the strangest of the customs. These were partly alchemical, based on ancient medical notions. They included the avoidance of cereals, and the eating of cinnabar (sulphide of mercury), which, be it noted, is a dense red substance used as vermilion pigment. They concern us little here. The only special points to be mentioned are that among the mystical foods and herbs producing spiritual benefits are a certain magical mushroom – of an inverted conical type like the Chanterelle – saliva, and dew, which is the saliva of the breathing earth, the body of Yin.

The sexual practices upon which spiritual success depends consisted basically of frequent and continuous sexual intercourse without any orgasm at all, whilst absorbing as much as possible of the energy of the opposite sex. It was best, especially for elderly practitioners, if the chosen partners of the opposite sex were young and vigorous, for then they had most Yang or Yin to release in orgasm (compare the story of the old King David). There are numerous stories in Chinese literature and legend concerning men and women who retained life and vigour by this means for vast periods of time – though never, perhaps, a true eternity. The legendary Queen of the West, Hsi Wang Mu, is supposed to retain her beauty and longevity by coupling continously with young boys who give her in their semen their Yang essence. I have not seen a work of Chinese art which shows her *in coitu*, but she *is* often shown sitting or standing with one of her sexual companions beside her. Hsi Wang Mu is the Queen of the mythical Peach Garden in the Western K'un Lun mountains, to which allusion – albeit sentimental – is made in the famous poem by Tao Yuan Ming (d. AD 427) *Peach Blossom Spring*. We shall discuss this important concept later on.

Certainly these religious sexual practices were not confined either to men or women alone. Indeed there are many stories of women practitioners, legendary and real. But far the greater part of the symbolism is developed from the masculine point of view, and it may be most convenient for me to adopt this standpoint. Thus, the man would retain his semen, the concrete substance of Yang gathered from his whole body, throughout a vast number of intercourses, during which the Yang was believed to be increased and activated. He would pass it up the channel of his spine, by meditative effort, and collect it in his head. At the same time he would absorb all the released Yin from his female partners that he could obtain by any means, unite it with the Yang, and so join himself to the cosmic force (Te) of the Tao. A considerable sage would require a large number of partners for his practice. One alone would never be able to supply the necessary Yin-juice. The Yellow Emperor is said to have become an immortal through having intercourse with twelve hundred women. The value of his partners to a man would always depend directly upon the genuineness and vigour of their sexual response.

The whole imagery of the feminine effluvia, represented by the clouds on the cosmic scale, is very important in Chinese art. One passage quoted by van Gulik from a Taoist text well known in Ming times, describes the Yin juices produced by the body of a woman upon which the wise man will nourish himself. These

149

229

XX Porcelain vase, painted in underglaze blue and overglaze green, purple and yellow enamels. A complete Taoist allegory. K'ang Hsi period (1662-1722)

juices are called the 'great medicine of the three mountain peaks' (a significant title). The first juice, from the Red Lotus peak, is grey and comes from the 'cavities' under a woman's tongue. It moistens a man's viscera and generates vital essence and new blood. The second, from the Double Lotus peak, is white and comes from her two breasts. The best comes from the breasts of a woman who has not yet borne a child, and who has no milk. To drink it helps the circulation of the woman's blood, and moves her to the pleasure which prompts the other secretions. The lowest peak is the mons veneris, called the peak of the Purple Fungus, otherwise the Mysterious Gateway, or the Grotto of the White Tiger (emblem of female energy). Its juice is red, analogue of the mystic cinnabar of the earth, and emanates from the depths of the vagina only when the woman is at the height of pleasure from intercourse. It can be drawn out by the man creating a vacuum with his penis, which can then absorb it. This last juice is the most important, the human analogue of the Yin effluvia of the earth itself, the clouds. Incidentally, for this reason *cunnilinctio* was much practised amongst the Chinese, as it provided an excellent means of imbibing this most precious fluid.

Sexual cryptography

I should mention that there are, of course, a very large number of other, non-sexual symbols involved in this erotic art; many depend upon rather banal puns, or specific literary references. But the image of the peach can best introduce the specifically sexual cryptography of Chinese art. In a sense, so far as he was concerned, the male

XXX   Taoist's sexual partners were simply female organs which nourished him with their juice. The peach was the standard image for such a sexual partner. The Chinese peach has a deep and opulent cleft, and visually suggests strongly the female genitalia while its generous sweet juice symbolizes the effluvia of the Yin. Throughout the history of Chinese art the peach has this significance. But because it is a symbol and not a sign it does not point directly at the female vulva itself but to ideas represented by it – ideas which as we have seen, possess a cosmic significance and nobility, and for which the female vulva itself is a symbol. The association in the mind between the vulva and the peach will enhance the dignity and significance of both actual female vulvas and peaches. So far as art is concerned the primary analogy which makes the symbol a valid one is a pattern of visual form; and unless both elements of the analogy are vividly present to the mind, consciously or semi-consciously, the symbol will have no meaning. So for us to understand the meaning of Chinese art of this kind, we must be sure that we experience directly all the components of the symbolism. We must assimilate the metaphor both visually and sensuously, awaking memories of our own in the face of the work of art.

One icon, that combines many Taoist sexual symbols together, is the figure of Shou Lou, the patron saint of longevity (it is probably based upon the traditional

154/177/178   idea of Lao Tzu). He appears as a happily smiling old man, whose skull is grossly enlarged by the converted Yang-semen he has stored in it. He often holds a peach in one hand; sometimes his finger is stuck into the cleft of the peach in an unmistakably sexual manner; sometimes the peach-cleft opens to display a stork – the standard Chinese symbol of celestial longevity. Sometimes he – or one of his alter egos, called Tung Fang So – holds the branch of one of Hsi Wang Mu's *176* peach trees bearing many peaches – indicating his multiplicity of sexual partners. He is often depicted in paintings as inhabiting the peach-gardens of Hsi Wang Mu, *155* and the peaches on the trees are painted a clear and unmistakably physical pink. In his other hand Shou Lou usually holds a staff, which may be a tree branch. But in a few extremely interesting cases the staff takes the form of a dragon which curls round behind and over the sage's head. This can only refer to the cosmic seminal Yang which has risen up his spine and invigorates him. There is perhaps an echo here of related Buddhist symbolism of cobra-heads which appears in late Khmer art.

The Taoist dietary, moral and sexual disciplines were held to create within the body of the sage the new 'cosmic personality'. This is called the 'golden boy' or sometimes the 'crystal infant'. He is the product of the fusion of Yang and Yin within the crucible of the sage's mystical physique. This 'boy' is a new body in the form of which the sage plays happily in the gardens of paradise. The playing children who appear in many paintings and decorative works from the Ming dynasty onward refer to this idea. Often the significance is sharply pointed by the *171* boys carrying peaches, or playing in a peach-garden. It is most likely that these boys are in some subtle way related to the boys who couple with Hsi Wang Mu in her peach-garden paradise. I should also mention that these boys often hold the characteristically shaped sceptre called ju-i, a name applied also to clouds, and patterns based on cloud forms. Such sceptres were given between friends as wedding and birthday presents. In sculptures and paintings Lao Tzu carries one as his *156* standard iconographic attribute. He is the reputed author of the Tao Te Ch'ing, the fundamental text of Taoism, and the prototype of the Taoist adept. The sexual meaning of this sceptre will be explained later.

The cryptic sexual symbolism invented by Taoism flourished extremely during the Ming and Ch'ing dynasties. It drew upon the store of significance gained by symbols during their long cultural past and a wealth of accumulated allusions to well-known legends and literature. As I have suggested, the classical method of Chinese thought has always been to avoid direct assertions expressed in abstract terms but rather to bring forward concrete figurative instances which convey the meaning either as examples or as analogies. Such symbols are often deliberately allusive and multivalent. During the later Ming and Ch'ing, customs established themselves which prompted the artistic elaboration of ancient symbols. In defiance of older purist aesthetics gentlemen began to set out on their desk, or on the table of the Confucius-shrine which every substantial house contained as a matter of course, various bibelots, many of which had been presents from their friends and associates. The ink-stones, water pots, brush washers and paper-weights they used on their writing tables, as well as their seals, became ornate objects of *vertù*. Their domestic porcelain was highly ornamented. Such exhibitionism, however much it was frowned on by the austere, gave opportunities to deploy an allusive imagery based upon traditional ideas for the private appreciation of a gentleman and his friends. And these small works of art in jade, stone, ivory, wood, glass and porcelain of which Western collections are full, are often highly sexual in their significance. They lie like erotic time-bombs on our shelves, waiting to explode at the touch of a little knowledge. There can be no doubt that through the centuries of Confucian obscurantism such oblique erotic communication between like-minded people was highly relished by the Chinese.

These works contain a large number of other symbols for the Yin and its physical embodiments. The pomegranate is one, especially the pomegranate whose skin bursts open to display the seeds among its reddish pulp, thus indicating female fertility. It appears on countless pieces of post-Ming porcelain, and other bibelots. The shell is another. Shells, in legend, may often turn into women. A red-fleshed melon or a closed peach globe refers to virginity. The peony, ubiquitous on painted porcelain, and a standard metaphor in erotic literature, presents an extravagant glorification of the vulva and labiae, which may be recalled by calligraphic finesse in certain erotic paintings. This association in Chinese tradition goes back to one of the ancient songs in the *Book of Odes,* which was learned by heart by every literate Chinese. At the Wei riverside festival in spring the boys and girls have intercourse:

> The boys and girls
> Gather there for their sport
> And a peony is the prize.

So the peony is also the flower of spring, and blossoming youth. The lotus was transferred from India to China by the Buddhists. In India it was a symbol both for the female genitals and the cosmic creative act of the female deity. The Buddhists used it to refer – not to a vague 'purity' as is sometimes said – but to the crossing of the boundary between existential realms. As the lotus emerges on its stalk from the mysterious region beneath the water into the air, so the transcendent Buddha appears in our world. So, too, in the Pure Land texts faithful 'souls' are born into the realm of paradise. There is a birth or rebirth symbolism involved. But the simile of the lotus for a lovely girl is universal. Gold Lotus is not the 'heroine' of the famous erotic novel Ch'in P'ing Mei without reason. For to the Chinese a woman's beauty depends as much upon her intimate as her public charms. Twining lotus-plants with their fertilized seed-boxes are common currency in Chinese symbolic expression, referring to a happy female household and its fertility. And the lotus pond, where play storks, egrets or herons – symbols of longevity – so often carved in ivory or stone, represents a similar idea.

We must go further in pursuit of Yin-symbolism. For Yin is called in the ancient classics 'the receptive' and the 'intrinsically female'. Of course the essence of the female is that it is receptive. Woman herself is regarded sexually as an unfillable receptacle, to whose appetite for Yang it is all too easy to fall victim. Therefore receptacles were always seen by Chinese eyes as essentially female (so they are, of course, by the unconscious perceptions of Westerners). Many Chinese vases, in fact, are virtually formalized images of the female genitalia. And we must recognize that pots and vases of all kinds are genital emblems of the Yin. There can be little doubt that the magnificent efflorescence of Chinese art-porcelain, with its symbolic ornament, sprang from the Chinese libido-charged interest in 'the receptive'. We can respond to this interest with our own feelings, though we may prefer to keep their real nature from ourselves. I illustrate an image which demonstrates perfectly

149 Chinese mandarin's robe, embroidered with sexual symbols of the Yang and the Yin. 19th century

150 Large Chinese jade bowl, with Yang dragons
amongst the clouds. 17th century

151 Hardstone statuette of a stallion, emblem of
masculinity. Chinese. 16th century

152 (*above*) Large blue-and-white porcelain dish decorated with peonies, female emblems. 15th century

153 (*below*) Small blue-and-white Chinese porcelain dish, decorated with the circular emblem of combined Yang and Yin, and with the trigrams of the Book of Changes. 16th century

154 Chinese hardstone figurine of Shou Lou, patron of longevity, with peach and dragon emblems

壽添海屋

乙未夏日壽道人祺畫

155 Part of a Chinese painting representing the Peach Garden of Hsi Wang Mu, with figures of Shou Lou and Lao Tzu. 17th century

156 (*opposite*) Part of a Chinese painting representing the Peach Garden of Hsi Wang Mu, with figures of Shou Lou and Lao Tzu. 17th century

157 Chinese jade disc of heaven, carved with figures of the male Phoenix and the female dragon carrying the ling-ch'ih fungus in its mouth. 18th century

158 Chinese hardstone carving of a goddess of longevity. She is surrounded by female symbols; roses (?), ling-ch'ih fungus, deer, and clouds—the female effluvia of the earth. 18th century

159 Chinese hardstone figurine of a deer, whose body is marked with plum-blossom – symbol of sexual pleasure – and who bears a version of the ling-ch'ih fungus. 18th century

160 (*far left*) Chinese ju-i sceptre of carved and painted wood. It is made up of female fruit-symbols. 19th century

161 (*left*) Chinese lapis-lazuli carving of the purple ling-ch'ih fungus, symbol of the feminine genital effluvia. 18th century

162 (*below*) Chinese hardstone carving representing a goddess holding the female 'receptacle' from which emerges the cloud-fungus, symbol of the female effluvia. At her feet a fiery-maned Kylin, symbol of the male Yang. 17th century

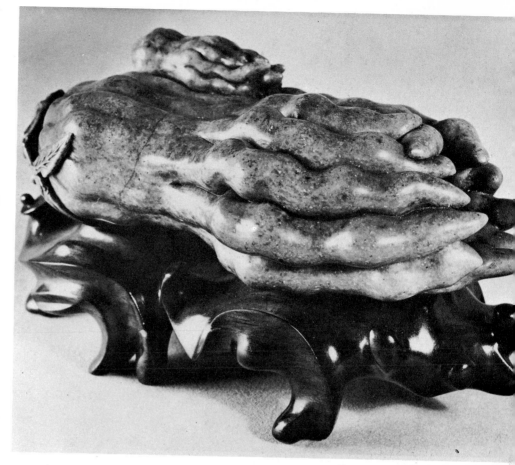

163 Chinese hardstone carving of the finger-citron fruit, emblem of the female genitals. 18th century

164 Chinese jade bowl, a female receptacle carved with peaches, peach-blossom, and a female dragon. 17th century

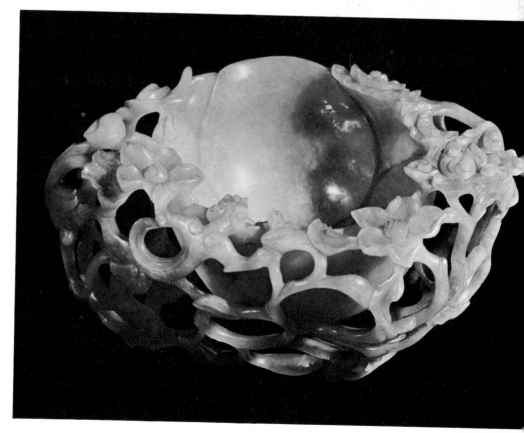

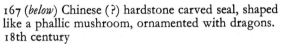

165 (*left*) Small Chinese jade emblem of the female vulva, carved with the cloud-pattern. 18th century

167 (*below*) Chinese (?) hardstone carved seal, shaped like a phallic mushroom, ornamented with dragons. 18th century

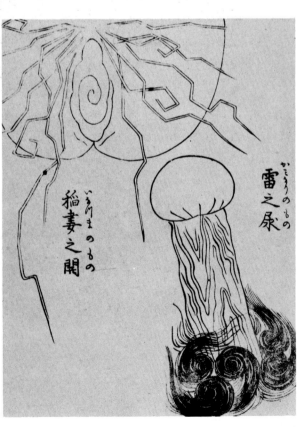

166 Illustration to a Japanese erotic book. The cloud-spiral representing the vulva, the mushroom with yang-flames representing the penis. 19th century

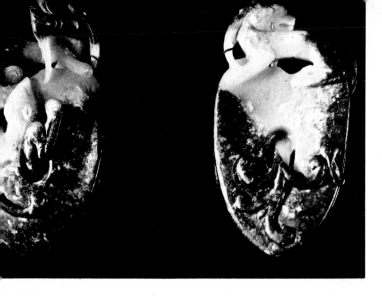

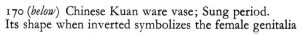

168 (*left*) Chinese small jade emblem of the female vulva, out of which creeps the female dragon. 16th century

170 (*below*) Chinese Kuan ware vase; Sung period. Its shape when inverted symbolizes the female genitalia

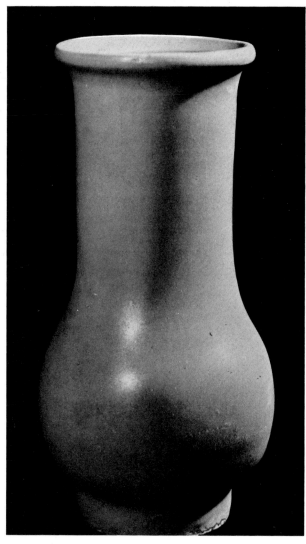

169 (*left*) Chinese vase of white earthenware; T'ang period. Male dragons bite the lip of the female 'receptive' vase

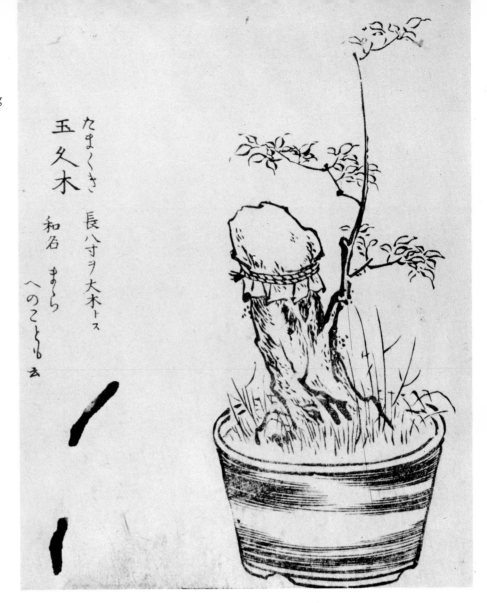

171 (*opposite*) Chinese painting of Taoist children, holding Taoist emblems, among which are a ju-i sceptre, peaches, and the flowering plum branch, emblem of sexual pleasure. 16th century

172 Illustration to a Japanese printed erotic book. Humorous conversion of a plum-tree trunk in a tub, into the likeness of the penis. 19th century

173 Chinese brush-washer in pink hardstone, with Taoist children. 18th century

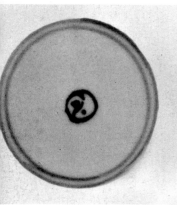

174 Famille verte saucer with male bird and female peonies. The mark on the foot (*inset left*) is a Yang-Yin symbol. K'ang-Hsi period (1662-1722)

175 Chinese ginger-jar, blue and white glaze, in the plum-blossom and cracked ice design, signifying sexual pleasure in old age. Ch'ing dynasty

176, 177 and 178 Miniature Chinese jade figures of Peach-bearing deities. 17th-18th centuries

179 Chinese porcelain 'cricket cage'. Women may have carried these in their sleeves, with singing crickets in them. Enamelled with erotic garden scenes in colours. 18th century

180 and 181 Chinese porcelain rice bowl painted with erotic figures. 19th century

182 Miniature Chinese porcelain couple in intercourse. 19th century

this identification for the Chinese context. It shows a feminine deity, at whose feet 162
gambols the animal emblem of the male Yang – a Kylin, in fact, an animal whose
meaning will be explained later. She holds a vase. From this vase emerges an
effluvium, which clearly symbolizes the Yin-juice. For it takes the shape both of
the common formalized cloud used everywhere in Chinese art *and* the magical
ling-chih fungus, as it appears in numerous carvings. We can recall that the most
intimate Yin secretion of the feminine body comes from the 'Peak of the Purple
Fungus', where lies hidden the 'Grotto of the White Tiger'. The vase held
by this goddess is its source, and so the vase is here consciously used to symbolize
the mystic female genitals. The 'Purple Fungus' is represented on one of our plates 161
by a carving of lapis lazuli, which suggests the same cloud shape. The external
'fungus of immortality' so continuously sought among the mountains by the
Taoist sages of legend must therefore be a symbolic Yin-bearing excrescence of the
earth, analogous to the clouds, a condensation of the essence of female Yin-juice. 158

The whole lavish Yin symbolism of fruit and fungus is summed up beautifully
in certain examples of ju-i sceptres, emblems of 'immortality' associated with Lao
Tzu and given as presents between Tao-minded friends. The shape of the sceptre
itself is a stylization of the fungus-pattern, suggesting unmistakably a 'flowing-out'
form. Some such sceptres merely have the 'cloud pattern' on their tops. Others are
carved with grape-bearing vines or Taoist legends. But I illustrate one carved with 160
a superabundance of Yin-emblems – peaches, bursting pomegranates, clouds and
the strange 'finger-citron' fruit, sometimes called 'Buddha's fingers'. This ambiguous fruit has a highly sexual suggestiveness. Its 'fingers' certainly resemble
penises; but on this sceptre they are braced out to suggest an open mouth formed
of soft, clutching tendrils. And in another piece they combine into a deeply sensual 163
image of the muscular vagina.

The receptive Yin-nature of the pot, vase or bowl is reinforced by further
symbolisms of a sexual significance. Certain types of Chinese vessel in T'ang, in 169
Yueh and Lung Ch'uan wares, and following them in later porcelains, show the
pot embraced or peered-into by a plastically modelled dragon, emblem of the
Yang. The number of post-Ming Chinese pots *painted* with dragons is indeed
legion. Another vessel I illustrate, of pinkish hardstone, probably used as a brush- 173
washer or water pot, shows the female receptacle embraced and played with happily
by Taoist 'golden boys'. Many other small receptacles show related symbolisms,
especially brush-washers of this kind into which the pointed brush was repeatedly
dipped. 'Writing' was a cant-word for sexual intercourse in Ming times.

A very common erotic flower symbol, highly ambiguous in meaning, is the
flowering branch of plum blossom, often called 'prunus' or 'hawthorn' in Western
books on Chinese art. Generally speaking, in all Chinese literature, plum blossom
is a universal metaphor for sexual pleasure. When it appeared amongst them the
Chinese called venereal disease 'plum blossom poison'. As erotic charms, the
canopies of the beds of women were embroidered with plum branches, and bed-
boards were painted with them. There is a bowdlerized and incomplete meaning
given to plum blossom in many reference works, which purports to explain its
constant association in a group with the pine tree and the bamboo – both of which
stay green in winter. Since winter is a standard metaphor for white-haired old age,
the joint symbolism of the 'three friends' refers in general to vigorous old age.

But we know now what vigorous old age signifies in the Chinese context. So it is not enough to identify the third of the 'friends' as simply the plant which flowers while the snow lies on the ground. It refers to a special kind of pleasure, just as the bamboo refers to a special kind of knowledge, not only in old age but universally. The pine tree provides Taoist nourishment with its kernels. Plum blossom pleasure provides its own kind of nourishment. The branches of plum-blossom against a ground of winter ice painted as ornament on ten thousand blue-and-white 'ginger jars' thus take on a new dimension.

171/172

175

172   One further frequent allusion of the 'flowering spray' is as a metaphor for the erect penis. The association of flowering sprays with peaches, pomegranates and lotuses on innumerable pieces of painted porcelain can thus be understood in both an erotic and a cosmic sense, with fresh resonances of meaning added to them. 'Libation cups' of rhinoceros horn – that famous aphrodisiac substance – may also be adorned with plum sprays, as they may with dragons, male or female. Likewise the icons of goddesses carry flowering sprays in their hands, in baskets or vases, symbolize the esoteric gifts of sexuality the goddesses bear with them. Similarly, since the full moon is used as a constant metaphor for the attractive feminine posterior we must recognize an extremely erotic connotation implied in those very common far-eastern pictures of a flowering branch silhouetted against or approaching the full moon. Once again literary sources demonstrate unequivocally that this meaning was both intended and read, often humorously, especially in Japan. Another frequent image for the male organ is the 'jade tree' or 'jade stalk'. The special significance here of the element 'jade' is obvious. Another name for the penis is 'the red bird', or just 'the bird'. In fact there is a close homophony between *tiao*, the old form of *niao* (= long tailed bird), and the normal word for penis.

164

158

Other emblems of the masculine are less equivocal. The dragon-pillar is an obvious one. Occasionally on a small scale this image can become assimilated to the male organ, as in the little ivory seal I illustrate. But the commonest Yang emblems are the various magnificent and semi-mythical creatures that are paragons of energy, light and brilliance. One particularly splendid symbol is the long-tailed Feng-Huang, identified with the gorgeously plumed male Chinese pheasant, the 'red bird' *par excellence* and often called the Phoenix. Like the dragon the Feng has his female counterpart, a female bird whose tail is short and lacks a proper crest. She often appears in the embroidered designs on women's robes. The lion forsakes on occasion his Buddhist significance as the Power of the Doctrine, and dedicates his flaming mane and tail to the impersonation of the Yang. The name of the turtle, who was invested with so much mythical significance by the Chinese in other directions – as supporter of the world, or as paragon of longevity amongst animals, possessed of immense reserves of vital energy – became so common a synonym for the penis, as well as connoting a man who connives at his wife's adultery, that it was banished for a long time from the language. His head in his carapace has suggested sexual ideas to many other peoples. Finally, the stallion is also an obvious image. The special Chinese slant it has rests on the legend that during the reign of a great and good emperor a 'jade horse' makes its appearance in the land. The numerous gift-horse figurines carved in jade may have been understood to offer delicate congratulation to the reigning monarch. Some, Confucian beasts,

167

157

lack sexual organs altogether. But others, more uninhibited, lift their hind-legs to display extravagantly developed members – no doubt a still more effective compliment to the Yang of the recipient and perhaps his emperor. Another animal symbol of sexuality is the deer, whose pulverized horns, like the 'horn' of the rhinoceros, feature prominently in those recipes for aphrodisiacs with which Chinese medicine is so largely concerned – even today. The deer is the creature ridden by Lao Tzu in many of the sage's icons, and is often represented alone – not because he is a beautiful Bambi, but because he incarnates the power of sex. Sometimes he bears on his back an emblem of the ling-chih, or carries it in his mouth. Finally I must mention the extraordinary compendium of the Yang animals that was assembled in the figure of the Ch'i lin (Kylin) or 'unicorn', who appears on many pieces of porcelain. In earlier examples he has a dragon-like head, with one or two horns, a scaly body, shaped like that of the deer; at other times he more resembles the Buddhist lion, his bushy tail flames, and flames spring from his shoulders. He, too, is said to appear during the reign of a supremely good emperor.

In the symbolic repertoire of the cryptic bibelots there are images for sexual conjunction. Sometimes male and female dragons circle around a pi disc; sometimes a male Feng-Huang plays with a female dragon, who holds a ling-chih cloud-fungus in her mouth. But far the commonest cosmic image is that in which a single dragon or a pair of dragons sport with a round jewel (often called a pearl) among the clouds. The jewel is frequently combined with a symbol for the lightning-flash. This motive is much used on the penis-rings referred to in the next chapter. The Dragon, the persona of heaven, source of the fertilizing 'rain, among the clouds' which are the female effluvia of the earth, alludes to the cosmic sexuality familiar to us by now. The jewel is probably a reference to the Tantrik Buddhist term *Vajra*. Tantrik Buddhism, whose sexual rituals are discussed in the Indian section of this book, is called *Vajrayāna*, the way of the *Vajra*. And *Vajra* means diamond, male organ, and bolt of lightning. The pearl among the clouds is most likely a Chinese echo of the 'mani padme', 'the jewel in the lotus', 'the male in the female' of Tantrik Buddhism as we knew it until recently in Tibet. The dragon's jewel thus represents the spiritualized male sexuality, semen converted into cosmic Yang. The dragons do not 'play' with it. They 'possess' it; or rather it is synonymous with their nature, perhaps even with their breath. Tantrik Buddhism did make its way into China, where it had a large following during the Six Dynasties and T'ang, then later under the Mongol Yuan. Later it was, however, successfully 'liquidated' by the Confucian hierarchy, just as it was in Japan, where a castrated version was allowed to survive as Shingon. Nowadays neither the Chinese nor the Japanese speak of it. It is all supposed never to have happened. Its art has vanished. In China old memories of Tantrik Herūkas and Dākinīs may survive as an element in the scabrous tales – sometimes illustrated – told with relish about fantastically endowed monks and their amorous escapades. No doubt there is a strong ingredient of realistic fantasy as well, for monks and nuns have been common targets for sexual speculation the world over – not without reason.

Other images of sexual conjunction occur, for example, in jade belt or cord fastenings which are made in the form of a shield-shaped plaque, pierced with a slot meant to suggest the vulva, through which a small female dragon sometimes

151

158/159

162

157

149

165/166/168

251

creeps to meet either a male dragon or a Kylin. The encounter of the male Feng bird and the peony occurs quite often. This, of course, still has cosmic connotations; but the connotations of fish are human. Normally the fish – usually the red carp – is not only a symbol of but a charm for fertility. (It can, in other contexts, symbolize success in the official examinations.) A fish emblem – of stone, wood, metal, pottery or paper – is put in the place where the woman who wants children is to have sexual intercourse. But the fish features again in purely sexual images so common that it must be present at the back of every Chinese mind, and is referred to in many pieces of painted porcelain. 'The fish playing among the water plants' is a synonym for the intercourse of the sexual organs, whilst the happiness of a pair of lovers is always indicated by a pair of fishes, either as wish or charm.

Erotic elements in landscape

In view of the ubiquity of these elements of symbolism we must look into the speculations and imagery involved in what are always accepted as the highest flights of the Chinese artistic spirit, the landscape paintings. I do not – obviously – wish to suggest that these have only or merely a sexual meaning. This would be totally absurd. What I must suggest is that unless the deep laid sexual *element* in their cosmic meaning is assimilated they can never properly be appreciated. For they are not intended as mere pleasant rustic scenes, but as full-fledged images of the Tao. For the 'mountain-water' pictures of Li Chen, Kuo Hsi, Mu Ch'i, Hsia Kuei, Wang Meng, Tao Chi and a hundred other masters present images of the mutual interrelationship of the Yang and the Yin, imbued with all the resonance of the sexual analogy between world and man. The mountain is the image of heaven, Yang, the bright, whilst the valley with its effluent mists is the image of Yin. From one down into the other flows the fertilizing water of heaven, in its streams and waterfalls. A stereotyped image of the mountain bedded in the abysmal *149* waters forms part of the imagery of, for example, imperial robes. And since the body of the earth is an analogue of the body of man, we can now perhaps grasp the sublime meaning to the Chinese of the ideal hermit-sage, the Shan-jen, the 'mountain man'. Whereas the ordinary adept nourishes his Yang and Yin by intercourse with concubines, maids and courtesans, the mountain-man, whose affectionate but detached viewpoint the painters of landscape pictures always adopt, nourishes his by involving himself intimately with the cosmic sexual process. His Yang he nourishes by his proximity to heaven on the mountains, and, as a thousand poems testify, by joyfully submitting to the rain. The feminine effluvia of the earth replace for him the female juices of the homebound adept's feminine household. The mist and clouds rise up for him to inhale at the right time of day. He eats the milky mushroom in which the Yin essence of the earth is condensed. The red cinnabar he consumes contains the red essence of the rocks of the earth's body. And so by this, and other related symbolic practices, he becomes one with the web of forces of which the universe is woven. The sage's sexual life does not stop. It just changes, and is enhanced. The great painter of landscapes is he who has animated his own double-sexed spirit in conformity with that of the cosmos, and is thus able through his brush to transmit to those who study his pictures a true experience of Yang and Yin working as Tao. What he transmits is not there simply to be looked at, but to be physically absorbed as a transcendent sexual gift.

8 The Overt Tradition of Chinese Erotic Art

The expression of movement

The Chinese themselves never regarded any kind of purely illustrative art as being of great aesthetic significance. Their highest appreciation was reserved, after calligraphy, for the 'mountain-water' landscape painting in which the totality of their philosophy was implicated. Then came the plant, flower and rock painting, in which these significant objects could most readily be invested with their symbolic attributes by means of the living brush. Human figures and figure-painting could enter this second category, if their inspiration was heroic. The great Zen monk-painter Liang K'ai (*c*. AD 1200) raised his brusquely painted figures of Zen patriarchs, and of the great poet Li Po, to the status of metaphysical expression. In this he followed a Zen tradition running back through his master Mu Ch'i to the legendary Shih K'o (tenth century AD) and Kuan Hsiu (*c*. 900). But such achievements in figure painting were exceptional. Generally speaking, from T'ang times onwards the many pictures of historical events, beautiful women, Confucian heroes and heroines, deities and religious tales which were painted, were regarded as little more than a cut above journeyman work. Fine calligraphic qualities alone could redeem them. Sexual and erotic pictures belonged in this category. And in so far as they are good by Chinese standards, they are good by virtue of their calligraphic élan. This, in itself, is very important for our appreciation and understanding of them.

The whole of Chinese painting rests upon calligraphy, the art of the moving brush. The artist's brush itself moves in response to the motions of his spirit. If he is a great artist, in tune with the cosmic motions of the Tao, his brush will capture and reflect the cosmic motions. He will be able to express 'the spirit of forms', not their mere outward likeness. And in Chinese culture this spirit is always a spirit in *motion*. Forms are not defined, either in philosophy or art, as eternal fixities, as permanent established areas or volumes which are intelligible only in spatial relation one to another. Western art at its greatest has always sought to root its forms in the eternity of ideal categories, by means of concepts of proportion, area and volume related to the ideal, immutable figures of Euclidian geometry. It has always sought to transport its images outside of time and change into an ideal eternity which Western culture recognizes as the essence of reality.

The Chinese conception of 'reality' and artistic 'realization' has always been totally different. The Chinese have always perceived the real as an immense web of movement and change. All apparently static and unitary objects are seen as patterns (li) merely apparent in the process of continuous evolution. The patterns themselves are far less 'real' than the uniqueness and individuality of the actual events which suggest them. The unrepeatable uniqueness – even eccentricity – of the artist's brush-stroke reflects reality more truthfully than the underlying pattern it may suggest. And when, for example, Liang K'ai has portrayed the sixth patriarch of the Zen sect tearing up the sūtras, he has sought to capture in his brush strokes, not the ideal volumes of the figure, but the movements it makes, and the spiritual movements of the subject. Motion and its qualities are the essence of his artistic realization.

The humbler artists of erotic figure art share in this same outlook, even if they may fulfil it with less success. They may remain more closely tied to the primitive *194* conception of drawing by mere outline, but their outlines convey qualities of movement rather than static volumes. We must therefore be prepared to read the lines of which the subjects are composed in sequence, along their length, so as to grasp their qualities of movement – sexual movement, in the best examples. Especially in the Japanese ukiyo-e erotica, themselves originally inspired by Chinese prints, do we find pictures which set out to convey not only the movements made by lovers, but also the moving spirit of erotic sensation.

The cultured Chinese always sought his sense of cosmic awareness in the first place in the presence of wild nature, among the mountains, valleys, streams, of his own country, with their clouds and rain. But since the affairs of life, official position and business concerns demanded that such men lived mostly in cities or large towns, they equipped their homes with gardens which were works of land-scale art, symbolic of those elements of wild nature from which they were – temporarily perhaps – cut off. Chinese houses of substance are based upon a pattern of enclosed courtyards, whose privacy is supposed to be conducive to harmony, both personal and domestic. Within this system of courts, the garden with its hillocks, artistically clustered rocks, trees and shrubs was included. Within it were often located pleasure pavilions from which the garden could be enjoyed. And such enjoyment was a kind of substitute for the enjoyment of wild nature. These pavilions, and the house-rooms themselves, were often equipped with elaborately rustic furniture – uncomfortable to the Western frame. This, too, was meant as a reminder of the operations of the Tao, whose vast sequences of time and change have sculptured the rocks, the mountains and ancient trees into their gnarled, eroded forms.

Such gardens, their pavilions and garden-rooms are the commonest setting for *184* Chinese erotic pictures. The setting itself connoted the Chinese concept of the ultimate pleasurable environment, whose distant undertones are cosmic. Time and again the pictures show a pair of lovers embracing on a rustic bench, shaded perhaps by a vast banana tree. The girl may lean negligently upon a fantastic rock whilst her lover approaches her from behind. Perhaps the two play the flute twined together on a dais. And if they are making love indoors, a vista of the garden will usually be visible through one of the windows, while a landscape screen or hanging scroll may remind them of the final meaning of their copulation. They act out on the human scale the union of Yang and Yin which weaves the stuff of the world. Sometimes a solitary girl may appear in the garden experiencing the arousing of *183* her Yin, perhaps caressing her own genitals, whilst she is in the presence of one of the standard emblems of the Yang, such as a Feng-huang bird.

Legend and literature illustrated

Many of the erotic pictures which survive are in the form of late Ming and Ch'ing woodcut illustrations to novels and stories, most of which contain long erotic passages. The most famous of these is Ch'in P'ing Mei, which has been translated into English (with passages in Latin!). But as yet none of the sets of illustrations has been published along with the translated text. In such illustrations the erotic situations are faithfully recorded – for example in Ch'in P'ing Mei, Hsi Men's tying up of Gold Lotus's feet to the pillars of a pavilion, whilst he embraces another girl and bombards Gold Lotus's vulva with small fruit, all three drunk and laughing. All kinds of erotic indulgences are represented. For, to some extent, it was the function of such novels to present the *non plus ultra* of sensual enjoyment taking place within the privacy of the courtyards of a wealthy home, or in the well-appointed houses of accessible ladies. But it must be remembered that even the most famous erotic novel, Ch'in P'ing Mei, is in fact a Taoist cautionary tale. The 'hero' is not only a villain, a thief and murderer who enjoys temporary success, he is also the very type of sexual spendthrift. He never conserves his semen; he spends his store of Yang in continually repeated ejaculations, and dies at last miserably, killed perhaps by the last ejaculation Gold Lotus draws from his body, misunderstanding the condition of priapism with which he is afflicted. For, as Taoist theory has it, the vulvas of women, as well as being the gateways to immortality, can also be 'the executioners of men'.

There are, and have been as the literary sources tell us, many pictures which represent the correct, heroic eroticism of emperors and sages, some of them in the form of independent paintings by considerable artists. Van Gulik has recorded text which refers to such old pictures of pre-T'ang times. For example, a legendary emperor is represented engaged in intercourse with one of a group of ladies. Some of them help by holding the head of the consort who is favoured with the imperial attentions, whilst others assist the action by pushing the imperial posterior. According to the religious prescriptions such intercourse should normally result, for the man, in ejaculations of a number suitable for his age, and the time of year (far fewer in winter than summer). Of course all his intercourses should *186* naturally be consummated by feminine orgasm. Thus many pictures follow the heroic pattern, in that they represent a man in relationship with several women. For, at the domestic level, the handbooks of sex recommended that the master of a house should not run the risk of causing discontent amongst his feminine household by shutting himself away to have intercourse with any particular member. His relationship with a new member, or with a temporarily favoured member, should be carried on in the presence of the others, who should be accorded their turn to avoid jealousy. Such multiple sexual relationships were the subject of *120/188* fantasy-speculations in Chinese art just as they were in Indian. For numerous pictures and prints were made which illustrate various forms of the *non plus ultra* of masculine sexual pleasure. The hero, for example, reclines, whilst he receives the attentions of several women; one engages his sexual organ in normal intercourse; the others satisfy themselves with his fingers and toes. The same image appears countless times in Indian art. It is, of course, certain that in the flourishing brothel quarters of old Chinese cities, as more recently in the

183 Chinese album painting in colour. Girl stimulating herself sexually on a flowering tree in a garden. 18th century

185 Chinese album painting in colour. Woman satisfies herself with a dildo taped to her foot, watched by her lover. 18th century

187 Chinese album painting in colour. *Fellatio* in a garden room. 18th century

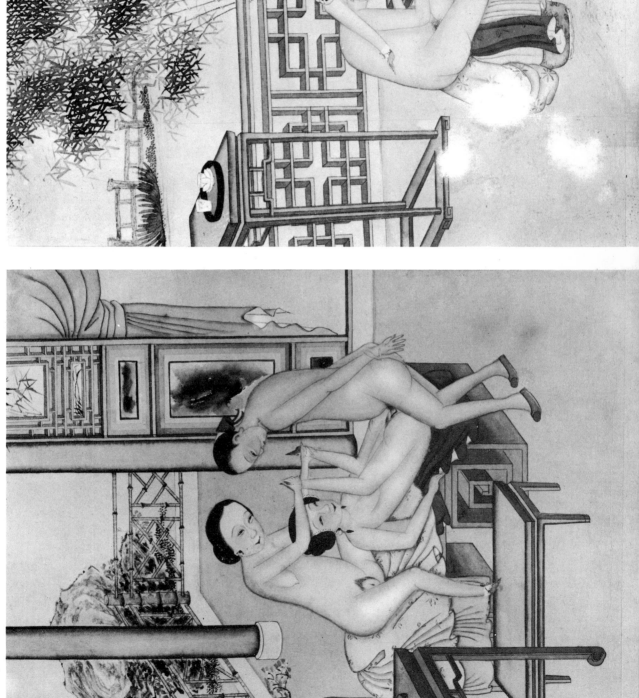

184 Chinese album painting in colour. Woman arousing her sleeping lover in a garden pavilion. 18th century

186 Chinese album painting in colour. Man and two women in sexual intercourse. 18th century

188 Chinese album painting in colour. Man and two women in sexual intercourse. 18th century

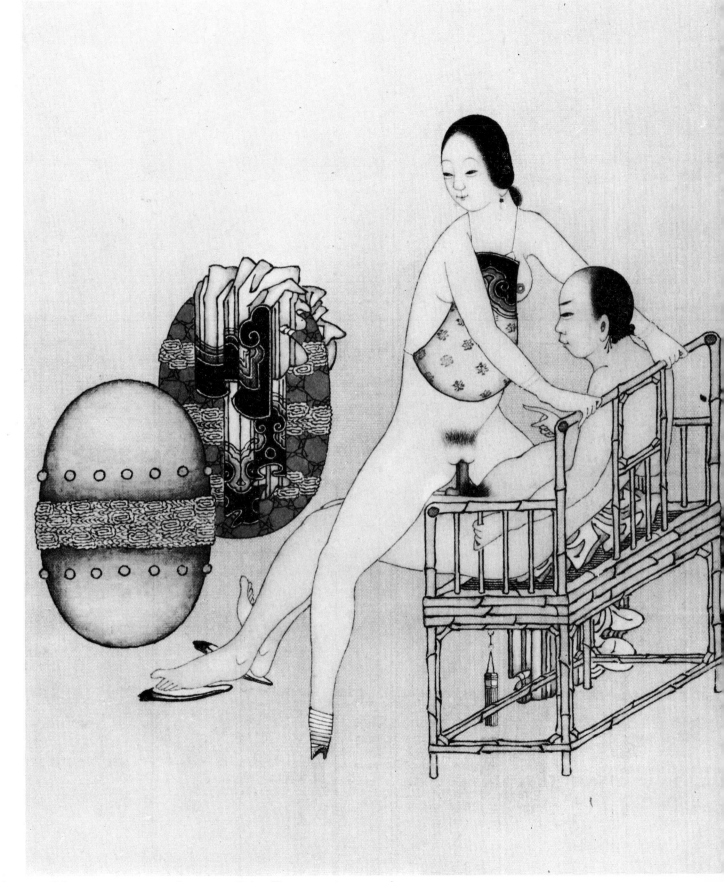

189 Chinese album painting in colour. Pair of lovers. 19th century

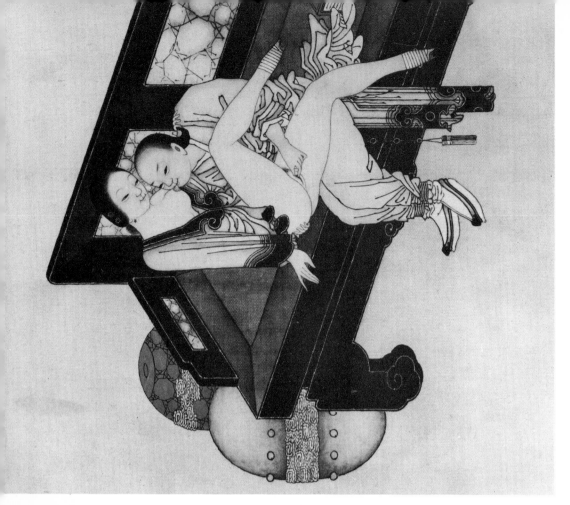

191 Chinese album painting in colour. Pair of lovers in preliminary caresses. 19th century

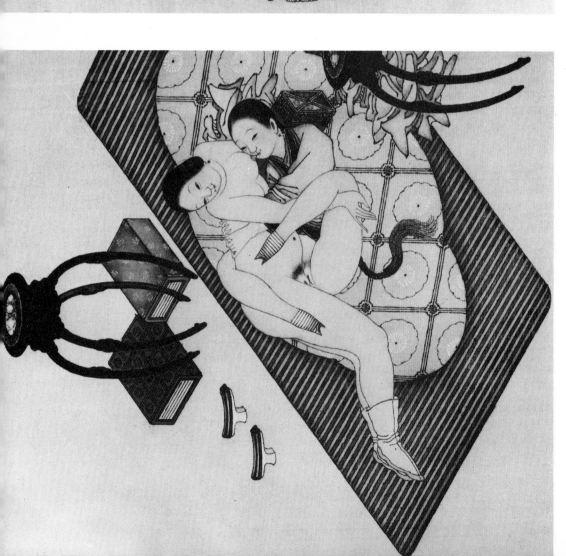

190 Chinese album painting in colour. Tribadism. 19th century

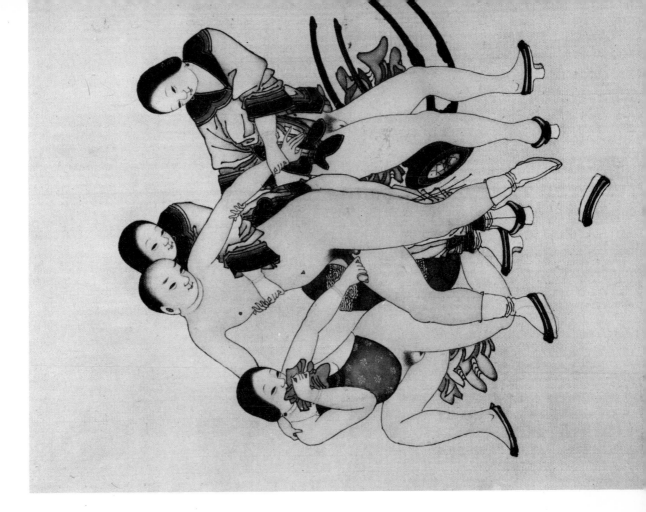

193 Chinese album painting in colour. Man desired by three women.
19th century

192 Chinese album painting in colour. Pair of lovers in a boat.
19th century

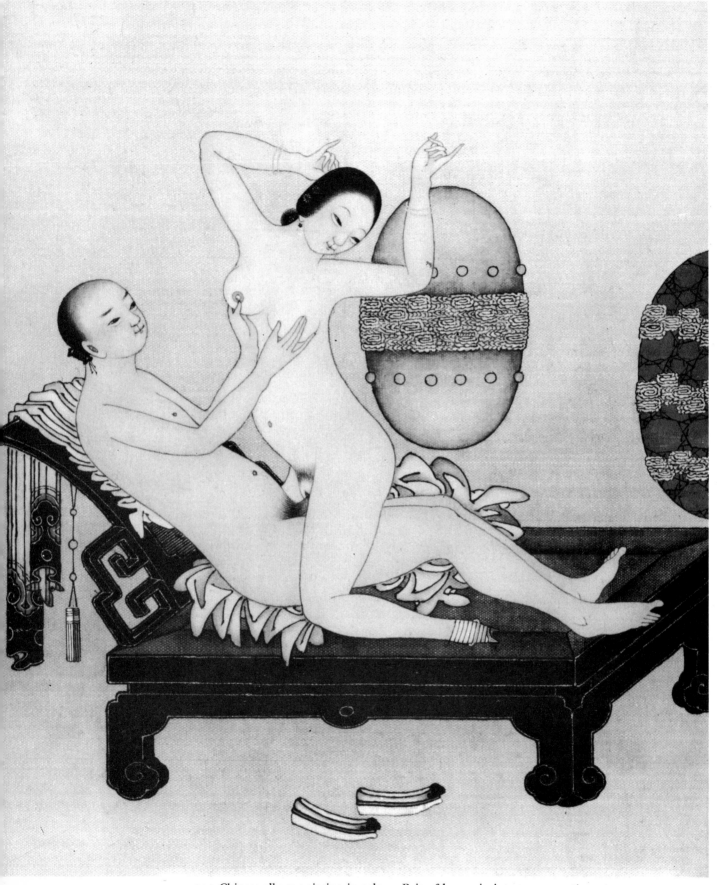

194 Chinese album painting in colour. Pair of lovers in intercourse. 19th century

'flower boats' of Chinese watersides, such pleasures were indeed freely available. *192*

In view of all that has been said about the medical and metaphysical importance to the Chinese cultured gentleman of sexual intercourse it is natural that the high-class courtesan and the prostitute both enjoyed a respected place in Chinese society. The courtesan, like her sisters in many other countries, was usually an accomplished artist in her own right, proficient in music, poetry and brush work. She provided intelligent and aesthetic entertainment for scholars and officials whose interests were not catered for by vulgar festivals. In fact through the *187* centuries many such men often kept one or more courtesans as temporary, or even permanent members of their households, as well as patronizing others. Their skill in the art of love was appreciated as highly as their skill in the other arts. At the same time, since sex was regarded as a normal human activity, the prostitutes who exercised their erotic skills in the brothels of the cities and towns were usually regarded as valuable members of society. For multiplicity of sexual partners for a man was an ideal which could best be met with their help. It is interesting that a scene set in a brothel, portrayed in one of the surviving sets of Ming woodcut prints, contains a stork – the Taoist symbol of longevity, as well as the canonical rock emblematic of the Tao. Such pictures were obviously intended to perform the same function as similar representations in India – to enhance the mental imagery and ritual value of the sexual act, as well as promoting its proper performance.

Erotic manuals

This same function was the purpose of perhaps the largest and most important class of erotic pictures, the illustrated manuals of sexual practice, upon which the other kinds of erotic art were originally based. Unfortunately, for reasons which have already been made clear, the history of the art of these manuals, and the whole history of erotic manuals before Ming times (*c.* 1500) can only be written from references to them in literature. No actual works of erotic figure art earlier than Ming survives for us to study.

We know that during the Former Han dynasty written manuals were in free and wide circulation. The official Dynastic history gives a list of eight major texts concerning 'The Art of the Bedroom', which follows the list of medical works. The texts seem to have conformed fully to the orthodox Taoist teachings concerning sexual practice that I have described. For the note at the end of the list reads (according to the translation of van Gulik, whose translations are used in what follows):

> 'The Art of the Bedchamber' constitutes the climax of human emotions, it encompasses the Supreme Way (Tao). Therefore the Saint Kings of antiquity regulated man's outer pleasures in order to restrain his inner passions, and made detailed rules for sexual intercourse. An old record says: 'The ancients created sexual pleasure whereby to regulate all human affairs.' If one regulates his sexual pleasure he will feel at peace and attain a high age. If, on the other hand, one abandons himself to pleasure disregarding the rules set forth in the above mentioned treatises, one will fall ill, and harm one's very life.

Unfortunately none of the actual books listed has been preserved. However we do know that illustrated manuals existed in the Later Han; a poem written early in the second century AD, an epithalamium by Chang Heng, conveys the bride's feelings towards her new husband. First telling him how she wishes to offer him comfort as though she were his mattress, and then silk coverlet and canopy, she says:

> Let us now lock the double door with its golden lock,
> And light the lamp to fill the room with its brilliance.
> I shed my robes and remove my paint and powder,
> And roll out the picture scroll by the pillow's side.
> The Plain Girl I shall take as my instructress,
> So that we can practise all the variegated postures,
> Those that an ordinary husband has rarely seen,
> Such as taught by T'ien Lao to the Yellow Emperor.

Several interesting points appear from this poem. First, the book mentioned is one in the official Han list, so it is quite possible that if *one* was illustrated, so may all have been. Second, the Plain Girl is mentioned. She is one of three such characters – the others are the Dark Girl and the Elected Girl – who appear as the female instructresses in the conventional dialogue form used in early manuals of many arts, besides the Art of the Bedchamber – War, for example. The Plain Girl becomes an important Taoist vehicle of sexual wisdom. She seems to be related to a figure in an old fertility cult, whose emblem was that common symbol for the female genitals, a shell. It is as a magical shell that she first makes herself known to a poor but virtuous man, whom the Heavenly Emperor is concerned to protect. The story is given in a Chou dynasty commentary on the Book of Mountains and rivers. The Plain Girl's handbook is said to have helped men and women towards immortality by sex.

184   The poem also shows that the illustrated manuals of sexual postures were used even in Han times, as we often see them being used in late pictures, as stimuli to the varying and prolongation of intercourse. Another poem by Chang Heng runs as follows:

> There is a girl, a worthy companion of Hsi-Shih
>   (a famous beauty)
> Tall, and of handsome appearance,
> With a soft and finely chiselled face,
> Full of languorous charm
> Her figure as faultless as a sculptured statue,
> Waist as thin as a roll of silk,
> With a neck long and white as a treegrub
> Of extreme elegance and wholly fascinating,
> Of gentle nature and modest behaviour
> Yet of luxurious and alluring beauty.
> With jet black hair done up in a chignon
> So shining that it could serve as a mirror,
> With a mouche that stresses her winning smile,
> With clear eyes, their moist gaze limpid.

With white teeth and red lips
And her body a dazzling white colour –
When then the red flower shows its beauty
And exhales its heady perfume,
While she is staying with you in the night
And you feast and sport with her,
Pointing at the pictures you observe their sequence,
While she keeps being bashful and ashamed
And coyly protests –
Such are the delights of carnal love . . .

The postures themselves would, of course, have been similar to those given in numerous later texts, copied no doubt, from the earlier, and to those contained in the repertoire of the sexual manuals of other countries. They do not need to be described here. The Chinese texts give as well elaborate instructions for the rhythms and qualities of strokes the man should deliver with his penis. This is an aspect of intercourse – the aspect of movement, it should be pointed out – which does not receive the same attention in the erotic literature of other peoples. Perhaps I should point out, as well, that the Chinese, like the Indians, are accustomed from birth to sitting on the floor, or on a dais, so that they have flexible knees and hip-joints. Thus many postures and movements are possible or at least comfortable for them which would cause normal Europeans considerable anguish. It is worth noticing that in these Han texts, as in much Taoist literature, the woman is regarded at least as the man's equal in the sexual partnership, and can even be his superior, in so far as the Plain Girl and the Dark Girl are presented as being the teachers of emperors. This was a point which aroused the resentful anger of strict Confucianists, who were committed to the subordination of women.

In fact, this mutual hostility reached extreme proportions towards the end of the Han dynasty, when the Taoists banded themselves together under a high priest called Chang Chueh into an organization known as the Yellow Turbans. The Confucian administration only suppressed them at the cost of its own power, for the Generals who did the suppressing ended by destroying the Han dynasty itself. However, we know something of the Yellow Turbans' sexual practices, for a Buddhist monk recorded what he knew of them a hundred years after their military defeat, when their customs were still remembered and still practised. The author, who is of course hostile to the practices himself, writes:

The Taoists wantonly practise obscene disciplines from the Yellow Book, which include 'opening the gate of life', 'embracing the Adept's infant', and 'making dragon and tiger sport together': also the art of sexual intercourse of 3 – 5 – 7 – 9 (a rhythm of alternating deep and shallow strokes), and the Heavenly and Earthly net as taught in the Yellow Book, whereby men and women indulge in promiscuous sexual intercourse like birds and beasts.

This *Yellow Book,* the manual of the sect, is recorded elsewhere as elucidating the above practices with the addition: 'Open the red gate, insert the Jade stalk. Yang will imagine the Mother of Yin white like jade, Yin will imagine the Father of Yang fondling and encouraging her with his hands.' This extraordinary and deeply illuminating passage offers a profound image of the psychological aspect of the true erotic process. The male and female energies when they are aroused in each partner promote a divine personification of their sexual counterpart which is projected upon their human partner. Surely this is one of the most important functions of all erotic art, whether it be called pornography or not – to provide the patterns for personifications that divinize the act.

Repeatedly throughout Chinese history such Taoist sects with colossal followings, their practices based on the *Yellow Book*, have challenged the Confucian ethos. Taoist 'monasteries' supplied the milieu. They have repeatedly suffered bloody repression; but they have survived. As one renegade adept wrote:

> We were . . . taught the practice . . . according to the *Yellow Book*, and the 3 – 5 – 7 – 9 method of sexual intercourse. In pairs of 'four eyes and two tongues' we practised Tao in the Cinnabar Field . . . Husbands exchanged wives, all for carnal pleasure; they were not ashamed to do these things even before the eyes of their fathers and elder brothers. This they called the 'True art of obtaining vital essence'. At present the Taoists regularly engage in these practices, in order thereby to attain the True Way.

So too, it should be remembered, do the Shāktas of Bengal. Even as recently as 1950 the Taoists, with the same sexual practices, were reported as being once more repressed. It is certainly true that extravagant claims were made at the popular level for the results of elaborate and difficult sexual practices, including immortality, immunity to disease or weapons. But true Taoists always knew that sex must form part of a much wider code of practices, and should be carried out as a true erotic experience, rather than a mechanical ritual, however elaborate. And, in fact, Confucianism did not disapprove of the Art of the Bedchamber as such, so long as it remained a private matter, and women were not encouraged to claim rights above their station. Only when it entered into the public arena, laying claim to an absolute validity and threatening established social custom, was it resented and suppressed.

In all the erotic manuals which supplied the materials for illustrations, as in all other Chinese cultural manifestations, the antiquity of the ideas and practices was much emphasized and valued. We thus find that, so far as can reasonably be ascertained, the basic patterns and ideas they contain are constant, varying from text to text mainly in matters of detail. They deal with the subject under the following general headings. First there is a discussion of the cosmic principles involved, followed by an affirmation that both man and woman must be properly aroused in their Yang and Yin natures, desiring each other equally. Great attention is paid to the love play preliminary to intercourse, and this is often illustrated. Stroking, kissing, and mutual caresses must never be neglected. Nor must the artistic *tendresses* of penetration ever be ignored. The actual postures of intercourse number about thirty, and are given such typically Chinese poetical names as 'Reversed Flying Ducks', 'Low-branched pine-tree', 'Wailing monkey embracing a tree', 'Cat and mouse in one hole', or 'Bamboos near the altar'. These postures are of course meant to be adopted in sequence, so as to make up an artistic whole, and they supply the main bulk of the illustrative material. The movements to be

268

XXI Famille rose plate-dish. A pair of women sit in a garden surrounded by female emblems, such as lotus, cloud, fungus etc. The male Feng bird flies into the garden down to them. The storks of immortality appear in the border. An allegorical representation of domestic Taoism. Late 18th century

made are carefully described, and, as I have pointed out, the illustrations attempt usually to suggest the moving qualities of the sexual act:

> Deep and shallow, slow and quick, straight and slanting thrusts, all these are by no means uniform, each has its own characteristics. A slow thrust should resemble the movement of a carp caught upon the hook; a quick thrust should resemble the flight of birds against the wind. Inserting and withdrawing, moving up and down from left to right, interspaced by intervals or in quick succession, all these movements should be properly correlated. One must apply each of them at the proper time and not always stubbornly cling to one style to serve one's own convenience.

There may be more precise descriptions of movements – for example, nine styles of moving, six styles of penetration, all of them described with poetic metaphors: 'Flailing to right and left like a brave general breaking the enemy ranks', 'like a sparrow picking rice grains', 'rising then plunging low, like a big sail braving the gale', 'prying open an oyster to get at the shining pearl inside', 'like an iron pestle descending into the mortar'. Such a sense of movement is deeply entrenched in the Chinese calligraphic style of representation.

The handbooks then continue with instructions as to how the man should, when he wishes, inhibit his orgasm, and draw forth from the depths of his partner's vagina the Yin fluid; how he should ensure conception by means of directional and seasonal magic; how a woman should conduct herself once conception has taken place with elaborate prescriptions for pre-natal care. Various auxiliary practices may be described and illustrated, such as preliminary *penilinctio* and *cunnilinctio*, or *coitus per anum,* both heterosexual and homosexual. Then various appropriate medicines are described, including aphrodisiacs and those used for such purposes as enlarging or shrinking the genital organs of both men and women, and curing impotence or frigidity. The later handbooks may also include passages describing the 'yogic' technique for making the Yin and Yang together combine within the body of the practitioner, and ascend to his 'brain'.

Sexual devices

One feature of some handbooks, often referred to in novels and other literature, and very often represented in the art, is the use of sexual implements of various kinds. Men often wore jade, ivory or bone rings around the root of the penis for the purpose both of maintaining the erection for a long time, and of inhibiting the orgasm by compression of the urethra. These rings were secured by ribbons or tapes passed between the legs and round the body. They were often carved with Yang-symbols, such as a pair of dragons with enlaced tongues and tails. There does not appear to be any reference to the use of penis pins or plaited collars as used in other countries, nor even to the common Japanese customs of binding the erect penis with straw or tape before intercourse, or of wearing an openwork enlargement of the penis (often jokingly called 'armour'). Feminine implements were common, for, of course, female homosexuality was accepted as normal for a poly-

190

271

XXII Famille rose plate-dish. A lady holds an open pomegranate. Her clothing is elaborated around the pubic region. One boy holds a lotus shaped like a ju-i sceptre, the other holds a ju-i. In a jar is a ladle, there are a coral stalk and peacock feathers in a vase, and 'writing' materials with books behind her. An idealized family woman, she wears the attributes of Hsi Wang Mu. Late 18th century

gamous society, and encouraged. There are many pictures of these in use. There

185

are a variety of dildos, made of different materials; perhaps the commonest was made of the stalk of a certain plant, which was soaked in hot water before use, so as to give it an agreeable warmth and swollen texture. Curved, double-ended dildos were made, to be used by two women at once; one woman, after inserting one end of the dildo into her vagina, would bind it to her body with tapes, and would then embrace her partner and introduce the other end into the partner's vagina. A more sophisticated implement was made, which was specially designed to procure prolonged gentle sexual pleasure. This took the form of a small hollow sphere of very thin silver, containing a metal ball, which was inserted into the mouth of the vulva. Any movement of the body causing the ball to rattle inside its container produced a sexual stimulation. It is possible that another similar implement is represented in art, though not described in text. This consists of an hourglass-shaped membrane, with a constricted neck, partly filled with mercury. The upper globe is inserted into the vagina, the lower globe remaining outside. Pressure of the thighs, even in walking, can squeeze the mercury from the outer globe into the inner, thus producing a continuous gentle stimulus.

One extraordinary Chinese custom, certainly intended as a sexual gesture, must be mentioned. This is the custom of binding the feet of women, which probably began just before the opening of the Sung dynasty, as a court custom, and has only recently been abandoned. After Sung times bound feet become an essential mark of every high-class lady, and of every sexually attractive lady represented

189/191

in visual art. What foot-binding involves is this. Virtually from birth the feet of girls are bound in tight bandages so as to compress the toes and arch of the foot into a tiny, pointed hoof-like shape. In the course of time the bones are deformed and take on this shape permanently. The bandages are always worn, even in old age, and they are never removed in the presence of anyone. In fact the Chinese woman reserves for her bound feet the same extravagant modesty the Western woman reserves for her 'red flower'. When, in an erotic illustration, a woman's foot-bandages are shown as loose, this should always be interpreted as conveying a kind of abandon which is only possible to a woman in a situation of deep intimacy. In rare examples a woman with loosened bandages is shown caressing her lover's penis with her feet. This represents a very special favour indeed. Never are the feet actually represented as completely uncovered.

Precisely why the bound feet should have come to occupy such a central place in erotic culture is unexplained, but it is a fact that they became the erotic focus of interest in all Chinese female imagery, with a vast amount of literature devoted to them. The tiny embroidered shoes, and draped silk leggings in which they were clothed also became the objects of an elaborate fetishism. Certainly the taboo and the sexual interest are psychologically interdependent. Perhaps the best 'explanation', psychosymbolism apart, of the origin of the taboo has to do with status. For a woman with bound feet cannot walk far – she must be carried in a chariot or litter – nor can she do any kind of menial or coolie work involving carrying weight. The bound foot might thus be one of many similar status-marks known to anthropology. And since the woman with bound feet has to walk with small, delicately tripping steps, such a gait became the epitome of sex-appeal. She cannot dance properly, of course. And this may well be why though we hear of many great courtesans of T'ang times who were superb dancers as well as poets and musicians, in Sung times and after dancing more or less disappears from the list of the courtesan's accomplishments.

Paintings and print albums

The history of the erotic art based on the handbooks, and carried through in the illustrations to novels and other literary works can only be traced with any accuracy from the Yuan period (1368–1487) onwards. References to illustrated versions of the Plain Girl's classic are made in T'ang literature. But most important perhaps is the censored reference made by the Ming artist and collector Chang Chou to a painting he saw by the T'ang painter Chou Fang. Apparently this exemplary work, which depicted an emperor having intercourse with one of his ladies, whilst other ladies attended, was meant as a work of art in its own right, independent of any text, and with no educative purpose. In this it must rank as perhaps the earliest such work recorded. The Ming critic remarked of the picture that the chief lady was shown as very beautiful, her vulva moist and rosy with erect clitoris, 'so that her passionate thoughts are well expressed'. He also notes that seals indicated that the picture had been in the collection of the Yuan artist Chao Meng Fu, himself a noted painter of erotic subjects.

Under the Yuan (Mongol) dynasty sexual life in China seems to have enjoyed something of a florescence after the confusion and puritanism of the Sung. Marco Polo records that in the Khan's capital there were at least twenty thousand courtesans and prostitutes. Many of them were involved in the world of the theatre, as actresses; and stories of their lives have been preserved in a treatise named *Records of the Green Bowers*, as the houses of love were called. This is the period, too, which seems to have witnessed the emergence of the novel as a literary genre, with all the opportunities it offered for illustration. It is significant that it was the foremost scholar-artist of the period Chao Meng Fu (1254–1322) who was noted as an erotic painter; whilst under the Mongol emperor Hui Tsung (1333–67) Tantrik Buddhism, complete with its paraphernalia of Herūkas and Dākinīs, sexual yoga, and images of Tantrik copulation, was established at the Court. This gave such practices a general vogue which carried them forward well into the Ming period. There is a text which describes how Tantrik metal images, in movable couples complete with sexual organs, were used as a means of instructing newly married couples of the royal family in the methods of sex, taking over, it seems, the role of the old manuals of the Art of the Bedchamber.

This Buddhist aspect of eroticism perhaps played its part in promoting the production during the Ming period of a novel very famous and popular in both China and Japan right down to modern times, called *The Prayer Mats of the Flesh*. It culminates in the admission of the hero as a Zen Buddhist monk, after a life of prolonged debauch, which his abbot explains to him was a metaphysical necessity before he could reach the proper spiritual state. An interesting episode in the novel revolves around the hero's method of arousing the interest of his scholarly and attractive but sexually ignorant first wife in erotic matters. He purchases an album of thirty-six extremely beautiful paintings of sexual postures by Chao Meng Fu, with accompanying descriptive poems. When she looks at it he explains that cultured people have always treasured such beautiful things, painted in full colours and mounted in fine silk, to prevent men and women losing interest in each other.

We know that this was indeed the case, in Ming times (1488–1643). For in that period both erotic paintings and woodblock prints were beautifully and carefully mounted in brocade. The figures they contained engaged in the 'flowery battle' were often painted with gold outlines in full colour. But it has been said that the skill of the early Ming artists was not adequate when it came to depicting the necessary nudes. The few such erotic works which survive, including painted porcelain cups and some monochrome woodblock prints, have relatively few crude formulae at their disposal to render the naked human body, although, of course, clothed figures – some with an erotic significance – were perfectly competently drawn. Certainly it is true that China never evolved elaborate aesthetic conceptions of the nude based on standardized systems of proportion, as European or Indian art did. But it is inconceivable that earlier artists as great as Chao Meng Fu and Chou Fang should not have been perfectly capable of arousing their ch'i for the task of capturing adequately the spirit of the forms of naked figures with their calligraphic lines. We must therefore assume that in early Ming times the older artistic patterns had been debased and lost their vigour.

180/181

Whatever the ultimate facts of the case may have been, the outcome was that a group of Nanking artists, scholars and business men of the late Ming period, disillusioned with the fare available, combined to produce a group of colour print albums which are the best surviving examples of the erotic figure-art of China, and which, almost certainly, prompted the sudden growth and flowering of the ukiyo-e in Japan. Coloured woodblock prints had been used for various purposes before this, at a relatively humble artisan level. But during the first half of the seventeenth century the technique was taken over by these Nanking connoisseurs, who produced a number of superb volumes, one of which is the famous *Ten Bamboo Studio*, a collection of colour prints of flowers, fruits and rocks, which is today still rightly famous. Between about 1570 and 1650 the erotic colour woodcut albums were produced, of comparable quality, bound between covers, or on long sheets folded concertina-wise. The earliest of them are still ineffective in their handling of nudes, and their figures may be only partly unclothed; but an impetus was given to later ones by the work of the great painter T'ang Yin (1470–1523). This artist had made a speciality of erotic pictures, including large sized and carefully observed nudes (though none is known to survive). He had painted numerous erotic albums – such as *The Six Extraordinary Positions* – hanging scrolls and long scrolls. His colleague and friend Ch'in Ying had done similar work. The figures that these two masters had invented were taken as patterns by the second generation of erotic colour print masters, and used as the basis for their compositions.

These colour woodblock prints were made by a most interesting and beautiful technique. The designs are linear, dispensing with any large areas of colour. And the different parts of the design are represented by different coloured lines – usually red, blue, black and green – printed on to the plain white ground of the paper. There is thus no single key-block, as there is in the Japanese ukiyo-e prints, so that the registering of the different colour blocks demanded an immense finesse. The printed calligraphy accompanying the pictures, which consist of fanciful poetic descriptions of the varieties of elegant entertainments illustrated, is also of very high quality. Thus, although there can be no doubt that these works are true descendants of the old educative posture-books, the manuals and Plain Girl texts in their general type and, possibly their format, their *raison d'être* has come to conform far more with the general aesthetic attitude of the Ming connoisseurs. These gentlemen had little truck with the ecstatic spirituality of the so-called Southern Sung Zen artists, or the thoroughgoing Taoist penetration of other great masters. They were still quite familiar with Taoist teaching on their subject, and probably knew at least some of the major classics of Taoist sexual mysticism. But their attitude was far more purely aesthetic than spiritual in the old sense. They were the people for whom the cryptic bibelots we have discussed in the previous chapter were made. They demanded of art elegance and pleasure – both with the classic overtones of established style and perfection of manner. The conduct of the gentlemen and girls portrayed in the woodcut albums in all the attitudes of pre-liminary lovemaking, entangled enjoyment, and satisfied mutual admiration was meant to show them to be paragons of sexual style. Their manners are perfect, their bodies and postures elegant in the extreme, their pleasures exquisite and poetic. Life, in short, as it should be lived.

Certain writers on this subject lament the 'lewdness' and 'depravity' that overtook both erotic manuals and novel illustrations during the Ch'ing era. And it is indeed true that the artistic quality of the numerous pictures and blockprints declined. This was partly a function of their wider distribution. But many of them continued to fulfil their traditional roles. There were posture manuals as well as mystic texts. In addition, a general, non-sexual function was ascribed to sexual images. They were used as apotropaic amulets. Stitched into a child's clothing they averted illness and misfortune; kept in a shop they averted fire. The only reason they could be so regarded must be that the cosmic reference of sexual intercourse was still present at the back of the Chinese mind. 'The proper union of Yang and Yin regulates all things.' At the same time the attitude of disapproval expressed by both Eastern and Western writers has undertones of dog-in-the manger resent-ment. For, as I said at the beginning, Chinese culture does not regard sex as some-thing to be ashamed of, and avoided. It is something natural, there to be enjoyed. If one is a person of high culture, with spiritual ambitions, one will not be content with journeyman pornography – not because it is pornography, but because it is of low-grade expression. If one is less educated, one is content with less, aesthetic-ally. Therefore below the level of Confucian censorship, and out of its reach, there flourished until recent times what can only be called an art of popular eroticism, an art which gives the common man, in his particular social milieu, an idea of what can be done, what has been done, and what is pleasant to do in the erotic relation-ship, without any pretence to the 'high-style' of the Ming aesthetic gentlemen. Pictures, prints, little porcelain figures, however crude aesthetically they may be, *182* have one great virtue, which visibly shines through them with a message for us, in the West. They convey an attitude both uninhibited and guiltless. They were made because the Chinese liked sex, enjoyed it, and like all sane men and women, *179* enjoyed thinking about it.

JAPAN

Introduction

There are a few generalizations which might be offered by way of preface to this section.

Normally the upper strata of Japanese society have been governed by an even stricter code of formal manners than our own. The basis of this code has been pure obedience. It was of prime importance to the rulers of Japan to preserve this strictly stratified society against its stresses and strains – which often erupted into appalling civil wars that raged sometimes for generations. Absolute self-immolating obedience to one's social duty was continually preached as the ultimate moral good. At the apex of the social structure were the Imperial House and the Dynastic dictator's house (called the Shogunate). Downwards, from grade to grade, extended the pyramidal feudal structure, the base of which was formed by the humble peasantry. There was a complex of rigid rights and duties between and in grades which was constantly strained by ferocious struggles for power. Great lords conflicted with each other and government officers in their pursuit of land and power. Emperors at first, and then the Shoguns tried to preserve order in the state by fostering a moral code based on a tendentious interpretation of Chinese Confucianism, with its conception of the state as a huge family to the head of which selfless duty was owed. The Shoguns converted this ethic into a cult of total loyalty, working through a rigid stratification of society. In this caste system the Samurai, professional warriors in theory, with an elaborate code of honour, had a privileged position. The system was based upon taxation in kind, and a studied calculation of each man's value within it, the medium of calculation being the staple commodity, rice.

Needless to say, this system was both open and subject to all kinds of manipulation and abuse. But the Japanese feudal hierarchy made centuries-long efforts to uphold the theoretical structure. One of the chief reasons for the frequent closing of Japan's shores to foreign contacts may have been to preserve the integrity of the social system. However, the merchant classes of the major cities became from the fifteenth century on increasingly wealthy in real terms, though not in terms of land. They thus became a potentially dangerous disruptive social force, a thorn in the flesh of the hierarchy, who often owed them vast sums of money, and confined them in psychological ghettos by restrictive legislation. In old Edo, modern Tokyo, the largest and most powerful such ghetto gave us the superb art of the Ukiyo-e, paintings and colour prints dealing with the life of the merchant pleasure-quarters, which Samurai were glad to patronise. For here, rather than in the formalized life of the nobility, was relative freedom to be found. It is significant that many of the great masters of Japanese art during the last four centuries have worked for mercantile rather than feudal patrons.

In earlier centuries freedom from stifling obligations and secular formality was usually found in Buddhist monasteries. These places, of course, had their own strict rules. But from the cultural point of view they were often able to shelter unconventional ideas, and unconventional art. Much that is most vital in earlier Japanese art sprang from monastic milieux.

Within this system sex and sexual relationships were strictly regulated. The relationship of wife to husband was theoretically one of strict obedience; and theoretically the wife (or daughter) owed no less strict an obedience to her husband's feudal overlord in both social and sexual matters. Such obedience was, in practice, frequently put to the test, sometimes on a casual basis, sometimes more seriously. The social code could demand that if a husband's existence became an embarrassment to the overlord in his enjoyment of the wife, the husband should remove himself honourably by suicide. This may have been rare. But the attitude of a woman thus possessed by an overlord was required to be nothing less than gratified submission – gratified theoretically by the opportunity to add to the comfort of the overlord.

This situation was fortified by the highly privileged status allotted to all members of the Samurai caste. The old law permitting them to try out their new sword-blades on casual passers-by was repealed a long time ago. But they did claim, partly by virtue of their status, but partly by that readiness to deal the death-blow which made them so valuable as retainers, the right to any woman of non-Samurai caste whenever they felt the urge. Peasant girls in the rice-fields were popularly imagined to be the prey of young Samurai. Such incidents provided subject matter for many Shunga. And no doubt this was indeed one of the less pleasant tribulations of peasant life in Japan.

Amongst the aristocracy at the Heian court (eight – twelfth centuries), as we know from the Tale of Genji and from Sei Shonagon's Pillow Book, love affairs were the normal game, just as they were at other courts the world over. And no doubt they were at the courts both of the Emperors and the feudal nobility in later times as well. But such affairs were in practice deeply tinged with status obligations. No doubt the flattery implied by a prince's choosing the wife or daughter of a more humble family as lover would influence the woman's attitude. But she would be under a strong obligation to comply anyway. Generally the spice of a true love affair of this kind depended on the cultural and social compatibility of the lovers. Custom demanded that they exchange poems, pictures and calligraphy. Too gross a conflict of aesthetic standard would never be acceptable. But as no upper class male would have the slightest difficulty in finding all the merely sexual satisfaction he required amongst the female members of his household, the cultural significance of the Heian love affair lay specifically in its aesthetic overtones.

Women, of course, were usually expected to play a subordinate role. Except at the indulgent Court the luxury of the love affair would have been a cause for grave scandal, probably for the death of the wife or daughter involved. And the moral basis for this would be the breach of the obligations of duty and obedience on the woman's part, if her lover was of equal or lower caste. In this case, he too would be in the gravest danger from the husband, unless he could protect himself. It

278

XXIII Utamaro: Woodblock colour print, from the album *Uta-makura*. Edo, 1788; *ōban*.
One of the most splendid works of the greatest master of late 18th century Ukiyo-e school

seems that Buddhist monks, far the greater part of whom were of Samurai origin, were particularly favoured as lovers by married women, largely, no doubt, because they had access to households, and women paid ceremonial visits to monasteries, but also because they were to some extent an *élite* outside and above the feudal structure; so that a sexual affair with a monk did not count as a duty-violation. There is no reason to believe that the licentiousness of religious orders was any less in Japan than it was in the European Middle Ages. Certainly monks were as apt and willing lovers in the Japanese popular imagination as they were in the European. They play the role frequently in art.

Once entered upon the sexual relationship of whatever kind, the Japanese imagination is not fettered by squeamish inhibitions. The conventions that are observed all have to do with the enhancement of the act of love itself. For the Japanese have no reservations at all about sex being a wonderful thing, of which the most possible should be made, by any available means. These means included all kinds of implements such as bandages on the penis, enlargements of the penis by means of hollow, fretted extensions, often called jokingly 'armour'. But most important of all were the fashionable costumes worn by the participants, and the ceremonious conduct observed. These added value and status to the act of love. It was no accident that during the great period of the Edo Ukiyo-e the courtesans were the leaders of high fashion, and their ceremonial skills were as highly cultivated as their erotic. The erotic art of Japan in the paintings and prints carries through in its own special terms this glorification of the act of sex.

There are several particular aspects of the Japanese art devoted to the hymning of sex which should be mentioned. First, there is the tendency for the participants to be at least partially clothed. The reason for this is not simply the fact that the Japanese shrank from the nude. The Japanese are accustomed to bath-time communal nudity. By itself nudity is ordinary, banal, lacking entirely in any special impact. There are, in fact, plenty of nudes in Japanese erotic art – people who happen to have cast off all their clothes. Clothes, especially beautiful clothes in the highest of fashion which were lovingly and accurately delineated, were always felt by the Japanese to offer the extra voluptuousness needed in emotively charged situations. This was not only for their suggestiveness by concealing here and revealing there, but for the opportunities they offered for the expression of feeling. The Japanese have always had a kind of sumptuary sense which few Westerners possess. On the Japanese stage, for example, the swing of a sleeve can move an audience to ecstasy. In the ceremonies of normal society garments were vividly employed to express personal feelings of a stylized character. In more intimate moments the drooping folds of the neckline, the swing of skirts, the suggestive multiple openings of the sleeve could be made to speak a subtle symbolic language of sumptuary gesture. And since, as I have pointed out in the section dealing with Chinese art, the essence of Far Eastern brush-painting is the movement it conveys, we must always try and read from Japanese garment-painting the movements which give this sumptuary gesture its deep appeal. At certain periods what matters is the grave and splendid formality of the folds, which serve as complex symbols of value and status. At other periods the linear evolutions serve as a kind of outward or theatrical demonstration of the complex feelings and sensations of the wearers, to express which the outlines of the body would be totally inadequate.

281

XXIV Shunshō: Woodblock colour print, from the album *Haikai yobuko-dori* (*The Cuckoo's Verse*). Edo, 1788; *ōban*. This album has also been attributed to Shunshō's pupil Shunchō. It was a popular work, and there are later imitations in the style of Shuntei, Utamaro II and Eizan

For, as Japanese art was always an art of contour, the expressive advantage of garments is that they offer for the artist's use a multiplicity of outlines along edges and folds, which the human body simply cannot offer.

The expansive linearism of Japanese painting has one further advantage in erotic representations. This has to do with apparent posture. The normal visual logic of volumes, as it prevails in much Western – and Indian – art, inhibits the variety of erotic representation. For the truth is that it is extremely difficult to make visible the genitals of figures engaged in sexual intercourse in an art oriented to the truth of volumes, without doing violence to the validity of the visual logic. Very few postures, and very few angles of sight in those postures allow the genitals to be seen. It is also true that the genitals are a natural focus of both sensation and interest in all erotic experience, actual or symbolic. Volume-oriented arts have solved this problem in various ways, more or less adequately. The Japanese solution, however, seems especially successful. For as Japanese art has no interest whatever in the three-dimensional structural actuality of volumes seen from a single viewpoint it is able to lay out in two dimensions whatever it wishes to include into its image. All that is necessary is that a linear logic be observed; and hence as much may be displayed of anything as is required for the artist's purpose, without a sense of dislocation. For the Japanese sense of location is fundamentally two-dimensional in the first place, allowing for the fusing together of aspects which could only be seen in actuality from a *sequence* of many viewpoints. The use of veiling garments helps here; because a complex of overlapping folds can form a bridge between exposed parts of the body without committing the artist to defining the precise bulk of the body-parts beneath the garment.

Finally, there is the question to which Dr Lane refers in his text – the Japanese fondness for representing both male and female genitals on a grossly exaggerated scale. There are many reasons for this, including the fact mentioned, that the genitals are a normal focus of sensation and interest. To represent them on a 'normalized' scale in an elaborate painting would deprive them entirely of their natural primacy in the symbolic scheme. Most erotic art enlarges the genitals somewhat. But the Japanese convention often seems to Europeans grotesque. It should be remembered that to Japanese eyes it is not grotesque, but normal. The same kind of attention is lavished upon the genitals in erotic art as is lavished on the garments in order to bring them up to the same high key of expression. The folds and ripples of the labia of the female vulva are multiplied and exaggerated into a linear efflorescence often resembling the petals of a peony. The collars, ridges, engorged veins and skin-pleats of the male penis sustain the same extravagant linear invention. Given the relative fixed sizes of brush-tip and page-format it would be impossible to lavish such expressive care upon the organs of sex without enlarging them. It is obvious that in real life the Japanese have been so casually familiar with the appearance of the genitals as a normal part of the naked human body that to raise these familiar objects to the status of an emotive and sensuous focus in a work of art demands dramatic treatment. It is not enough merely to expose the genitals, or even to exhibit them in an excited condition. They must be exposed with extravagant élan, and enhanced by vigorous artistic development, haloed in sinuous and singing brush-lines.

9 Preface

Eroticism in Japanese art

Shunga or 'Spring Pictures', is the term used by the Japanese to describe that branch of pictorial art that glorifies the erotic. The word 'shunga' may seem to have a dreamy, poetic sound to us abroad, but actually it signifies nothing more or less than 'sex pictures'.

To the Japanese, indeed, sex represented neither a romantic ideal of love, nor a phallic rite to the gods; it was simply the joyful union of the sexes: a natural function that represented man's greatest pleasure – almost, his *raison d'être*.

In preparing this, the first detailed, fully-illustrated account of shunga to be published, we have encountered a number of unusual impressions and scholarly problems that it may be of interest to outline here – together with certain general remarks on the Japanese attitude towards sex.

The fact that most of the great ukiyo-e print masters produced bold shunga has been cited by popular writers as a 'shocker' – as though this fact either on the one hand served to justify erotica, or on the other proved the artists themselves were morally depraved. Neither assumption is correct: the fact that a Freud or a Havelock Ellis should have devoted his life to describing sex neither makes the erotic justified or unjustified – nor does it say anything at all about the scholar's personal morals. The role of the shunga artist was simply that of an artistic popularizer of sex manuals: such comprised, at the most, a fifth of his work, and were approached in a manner differing only technically from whatever commission preceded them – a flower-viewing print, a New Year's card, a book of kimono designs, or an illustrated guide to penmanship for children. Some of the artists were, necessarily, better than others at shunga; some even took a special delight in the genre. But shunga was simply an integral part of the artist's recognized work.

Shunga – at least until the early eighteenth century – were thus considered but one normal function of the Japanese artist, no more improper or degrading than the painting of a nude or a classical love-scene would have seemed to a contemporary Western artist. True, the Japanese feudal government's 'austerity edicts' of the 1720s and following seem to have gradually altered this attitude towards shunga – at least bringing official censure to bear on their more widespread, popular publication; but there appears to have been little moral stigma attached either to their design or their purchase, on up to the time of the 'modernization' of Japan in the later nineteenth century.

Indeed, sex itself in all its forms and varieties was readily available to any Japanese male with the means or the inclination: thus Japanese erotic art had really but a secondary stimulatory function. Aside from its usefulness in sex education, shunga's place in Japanese art corresponded, to most intents and purposes, with Western nude painting. And when, in the later nineteenth century, Japan officially adopted the appurtenances – and, so far as convenient, the morals and customs – of Western, 'Victorian' culture, it promptly banned *both* shunga and the nude in art. To the Japanese authorities of the time, the distinction just did not exist: if shunga were pornographic, then so was the nude.

In viewing shunga it may be well to remember this analogy: to the adolescent or sexually underprivileged, shunga may prove stimulating, even aphrodisiac – as may nude painting, or any other art form even vaguely related to the erotic. For a dispassionate understanding of any erotic art form, of course, one should be not only a mature (and, let us hope, sexually happy) individual, but should also be versed in the artistic styles and conventions of the culture concerned. The latter is a particularly vital prerequisite in the arts of Asia. Here, the potentially 'objectionable' subject matter is rendered even more difficult of dispassionate appreciation, by the varied and exotic nature of each of the civilizations concerned.

Thus – while hardly a statement conducive to making friends in the Occident – the fact is that a good part of the intrinsic interest of Japanese art is quite lost to the connoisseur, collector or scholar who has little intimacy with the psychology, manners (and hopefully, the language) of Old Japan. As with a blind man, of course, other imaginative senses may well develop to increase the connoisseur's personal appreciation of a print or painting: we can see such developments pronouncedly in the writings of the early enthusiast Edmond de Goncourt – as well as in the modern critic J. Hillier. But if this is true of Japanese popular art in general, it is even more so in the case of shunga, where literary and legendary allusions contribute so much to the total effect of a print or illustration.

Edo art has been characterized (by K. Shibui) as 'of formal simplicity of expression but complexity of overlapping nuances; non-intellectual; erotic'. To miss this vital element of complexity of allusions is to miss the final effect of the print – at least, as it was planned by the creator, the artist himself. To regard the ukiyo-e print merely as a colourful, charmingly decorative art-form is to deny half of its content, half of its value. It may well be that for the average Western viewer, appreciation of ukiyo-e can never extend much beyond these 'colourful, charming, decorative' bounds. To deny that more than this exists, however, is to insult the original artist – as well as faint-heartedly to deny the ability of the Western mind ever to penetrate this fair, Oriental veil.

Function and form of shunga

The first impression one gets from reading the texts to the earlier shunga books is that the concept of family continuity was a strong one in Japan: procreation was thus a most serious affair. We are not trying to minimize the erotic nature of shunga when we suggest that a good portion of their audience were seeking practical advice in improving their sex life – whether for procreational or emotional reasons. True, there were a few medical texts available that treated of sex matters;

but these were generally Japanese editions of old Chinese works, phrased in Chinese style, and requiring some familiarity with classical medicine to be used meaningfully. Thus the shunga books, albums and scrolls proved the primary means of sex education throughout Japanese history – on even into the early twentieth century. (As late as the 1930s, surprisingly enough, it was still the practice among certain of the more traditional Japanese department stores to include a shunga volume in the corner of a chest-of-drawers purchased for a prospective bride.)

Viewed in this historical light, the policy of 'education by shunga' may be considered well ahead of its times. In the West, it is only in the present century that we find detailed, popular treatises on sexual positions and the like – which were already the staple fare of Japanese shunga books by the seventeenth century. And Western sex manuals have yet to reach the point where they feel justified in substituting creative work by major artists, for the usual coldly-scientific diagrams. In this sense, Japanese shunga works already represented, several centuries ago, the ultimate alliance of sexual science and art, which yet remains the unrealized ideal of Western sexology. Ideally speaking, after all, art, science, and life are but different aspects of a single humanity.

To judge, at least, from the authors' prefaces and postscripts to the earlier shunga books, their attitude was a most serious one. (Doubtless, they might even be considered too serious and conventional by the more enlightened thinkers of today.) Typical is the postface to Sugimura's shunga book *Raku no uwamori* (*The Best of all Pleasures*) of 1687: 'Excesses, in general, are the root of illness and foreshortened life; this is even more the case with iniquitous appetites in sex. The great will destroy their nation; the lesser will lose their homes and ruin their lives. Moderation should be the rule in all things.'

Parallel to the serious attention paid to family continuity, procreation and sex, was the rather strong belief that conjugal compatibility was influenced by natural or divinational forces. Thus, where there were numerous volumes (deriving from the Chinese *Book of Changes*) which provided divinational and astrological guides to human fate and conduct, there were also books of 'sexual astrology', which provided detailed, illustrated descriptions of the good and bad consequences of union between men and women born under compatible or opposing zodiacal 'signs'. Such beliefs were not really strong enough to outweigh other, more human factors – and were often, doubtless, more the concern of 'old grandmothers' than of modern young couples. Yet such concepts do flavour the popular thought of the times.

Another background element to shunga publication was the 'therapeutic' function sex played in certain hygienic philosophies derived from China. In these doctrines, sex (like sports or exercise today) was considered to have a definitely beneficial effect on health and longevity. This attitude towards sex never achieved very striking popularity among the Japanese – to whom sex doubtless seemed too natural a function to require such devious apologetics. But this prestigious, intellectual approval of sex from the Continent surely smoothed the path for erotic publications – and especially so among the ruling samurai, who might otherwise have more actively restricted them.

The specific subject matter of Edo Period shunga is practically limitless, and our illustrations can give only a brief suggestion of the variety. It is worth noting, however, that shunga often bore a very close relationship to the popular literature of the time – not only when they illustrated it directly, but when they emphasized certain literary scenes or situations currently in vogue. Thus, when literature took as its setting the pleasure-quarters, and as its heroines, the courtesans, so did shunga. Later, when love stories and scandals featuring ordinary maidens – or pederasts, or geisha, or even bestiality – flourished, these immediately found their reflection in the shunga books and print-albums. With the official banning of foreign travel after the mid 1630s, tales of a hero's shipwreck to a distant Island of Lusty Females flourished, as did shunga depictions; the 'outlandish' Dutchmen of Nagasaki appear in the shunga about concurrently with literature and other forms. There is, of course, nothing strange about this: the same artists who produced the usual prints and book illustrations did the shunga, and some of them even wrote their own book-texts and print-dialogues for the latter. There were even cases where especially notable shunga works created vogues of their own, which diffused soon into less erotic art and literature.

Shunga, at any rate, were a clear reflection of the tastes and manners of their times. They have their own conventions and exaggerations, but a worthwhile history of Japanese morals, customs, and popular thought could easily be written from them alone.

One interesting aesthetic problem arose in the selection of our illustrations. No shunga artist worth his salt simply presented page after page of pictures featuring coitus alone. He varied both his poses, his viewpoint, and the degree of eroticism employed. Thus, if two illustrations featured various advanced stages of love making, the third scene, as often as not, presented a more idyllic view of young lovers, perhaps only 'holding hands'.

Ideally, therefore, every artist should have been represented here in at least two such series of three or four prints each, to reveal his true mastery of the mood and continuity of erotic response. Space has not, unfortunately, permitted such a comprehensive showing. At the same time, many of the Japanese print artists have been almost *over*-published in their customary oeuvre, while neglected in their shunga work; and the 'presentable' cover-sheets to the various major shunga works have already been rather widely illustrated, by ourselves as well as others.

For these, we hope valid, reasons, it has been necessary rather to over-concentrate illustration on the more extreme (though predominant) elements of shunga. These are typical of shunga *per se*, but present an unrelieved picture of eroticism which is not necessarily the case with the original, complete books or albums. The intrinsic variety of the various artists presented will doubtless preclude any danger of monotony. But it should be emphasized that nearly all Japanese shunga were originally designed as part of a unified series – a book, an album, or a scroll – and it is no small wonder that the detached fragments presented here show up as impressively as they do.

By their nature, shunga tended to utilize certain formats more than those most frequent in non-erotic Japanese art. Thus, in the field of hand painting, *kakemono* (hanging scrolls) are of course rare, where the more intimate picture-scrolls and albums predominate – just the opposite of the case with non-erotic paintings. Erotica seldom appeared on panels and screens – though these did sometimes exist in the houses of assignation. (We have seen examples – admittedly rare – of *tsuitate,* single-panel screens, which, when the frame was removed, opened up into two-panel screens with shunga on the inner side, and innocent landscapes, calligraphy or bird-and-flower paintings on the outer surface.) With the prints, too, single-sheet shunga are practically nonexistent: they were normally folded once and mounted in a series of twelve as an album; or, rarely, mounted end-to-end as a picture-scroll, or issued as unmounted series in an envelope. (Once dismounted, of course, such album-plates are hardly distinguishable from independent prints – other than from the fact that they usually lack artist's formal signature or publisher's seal.)

Indeed, for the first four decades of printed ukiyo-e, *c.* 1660–1700, there were few separately issued ukiyo-e prints even in the non-erotic field. Other than some rare *kakemono*-prints of large size, and a few albums or scrolls of historical-genre subjects, all of the extant 'presentable' prints that grace the museums of the world today – by such early masters as Moronobu, his pupils, and Sugimura – are the so-called 'cover-sheets' to erotic albums: the prints (usually two or three in number) that were interspersed through most of the shunga books for variety's sake. From an historical point of view, it is most unfortunate that dealers – and even some prudish collectors – have customarily detached these 'frontispiece' prints for separate sale: the albums and scrolls must be seen in their original setting for proper appreciation, and both the erotic and the non-erotic suffer from being removed from their context. (Doubtless far worse is the dealers' practice of having shunga prints drastically retouched – sometimes even by means of newly-carved woodblocks – to cover over objectionable pubic details.) Given, of course, the choice of the public seeing only censored plates and bowdlerized fragments, or nothing at all, we must doubtless temper our complaints of such vandalism.

The artists themselves, however, felt no need to apologize for their work in erotica. Indeed, it is a curious fact that the shunga artists often signed their erotica, while neglecting to affix their names to much of their more ordinary work in the same format. Such masters as Harunobu and Utamaro even publicly disdained production of portraits featuring the Kabuki actors (social outcasts, according to government reckoning and to Confucian doctrine, at any rate), but took great pride in their shunga work – producing, indeed, some of their finest achievements in this genre.

The illustrations

To turn to certain matters of more specialized interest: although some care has been taken in the matter of attributions, we do not wish to be dogmatic. Experience has shown that, in woodblock prints, for example, the 'stylistic' influence of the engraver has been underestimated. Thus, an experienced (and sympathetic) engraver working from the sketches of an artist's pupil may sometimes give us the impression that we are viewing the master himself. And an unskilled engraver (*or* one accustomed to handling the work of a quite different artist) may sometimes lead us to suspect we are viewing the work of a pupil – or even of an imitator.

(A famous letter of Hokusai's thus complains to his publisher of the engraver's giving his prints facial features in the quite different, Toyokuni style.)

In order to simplify the captions, the following method is used: signed work is so noted; for unsigned but reasonably certain attributions, simply the artist's name is given; in cases where identification is less positive, the notation 'style of' is used.

And a cautionary note regarding shunga paintings: it should be remembered that, just as the classical scrolls were copied assiduously on into the late nineteenth century so were the early ukiyo-e manuscript works copied in the following two centuries, even after *printed* ukiyo-e had taken the creative lead. That is to say, the affluent public for the expensive hand-scrolls remained even after woodblock printing had made the genus more cheaply and widely available. And though the ukiyo-e print artists sometimes thus did original and creative painted scrolls for their more wealthy patrons, the artisan-copyists and artists' apprentices of the period tended, rather, to copy the masterpieces – often no longer extant today in the originals – of the earlier, classical masters.

These are, of course, features found throughout Far Eastern painting. But they do render the art-scholar's task a complex one, since it is usually impossible to authenticate such paintings accurately through photographs alone – and the originals are, understandably, sometimes difficult of access. The unfortunate fact is, that most publications dealing with shunga, both in Japan and in the West, have been the work of casual sexologists or amateurs, and many of the paintings and even some of the prints, reproduced, have been late copies or outright forgeries. Shunga is yet a pioneer region in art studies, and will doubtless remain so until prejudice against its subject-matter diminishes, either in Japan or abroad. In the present preliminary study, we have at least tried to indicate surmised date of execution in cases where late copies had to be illustrated in place of lost or unavailable originals.

We must hasten to add that such original, early works may well yet be extant: indeed, the prime difficulty in any study of Japanese erotic art is the difficulty of making any comprehensive survey of the originals. Doubtless, several decades of assiduous search in Japan and abroad would serve to unearth the major extant treasures of shunga painting. But it would have to be energetic, original research, for no guide to this treasure-house yet exists in any language.

Our own attention to shunga has been as a necessary adjunct to our general ukiyo-e studies; but even in this latter field, our attention has hitherto been directed more to prints and book illustration than to painting. Here exists, clearly, an area for virgin research in one of the great erotic treasures of world art. The keys to its understanding are not available to the casual observer, however; they require a firm understanding of Japanese classical language, literature, customs, art-history and connoisseurship – each in itself a lifelong study. But of all these, that art of expertise in the Shunga field is surely the most difficult, for this has yet to be explored in Japan itself.

It is commonly said that nearly all of the ukiyo-e artists produced shunga, and this statement is probably accurate enough in general. As a matter of fact, however, no one scholar of ukiyo-e has ever studied carefully even a bare majority of the shunga now extant; and once more detailed investigation and publication in this field becomes possible, we shall doubtless have to revise some of our basic ideas on the relative productivity of the various artists. For our present purposes, however, we have chosen to concentrate on works actually available to us for study. The absence of certain artists – ukiyo-e or other – from our account does not, therefore, necessarily mean that they did no shunga work, but simply that we have not had the opportunity to trace such, either in the original or in photograph or reproduction. Thus, while we may doubt that such a specialized artist as Sharaku ever produced (or at least, ever published) shunga, it would be unwise to make any such categorical statement at the present stage of our knowledge.

The student of ukiyo-e in general will usually find that despite the literally hundreds of books and catalogues available on the subject any original, 'definitive' study will prove already incomplete by the time it is published. Such fallibility must be accepted as the rule, rather than the exception, in the shunga field, where publication is rare, and really reliable studies are, alas, yet to be made even in Japan, despite the avid body of collectors there.

Unlike the case of Old Japan – where the government had been generally complaisant towards sex expression, whether in life, literature or art – modern Japan rose in the midst of the Victorian Age, and adopted, all too literally, most of the supposed sexual repressions of the late nineteenth century Western society which it took for its model. Both the European nude and the Japanese shunga were banned without distinction. More recent education has removed the more prestigious nude from 'beyond the pale', but the true nature of traditional shunga is both unknown and misunderstood by the very agencies who must regulate them – the police and the courts.

Needless to say, such banning and restrictions have greatly impeded the progress of Japanese studies in their own erotic art. There are numerous (though generally fragmentary and inaccurate) bibliographical studies, only obliquely illustrated; and there have been a few generalized discussions of shunga, lacking in any meaningful illustration at all. But the fact is that, so far as published works go, the student of ukiyo-e shunga would do better – despite their excessive historical and artistic inaccuracies – to study the few unexpurgated portfolios published in the West, rather than search through the total bulk of what has appeared in modern Japan. For any really worthwhile research, however, there is no alternative but to seek out the originals, scattered through the private (and a very few public) collections in Japan and in the West. For this reason, anything like definitive research on most of the details of Japanese erotica will doubtless remain virtually an impossibility for the present generation.

In the limited space available to this monograph, we have been unable to speak, other than in passing, of the general background of life and art in Old Japan. For details on the history of Japanese genre painting and prints, Edo society, Kabuki and the Yoshiwara, the reader is referred to our earlier *Masters of the Japanese Print*. And although space-limitations have not permitted the inclusion of detailed captions to the plates, a brief note has been appended whenever it was thought that the subject matter might not be obvious to the Western reader.

For the specialist, the following general note on print sizes may be appended: Average print sizes: *ōban* – 10 x 15 inches; *aiban* – 9 x 13; *chūban* – 7½ x 10; *koban* – 5 x 5½; *hashira-e* – 29 x 5.

Book sizes: *ōbon* – 11 x 7½ inches; *hanshi-bon* – 9 x 6½; *chūbon* – 7½ x 5½; *yoko-bon* – 5 x 7¾.

Scroll sizes: average height – six to fourteen inches; length – from twelve to forty feet.

Although the omission of footnotes may prove an inconvenience to scholars, it must be noted that these would consist almost entirely of references to the Japanese originals – for there is surprisingly little accurate information on this subject available in Japanese secondary sources, and none at all in Western languages.

A final word should be said here about the important place of book illustration in shunga, and in ukiyo-e in general. Some criticism was raised, by print collectors, at the space given to ukiyo-e illustration in our earlier *Masters of the Japanese Print* – on the grounds that no single book-plate can equal the artistic quality, or at least, impressiveness, of an independent print. This we do not doubt. But we do feel strongly that few if any single prints, indeed, can match the wonder of viewing at leisure a series of several dozen integrated illustrations by a master such as Moronobu. The effect is cumulative, and being divided over a period of time, is more lasting than that any single print can produce.

By the same token, even the finest single illustration, torn out of its context, will never equal even the average independent print. But this does not mean that we must choose our plates solely on the basis of isolated photographs spread out on a table in front of us. Inevitably, we associate each plate with the book or series in which it originally appeared. And we must simply plead that we are dealing here primarily with the *originals* – of which our plates are sometimes but fragmentary approximations.

After all, we do not eschew publishing illustrated books on architecture or sculpture – just because these subjects are less suited than prints or paintings are to two-dimensional reproduction. Nor, by the same token, can we neglect book illustration just because random samples cannot even begin to reveal its total charm. The beauty of the Japanese picture-book lies in its cumulative effect: it represents a kaleidoscope of lively yet integrated scenes and impressions – as against the print's single, stationary tableau.

To be sure, one of the characteristics of Japanese shunga is that there are few independent, solitary works: whether print or painting, the original came as part of a set or series, a book, an album, or a scroll. In this broad sense, *all* shunga is illustration. Nevertheless, the shunga scroll or album most often represents a series of twelve rather unrelated tableaux – as opposed to the book illustration *per se*, which represents a more conscious effort on the artist's part to create a continuous artistic unity. The *publishers* of Old Japan may well have spent their greatest efforts on the prints and albums; but to the ukiyo-e artist, one feels, the book illustration represented an even greater, sustained effort of creation.

Our earlier *Masters of the Japanese Print* attempted to present the overall story of these 'Pictures of the Floating World' – the prints, paintings, illustration, and shunga. In the present monograph, we have tried to shed further light on the least understood of all of these genres, shunga. In the future, we hope to fill out the story even further with monographs on ukiyo-e book illustration, and painting –

together with a more detailed view of the prints of the 'Primitive' Period. Only when *all* these aspects of ukiyo-e have been studied thoroughly may we pretend to know something of this fascinating eddy of Japanese art, this pageant of Edo life and civilization in miniature.

10 Early Japanese Erotica and the Yamato-e painters

The earliest works

We can speak here only in passing of the prehistoric periods of Japanese erotic art – the Neolithic Age, and the early Iron Age (the 'Burial-mound Period'). Sexual art now extant from these early times comprises principally the phallic symbols and fertility images of primitive religion and tribal rites – clay amulets and relief work, stone staffs, wall-carvings, *haniwa* (clay grave-figures), stone amulets and pottery, featuring figures with prominent sex organs, or sometimes even engaged in conjugal intercourse.

With the sixth century AD these beginnings of native Japanese art were practically smothered by the wholesale import of Buddhism and its art from the Asiatic mainland – an artistic tradition which, though filled with images and iconography, treated but rarely of the erotic.

Indeed, one of the characteristics of much of Far Eastern Buddhist art is the asexual nature of its images – emphasis placed upon idealized depictions of the various deified Buddhas and Bodhisattvas, rather than upon the historical Sakyamuni and his followers. If any notable erotic strain is to be found in the earliest Japanese Buddhist art, it must lie in the idealized, *feminine* depiction of deities which most often, in China and Korea, had been *male*. Without meaning to strain a point, one can reasonably imagine the sexual attraction these lovely, increasingly voluptuous and feminized figures must have exerted on the abstemious monks who daily worshipped them.

From the virginal innocence and other-worldliness of Suiko Buddhist sculpture in the early seventh century to the voluptuous, this-worldly femaleness of Tempyō and Heian Buddhist sculpture and painting of the eighth century and following, the ideal of female beauty saw mutation with the times and with their changing religious emphasis. The depiction of true female deities likewise increased – Kisshōten, Benzaiten, Marishiten, Gigeiten and others; and the numerous female deities of the native Shintō religion also found artistic expression from the early ninth-century Kōnin Period and later.

The semi-nude appears in such Suiko Period Buddhist sculpture in wood as the Miroku statues of the Chūgūji and Hōryūji temples; but the most noted works of this class are the so-called 'Nude Bentens', the curious seated statues of the Goddess Benzaiten at the Kamakura Hachiman Shrine and the Enoshima Shrine. These wooden sculptures date from the thirteenth century (the first bears an inscription dated 1266) and though doubtless originally designed to be clothed, feature completely nude forms, including carefully-delineated depictions of the vulva.

In the meanwhile – though little recorded in art histories – native elements of

195 Graffito. Sketch in sumi on wooden base of early 7th-century sculpture. Horyuji temple, Nara. (Woman at top, phallus below.) This is one of the very earliest shunga, located on an image in a revered temple

196 (*below*) Frontispiece to an early illuminated Buddhist scripture scroll. Painting in gold on indigo paper. From the so-called *Hidehira Tripitaka* (*Hidehira Issai-kyō*), dedicated by Fujiwara Hidehira in AD 1176. Chūsonji temple, Hiraizumi.
One of the earliest known examples of erotic pictures included in a religious text. Image reproduced in negative reversal for greater clarity

197 and 198 (*left and top*) From the
Brushwood-fence Scroll (Koshibagaki-zōshi).
Painting in colours on paper. From a 13th-
century version of the 12th-century original,
now lost.
These illustrate characteristic examples of this
well-known and much-admired style of
painting, but in the erotic vein, and preserved
only in a copy

199. ....*go no sōshi*). Painting in colours on paper, dated
1321. Sa..st example of an actual erotic scroll in Heian court
style know............urvive, preserved in.........mple

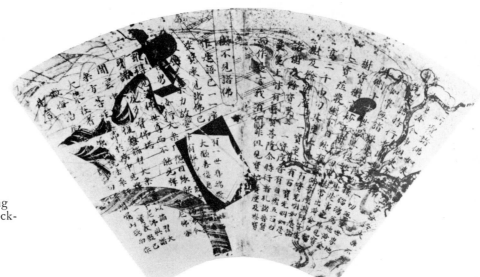

201 Early sutra-fan-painting. Painting in colours on paper, over a woodblock-printed outline, twelfth century. Restored. Shitennō-ji temple, Osaka

202 From the *Phallic Contest Scroll* (*Yōbutsu-kurabe*). Painting in colours on paper. A mid 19th-century copy ascribed to Tasaki Sōun (1815-98), after an original, now lost, of the 12th century. This gives an insight, social and perhaps historical, into an interest of the Heian court; it is in one of the classic styles of Heian Buddhist art

205 (*opposite*) From a shunga scroll of twelve scenes in Muromachi style. Colours on paper. Genroku period (late 17th century). Court rank was indicated by the style of headgear, which was hence worn by courtiers at all times. This illustrates the type of erotic scroll without a story line, which developed in the Tosa-kano school of painting

203 (*left*) From the *Brushwood-fence Scroll* (*Koshibagaki-zōshi*). Woodblock print in shades of sumi by Maruyama Ōshin (1790-1838), copied from an early original in that artist's collection. From the *Kagetsu-jō* of 1836, an album of plates in chiaroscuro manner, by leading Kanō, Tosa, Maruyama, Shijō and other neo-classical artists, after early shunga models

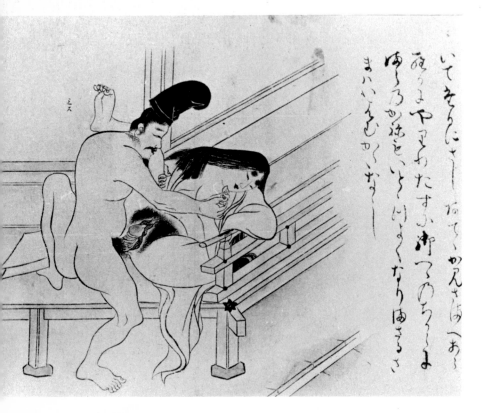

204 (*left*) From the *Brushwood-fence Scroll* (*Koshibagaki-zōshi*). Painting in colours on paper from a copy, by the artist Keitoku, bearing the date 1800—after an original, now lost, of the 12th century

Two works derived from the early, classic scroll, now lost. They illustrate the importance of and continuing interest in the original masterpiece

206 (*opposite*) Early Ukiyo-e School: From a shunga scroll of twelve scenes (incomplete). Colours on paper. *c.* early 17th century. The calligraphy is a later addition.
An outstanding example of painting of the early Ukiyo-e school

207 From the *Priest in the Bag Scroll* (*Fukuro-hōshi ekotoba*). Scroll in colours on paper from a copy (*c.* mid-18th century) after an original of the 14th century. Since the early original scroll after this famous tale is lost, we must depend on copies like this one for an insight into its qualities

209 Kambun Master: Detail from the *Yoshiwara makura-e* (*Yoshiwara Pillow-pictures*), an early shunga 'Courtesan Critique'. Woodblock-printed book with hand-colouring; Edo, dated 1660; *yoko-bon*. This belongs to the first extant generation of printed books containing shunga

208 Anonymous: From the *Kōso myōron*, an early sex manual. Illustration and printing in Kōetsu-book style. Woodblock-printed book, early 17th century: *ōbon* size. From an illustrated adaptation of a Chinese sexo-mystical text

210 Kambun Master: Woodblock print from a series of twelve.
Edo, early 1660s; *ōban* size.
One of the masterpieces of the first great, but anonymous, master
of the Ukiyo-e woodblock print

phallic worship had persisted depite the widespread importation of Buddhism. Popular festivals sometimes featured phallic deities, and the generally superstitious nature of the times led to the development of sexual rites and folklore which are featured from time to time in the literature and records of the Heian Period.

Buddhism itself, particularly the esoteric Shingon Sect, also harboured certain sexual deities (derived from India via Tibetan and Chinese Lamaism), the best-known of which is Kangiten. Derived from the Hindu Ganesha, Kangiten is depicted most strikingly as a male and female pair in standing embrace, featuring human bodies but elephantine heads. The earliest such dated statue of Kangiten bears the inscription 1197. Shrines to this deity (popularly known as 'Shōden-sama') are still prevalent throughout Japan – that at Matsuchiyama, near the Yoshiwara, being well known. Their icons are generally treated, however, as *hibutsu* ('secret Buddhas'), and thus seldom displayed publicly.

Of the 'Household Deities' – the 'Seven Gods of Luck' we find so commonly in the later ukiyo-e, – Bishamonten and Daikoku are also sometimes depicted in early sculpture in dual sexual forms, similar to Kangiten. Further, one branch of the aforementioned Shingon Buddhism, the Tachikawa Sect – a development of the later eleventh century – combined strong elements of *Yin-Yang* shamanism and phallicism with a most positive attitude towards sex, and exerted considerable influence throughout Japan until its formal banning in the fourteenth century.

Our interest here, however, centres principally on *shunga* ('spring-pictures'), the erotic in Japanese painting and the graphic arts.

Fragmentary evidence would indicate that the earliest Japanese shunga were a diversion of Buddhist artists and artisans, graffiti sketched for relaxation in the midst of more serious endeavours. For example, an early, amateur shunga sketch has been found on the base of a statue in Japan's oldest extant temple, the Hōryūji (early seventh century); and fragments of early shunga (displaying, interestingly enough, use of both male and female 'sex implements') are said to have been discovered during the dismantling and repair of the Senju Kannon statue of the Tōshō-daiji temple in Nara – a work of the late Tempyō Period (mid-eighth century). Although sex life, to judge from the novels of the period, appears to have been free enough 'on the outside' (at least among the upper classes), the austere life of a Buddhist monastery would indeed have provided a fitting need for such sexual outlets among the priestly artisans.

Sophisticated sex knowledge was evidently widespread among the educated classes. We know, for example, that shunga-illustrated sex manuals were prevalent in this period – the official Taihō Code of the year 701 even specifying that physicians were required to study such illustrated texts, *osokuzu-no-e* ('posture-pictures'), as they were then termed. And in 1288, the *Eisei hiyō-shō* ('Secret Essentials of Hygiene') – a Japanese sex manual which conveniently summarized the earlier Chinese texts – was even presented to the Throne.

Pictorial erotica was not, naturally enough, suited to wide exploitation in the more 'public' formats of Japanese art – *kakemono* (hanging scrolls), screens, panels or murals. It is thus only with the development of the *emakimono*, the lateral hand-scroll, that shunga found its first permanent art form in Japan.

The format itself derived from China, but the Japanese picture-scroll developed extensively just at a time when native forms of art and literature were finding their first full expression. Thus we can state, with only a little exaggeration, that the picture-scroll practically epitomizes the truly native pictorial art – the *Yamato-e* ('Japan-pictures') – of the pre-ukiyo-e period, from the twelfth to the sixteenth centuries.

All that saved that classic novel, the early eleventh-century *Tale of Genii,* from being a recitation of redundant love adventures was the taste and genius of the authoress – and the refined (if sometimes effete) taste of her complaisant society. In the centuries of war and political unrest that followed, it was as often as not the ribald (or the absurdly romantic) that fitted more the taste of the times. Such collections of medieval tales as the *Konjaku monogatari* (early twelfth century) and the *Kokon chomonju* (1254) – as well as the erotic verses of the Zen priest Ikkyū and of the *Inu-Tsukuba-shū* – resemble the *Gesta Romanorum* or Boccaccio in their enthusiasm for earthy humour of the bedroom, and it is this lively belly-laugh that most often flavours the early shunga scrolls of this period.

The first *non*-erotic picture-scrolls in native, Yamato-e style may be typified by two famous examples: the twelfth-century *Tale of Genji Scroll* (*Genji monogatari emaki*), in colourful but passive, formal, decorative style; and the twelfth–thirteenth-century *Animal and Figure Scrolls* (*Chōjū jimbutsu giga*), quickly sketched works of humour and abundant humanity. Whatever the form of artistic expression employed, Japanese shunga tended, most often, to the latter lively vein of depiction.

Certain human scenes in the *Animal and Figure Scrolls* are reminiscent of later shunga works, and provide a ready glimpse of what the early shunga scrolls, now lost, must have been like. (The distinction between shunga and the non-erotic is, after all, primarily one of *subject* – a distinction only of but minor importance in basic art studies.) Other noted twelfth-century works such as the *Scroll of Diseases* (*Yamai no sōshi*), the *Scroll of Hungry Devils* (*Gaki-zōshi*), and the *Hell Scroll* (*Jigoku-zōshi*) contain scenes – e.g. of hermaphroditism and sexual diseases, of parturition, of nudity and torture – of great interest to the sexologist as well as to the art student.

Yet in none of the publicly-known early scrolls does eroticism as such appear. The nude figure itself is seen – but only in the natural course of the events depicted. Indeed, the lack of interest in the nude *per se* may well help explain why Japanese erotica is so extreme in its sexual depictions: mere nakedness in itself held little erotic interest to the Japanese viewer; he demanded the full details of sexual intercourse – spiced with imaginative exaggeration – to receive any erotic stimulation worthy of the name.

We know from the *Tale of Genji* and other Heian Period sources that the picture-scroll as such was a most popular source of diversion among the nobility of the tenth and eleventh centuries: there were even frequent exhibitions, in the form of 'picture-contests' (*e-awase*) to see which owner's scroll or scrolls could glean the greatest number of votes. But despite the fact that dozens of such works must have been produced, hardly any are extant from this age. Thus it is not surprising that the shunga scrolls, too (necessarily, less widely produced and circulated), are lost from this early period, and scarce enough during the ensuing centuries of war and turmoil that followed – until the establishment of peace and stable government at the commencement of the seventeenth century.

Indeed, aside from the graffiti of the temple monks, the only near-erotic paintings we know today of the Heian Period are one or two 'bed-scenes' depicted in the frontispieces to the Chūsonji Buddhist sūtras of the year 1176; and a love-scene or two, found among the sūtra fan-paintings (featuring hand-colouring over a block-printed outline) of about the same time. The first example is notable in its retaining the innocently refined flavour of scriptural illustration, despite the erotic subject-matter – some indication of the naturalistic view of sex that must have prevailed at the time. The second example is remarkable in being so closely related in style to the earliest extant Yamato-e scroll, the *Genji* itself, as well as in its already featuring one of the characteristic conventions of shunga – the presence of a voyeur spying on the love scene (an element which, technically, introduces a needed variety into a series of basically similar erotic scenes; but which also may serve to suggest the basically humorous Japanese attitude towards sex and love-making). From such semi-erotic works and from literary and historical records of the time, we know that shunga art was already a firmly-established form in the tenth and eleventh centuries, and in style differed little from the other genre painting of the period.

Throughout much of the extant early literature of shunga appears the name of the Abbot Toba (Toba Sōjō: 1053–1140), best-known today as the legendary painter of the *Animal and Figure Scrolls*, and of the *Shigi-san engi*. Whether or not the Abbot actually painted these specific works is still a matter of scholarly controversy; but he was, in any event, one of the best-known painters of his time. Book XI: 16 of the aforementioned mid thirteenth-century collection of semi-historical tales, the *Kokon chomonju*, recounts an interesting anecdote concerning the Abbot, in which mention is made of even earlier shunga:

The passage in question features an argument between the Abbot and his leading art-pupil, in which the latter defends certain artistic distortions of his work in the following manner:

> Let my Master consider the *osokuzu-no-e* ['posture-pictures', i.e. shunga] of the older masters: the phallus is always depicted large, far in excess of the actual size. As a matter of fact, if it were drawn only in its natural size, it would hardly be worth looking at. Thus in its depiction is resort made to artistic exaggeration. And in my Master's own paintings is this principle often seen.

The story itself is apocryphal, and belongs to that category of anecdote which takes delight in the discomfiture of established authority. But it does offer further evidence that shunga was already a recognized art-form in the Heian Period – as well as confirming the fact that exaggerated depiction of the phallus was one of the artistic conventions of shunga, practically from its inception. Aside from its function in artistic expression, this latter, most striking feature of Japanese erotica was doubtless also akin to and derived from the earlier phallic worship – the phallus as an object of reverence and awe, the source of life and power. This fascination with the phallus was to persist throughout Japanese erotic art, long after its origins in folklore and primitive religion had been forgotten.

Osokuzu-no-e, the earliest Japanese term for shunga, has been the subject of much scholarly controversy, but it seems basically to originate in a book-title, *Osoku-zu* ('reclining-pictures', or 'posture-pictures'), an early physician's text, now lost, which was a medical guide to sexual postures – and later came to refer to erotic pictures in general. Just when shunga ceased to play a purely medical role and became more a subject for pleasurable appreciation and general sex education is difficult to determine. Painting in general, for most of this period, was intimately connected with expounding the Buddhist tenets, explaining the divine origins of noted shrines or temples, or illustrating famous tales. The idea of *any* work of art purely for its own visual sake was doubtless nonexistent. Indeed, it was probably not until well into the eighteenth century -- until the time of Harunobu or Utamaro, say – that a good part of shunga became truly independent of their educational function.

At any rate, semi-historical allusions to the early painters of shunga refer most often to the later Heian Period, and we may assume that such paintings existed as a recognized artistic genre by then – separate, that is, from the purely medical works on coital methods and postures, sexual stimulants and the like. Most likely shunga were considered but one customary facet of the genre-painter's craft, rather than as a special species 'beyond the pale'. The Heian Period (794–1185) is, of course, the age of the famous *Tale of Genji* – as well as of other noted novels and diaries – and it is interesting to note that even in the *Genji* one probable reference to shunga exists, where, in the Ukifune chapter, Prince Niou paints some erotic sketches to console his sweetheart the Princess Ukifune during his absence.

Erotic narrative scrolls

At this point we should be able to leave off theoretical discussions – references to shunga works no longer extant – and turn our attention to the concrete art objects that are our real concern. Such is, indeed, the case: but with the notable condition that, in dealing with medieval Japanese shunga art, the original versions are usually no longer extant – though often available in excellent copies, themselves of a certain antiquity.

Were our concern only with fine art as such, we should personally prefer to treat only of extant early works, and in strict order of extant antiquity. Our attention here must lie in part, however, in the historical development of shunga depiction and shunga subjects. This essay may, as well, interest sexologists and students of Japanese customs, who are less concerned than we are with artistic antiquity. Thus it seems our duty here to outline in historical order the earliest examples of shunga scrolls, even though we must often study and illustrate them in relatively late copies.

Probably the first shunga scroll cited by name in literary sources is *The Phallic Contest* (*Yōbutsu-kurabe*). Ascribed to the Abbot Toba, one early version of this scroll seems to have dated at least from the mid-Kamakura Period, and originally was preserved in the Tōji, head temple of the esoteric Shingon Sect in Kyoto. Its text was ascribed to the Shingon Abbot Jōken (1162–1231), of the Sambōin temple at Daigo; but the original work may well date back to Heian times.

In subject this famous scroll depicts an Imperial contest in which the most vigorous males of the Empire gathered at the court, disrobed, and displayed their phallic splendours to be measured by the judges. Then, the curtain was raised on the court-ladies, who had been viewing the spectacle from concealment, and who now rushed out naked to engage the winners in a contest of sexual powers. As might only have been expected, the ladies won, and were conferred the Imperial palm.

Aside from its obvious delight in the joys of sexual orgy, the scroll's satirical theme is that the most vigorous male is no match for the sexual resources of Woman. Beyond this, it may be surmised that, in the increasingly feminized Court society of late Heian Japan, the fast-rising might of the samurai classes – who were to conquer the Empire but a generation or two later – held a morbid fascination for the effete courtiers, both male and female. If the scroll bears any prophetic intent, it would seem to be that samurai prowess may indeed conquer the Court, but will be in turn quelled by the Ladies.

To judge from the late copies now extant, *The Phallic Contest* was executed in the more comic Yamato-e vein of the *Animal and Figure Scrolls* – likewise, it will be recalled, attributed to the Abbot Toba. The emphasis of the scroll is not so much on the erotic as on the comic side of sex relations between male and female. To the male who finds the resolute Japanese female both fascinating, and somewhat terrifying, the scroll's more philosophical overtones are apt to quell any priapic effect.

A companion-scroll, *The Fart-battle* (*He-gassen*), is not primarily erotic in nature. It depicts, rather, the ribald account of a legendary 'wind-breaking contest' between two groups of Imperial courtiers. Even to the modern viewer, it belongs rather in the class of 'earthy humour' than of shunga.

It is well to remember, though, that even in the prior *Phallic Contest* scroll itself – as in a rather large portion of shunga – the element of humour far outweighed the erotic; and it is highly doubtful that even *that* scroll had any priapic effect on the mature viewer, who would laugh before he ever thought of being sexually aroused. (On inexperienced adolescents, to be sure, the effect was doubtless a different one.)

The Fart-battle evidently formed a pair with the above-mentioned *Phallic Contest*, being ascribed to the same famous artist and calligrapher. This pair of picture-scrolls was, from the Kamakura Period on, known collectively as *The Victory-pictures* (*Kachi-e*) – the name deriving from the story, probably true, that they won first prize at an Imperial picture-contest held by the Consort of the Emperor Kameyama about the year 1270.

Coming to the *Brushwood-fence Scroll* (*Koshibagaki-zōshi*), we find the earliest scroll that could be termed truly erotic and aphrodisiac in nature. Here, for the first time, we are presented with a continuous story of sexual romance, displayed in increasingly fervid degrees from voyeurism to *cunnilinctio* on to full-fledged coitus in many, varied positions – all depicted in a voluptuous, colourful style calculated to stir the viewer's sexual instincts.

The original of this famous scroll is said to have been presented by her aunt to the Imperial Consort Kenreimon-in (daughter of the tyrant Kiyomori and later to be romantically linked with the hero Yoshitsune), on the occasion of her betrothal to the Emperor Takakura in 1172. As such, it may well constitute the first recorded example of the shunga scroll in its common function of sexual handbook for brides.

The Brushwood-fence Scroll (which is also known as *Kanjō no maki – The Initiation Scroll*) – a late Kamakura copy – exists in many versions, perhaps the earliest of which extant in modern times was allegedly sold abroad by its Kyoto owner some years ago. Various colophons exist, giving the paintings to the Kamakura masters Sumiyoshi Keion or Fujiwara Nobuzane, (as well as to later artists), and it is quite possible that both of these artists did a different version, no longer extant in the original. The text is ascribed, variously, to the Cloistered Emperor Go-Shirakawa or to Lord Fujiwara Tameie; and as with most of the early scrolls featuring text, the authors or calligraphers are usually personages of the highest rank in Imperial Court (or ecclesiastical) circles.

This, the most famous of all early shunga scrolls, depicts a notorious Court scandal of the year 986, fully confirmed in the historical records of the period. In the autumn of the previous year the Imperial Princess Nariko had been placed in the Nonomiya Shrine near the Capital, for the two-year-long ritual-purification in preparation for her State visit to the Grand Shrines of Ise, in the office of Vestal Virgin. Conditions were, from the outset, hardly auspicious: the Nonomiya Shrine itself had yet been only partially constructed; an inauspicious funeral procession (death being ritually unclean in the Shintō religion) had passed close by the holy group; and a day or two later, brigands had broken into the Shrine itself and stolen some of the Ladies' robes. Then, after some nine months of the Princess's official residence at the desolate Shrine, a rumour suddenly arose that the Vestal Virgin had been seduced by one of her own Imperial Guards – one Taira no Munemitsu, a well-known gallant who had assumed his post only the day before. Once news of the affair and of the Princess's defilement became known, she and her lover were dismissed from their Offices, and plans for the important State Pilgrimage postponed.

Although it would doubtless be convenient to presume that the earliest version of this scroll might have been executed soon after the actual historical events, there is yet no evidence one way or the other. The fact, however, of the fashion for such semi-historical narratives in the Kamakura Period suggests that the scroll may have been an original creation of this later period – based, doubtless, on still-current versions of the famous scandal of over two centuries earlier. Interestingly enough, however, although there are several historical references there is no early literary treatment of the affair extant – *The Brushwood-fence Scroll* combining in itself both the artistic and the literary foundation for our present knowledge of the notorious incident.

The scroll itself is devoted entirely to the first hours of this torrid, classical romance: it opens with the handsome warrior Munemitsu seen standing in splendid hunting-costume beside the brushwood fence that gives the scroll its name, as the Princess Nariko regards him, half-shyly, from behind a curtain. Stricken by her beauty, as she is by his manly presence, he creeps up to where she now sits by moonlight, on the verandah of the shrine, her long robes open in disarray, and engages first in *cunnilinctio* and then – divesting himself of his robes – continues with the many and varied coital positions that form the body of the scroll.

The Brushwood-fence Scroll is remarkable as the earliest known shunga work to devote itself wholeheartedly and in detail to the evolution of a single love-episode. Later ages were to demand greater variety in the subjects depicted within a scroll

– but with a resulting loss of the continuity of narrative mood that makes this work so effective. Seen in the pedestrian copies most often extant today, the scroll is indeed lacking in the ability to sustain interest through more than one or two viewings. The original Kamakura version of this work, however, must surely have ranked among the true world masterpieces of erotic art.

With the noted *Catamites' Scroll* (*Chigo no sōshi*), preserved in the Sambō-in temple of Daigo, we come to the earliest shunga scroll extant in its original version in Japan. Although the artist and calligrapher are unknown, this scroll bears the colophon date 1321, and is probably the only extant shunga work which, except for its subject, would be officially classified a 'National Treasure'.

The text to *The Catamites' Scroll* consists of a series of short and sometimes ribald tales of pederasty among the Buddhist monks of medieval Japan. The tales themselves (somewhat reminiscent of Boccaccio – who was in his youth at just this time) are generally humorous in vein, and the paintings are (it seems to us) rather too realistic and lacking in 'mood' to be considered truly erotic. Here, again, we should suppose the humour and human interest of the tales to have affected the early viewer more than the sexual content itself. (Though, it is perhaps perilous to assume such necessarily to have been the case to a monastic viewer, addicted to the perversions displayed therein.)

Whatever influence the subject matter may have on the viewer's appreciation of *The Catamites' Scroll*, however, it must be recognized as the earliest and most important single work of erotic art extant in Japan.

With *The Priest in the Bag* (*Fukuro-hōshi ekotoba*) we find yet another early shunga scroll whose content, though erotic, makes humour its predominant theme. Attributed to the fourteenth-century Yamato-e artist Korehisa (painter of the noted battle-scrolls, *Gosannen-kassen ekotoba*), the scroll is also known as *Uzumasa no maki* (*The Uzumasa Scroll*).

The intrepid hero of *The Priest in the Bag* is a Buddhist bonze who one day picks up three court ladies-in-waiting in his small ferry-boat, takes them to an islet in the midst of the wide river near Uzumasa (in Kyoto), threatens them unless they submit to him, and then violates them one by one. The ladies, however, are loath to return thus forlorn to their abstemious, cloistered life and, placing the lusty priest in a large bag, they smuggle him into their quarters. The ladies reveal the secret to their mistress – and the widowed nun-princess living in the opposite wing of the palace also learns of their find – and thus it comes about that all the ladies henceforth share in the lucky priest's amorous attentions. What had once been his greatest pleasure, however, becomes a source of no little suffering, for the ladies give him no rest at all, whether by day or by night. He waxes pale and gaunt and seems, indeed, on the point of losing his life, when the ladies, determining that rumours of his death would affect their reputations, at last set him free to return to his temple – his worldly possessions consisting of his robe and one parasol.

Although superficially somewhat resembling the earlier *Phallic Contest, The Priest in the Bag* is actually the first in a long line of Japanese erotic tales in which the hero (or heroes) finds himself captive in a closed world of lusty females, escaping only after losing his strength – and often his health – at their hands. Though commencing with the adolescent dream of unlimited sexual conquests, the tales invariably end with the hero sadder and wiser for his experiences. An anthropologist would doubtless find, in this literary tradition, vestiges of an earlier, matriarchal society.

Like so many of the early shunga scrolls, *The Priest in the Bag* is no longer extant in its original version, but seems to have been a work in typical Yamato-e style of the later Kamakura Period. The excellent copy illustrated here succeeds well in conveying the flavour of what must have been a later, Muromachi Period version – perhaps that attributed to the court painter Tosa Mitsunobu (*c.* 1430–1521), and owned by the ruling Tokugawa Clan until its loss in a fire of the mid nineteenth century. The scroll's style is open and uncomplicated, well suited to the tragi-comic nature of its subject.

Standardization of shunga subjects

One predominant element of construction we note in most of the above, early scrolls is that of pictorial and narrative continuity. Some sort of story is told, and the successive scenes usually lead to some kind of climax or dénouement. With the sixteenth century, however, the picture-scroll in general often tended to lose this story-telling quality, and become simply a series of detached tableaux on but vaguely related themes.

In shunga, the format became standardized on a set of, usually, twelve scenes (after the months of the year), each displaying a variant pose or position of love-making or coitus, but with no attempt at creating any continuity. This format may possibly date to a shunga work of this type ascribed to the aforementioned late fifteenth-century artist Tosa Mitsunobu, who seems to have been the leading shunga artist of his time. While the individual beauty and interest of each such tableau cannot be denied, one nevertheless feels that when the Japanese picture-scroll (erotic or not) abdicated its story-telling function, it lost a major element of its life-force.

205   Plate 205 illustrates a notable example of this type of Tosa/Kanō-style, non-narrative, text-less shunga scroll – a series of unrelated erotic tableaux, in which the vivid colour and variegated subject matter serve to compensate for the absence of story-line. It dates from the seventeenth century.

XXV   Plate XXV dating from about the same time, will also serve to indicate this general type. This particular scroll bears on its box the inscription, 'Brought with her by the daughter of the Yagyū Clan on the occasion of her marriage into the Yanagisawa Clan. Former collection, Yanagisawa Clan.' This is yet another reminder of the fact that such elaborately-executed scrolls often found their at least nominal justification as *yomeiri-dōgu* ('accoutrements for a bride's trousseau' – i.e. sex-instruction guides); and that such an original, painted scroll, even by one of the lesser artists of the time, would have cost the equivalent of many months' pay to the average manual worker, and thus was still limited to the wealthy – whether among the Court or Samurai aristocracy, or among the rising bourgeoisie.

Of the latter scroll, we reproduce here the opening *two* scenes (of twelve), both to show the typical format, and to indicate something of the artistic devices, both of subject, composition and colouring, used to provide sufficient variety so that the dozen views should not – at least, at the hands of a competent master – become repetitious. (As with all Far Eastern picture-scrolls, the paintings are designed to be viewed from right to left. For an idea of the format of the Japanese shunga scroll – and one of its contemporary uses – see also our plate 249 infra.)

Finally, we might note that early shunga depiction was not always limited to painters of the native, Yamato-e or Tosa styles. In the Tokyo National Museum, for example, is a late copy of a noteworthy shunga scroll ascribed to the master of predominantly classical, semi-Chinese-style painting, Kanō Motonobu (1476-1559). Again, an original, signed shunga scroll of yet another classical master, Hasegawa Sōtaku (d. c. 1611) is known to have been dismounted in the 1930s for subdivision among members of the 'Inten' group of modern painters. And it is worth repeating here that, though the genre quality of most shunga work dictated its execution by painters in predominantly native styles – Yamato-e, Tosa, and later ukiyo-e – no special stigma was attached either to the artist or the patron of shunga. Thus, an artist of *any* school might receive a shunga commission – but he would be most likely to execute his work after the manner of the native style that was best suited to this particular subject.

In surveying Japanese erotic art during its first millennium, we become all too conscious of the many gaps in our present knowledge. It should be emphasized, though, that the scarcity of early and medieval shunga has nothing to do with censorship or overt prudery. Where many medieval samurai carried an icon of the god Fudō into battle, others kept a shunga-scroll in their armour-box as a battle-charm – their own private kind of *kachi-e* ('victory-picture'). Shunga served in the handbag as a charm for getting rich; shunga in the storehouse were thought to guard against fire and termites. Shunga served physicians in treating sexually inhibited or frigid patients, young brides in overcoming their over-imaginative fears of the details of married life. Shunga were not, however, ever meant to be displayed publicly; like sex-life itself, they were for private, intimate consumption.

All but a few of the early shunga have disappeared in the wars, fires, floods and earthquakes that have been Japan's lot. Prior to the development of extensive printing in the seventeenth century, shunga circulated only in rare and expensive hand-copies, and principally among the wealthy Court-aristocracy and samurai. They served both as phallic charms, as earthy amusement, and as educational accoutrements to the trousseaux of noble brides; but their distribution was, necessarily, never as widespread as that of non-erotic art, nor was any massive creative force devoted to their production prior to the seventeenth century. Shunga were only an occasional sideline of the classical Court or manor artist, and it is not surprising that fewer than a dozen separate shunga themes remain extant today from these early and medieval periods.

Shunga found their first and most serious, unselfconscious flowering in these early eras; but their golden age was to come with the following, *popular* phase of Japanese art.

Ukiyo-e

While the pictorial art of the early seventeenth century was primarily a reflection of the Yamato-e or Kanō classical styles, the new taste of the times came gradually to be reflected in a fresh art-form, known today as *ukiyo-e* – 'pictures of the floating world'. It may be of interest to note here some of the changing connotations of the root-word *ukiyo* ('fleeting, floating world') which, indeed, well mirror the changing tastes and morals of the times.

Ukiyo first resolved from the medieval Buddhist concept of the grief-filled, evanescent world of illusion, to that of a transient, 'floating' world, and then, with the seventeenth century, to the meaning of the world of pleasure – the courtesans and the actors. At the same time, in some contexts *ukiyo* was used to signify the everyday, commonplace world. It is the latter two concepts – those of pleasure and of the genre – that most flavour the meaning of the compound *ukiyo-e* – pictorial depictions of that world. Let us analyse a few pertinent seventeenth-century uses of the word *ukiyo*, grouping these into three categories:

(1) *ukiyo-fū* ('floating-world manner'): stylish, fashionable. *ukiyo-sugata* ('floating-world form'): a stylish appearance. *ukiyo-mōyō* ('pattern'), *ukiyo-zome* ('dyeing'): a stylish kimono design or pattern. *ukiyo-nembutsu* ('prayer'): 'a stylish [i.e. frivolous] prayer' – said merely for the sake of form.

(2) *ukiyo-gokoro* ('floating-world emotion'): a profligate nature. *ukiyo-otoko* ('man'): a libertine. *ukiyo-gurui* ('madness'): a passion for harlots. *ukiyo-dera* ('temple'): a Buddhist temple whose priest kept a secret concubine. *ukiyo-bōzu* ('priest'): a Buddhist priest addicted to the pleasures of the flesh. *ukiyo-ningyō* ('doll'): an erotic type of doll, equipped with pudenda.

(3) *ukiyo-machi* ('floating-world quarter'): the demi-monde. *ukiyo-onna* ('woman'): a woman of the demi-monde. *ukiyo-zue* ('cane'): a type of cane affected by rakes on their way to the Yoshiwara. *ukiyo-ginchaku* ('purse'): a type of purse carried by the maidservants of courtesans. *ukiyo-bikuni* ('nun'): a type of wandering prostitute who dressed as a nun to ply her trade. *ukiyo-mono* ('floating-world fellow'): Kabuki actor; in other contexts: a rake.

Ukiyo-e – 'floating-world pictures' – the compound that immediately concerns us, will be found in all three of the above connotations. When we add to these the 'genre' meaning of *ukiyo* (e.g. *ukiyo-banashi* – 'floating-world conversation' – small talk, talk of mundane matters) we can formulate a synthetic but comprehensive definition of ukiyo-e, at least as the term was used in its formative period: *A new style of pictures, very much in vogue, devoted to the depiction of everyday, human life, but particularly of fair women and handsome men engaged in pleasure, or part of the world of pleasure; pictures, as often as not, of an erotic nature.*

(These usages do not preclude, it must be observed, the consciousness or sub-consciousness on the part of sensitive Edo artists and writers of the impermanence and precariousness of the 'floating world'. Some of its graphic depictions, even though all gaiety or luxury on the surface, seem to have an indefinable touch of sadness, communicating a vague uneasiness at the flight of time and the vanity of desire.) But in short, the term *ukiyo-e* was often synonymous with *shunga* – and this strong erotic element remained at the root of ukiyo-e throughout the two and a half centuries of its flourishing.

The ukiyo-e style itself had commenced in the more academic genre painting of the mid sixteenth century, depictions of plebeian scenes for the amusement of the wealthy art patrons. (It is possible that the *idea* of depicting such genre scenes may have derived from Ming painting. But the style and subjects were entirely Japanese.) Before a century had elapsed, ukiyo-e had developed into a unified style of painting, practised both by the semi-academic masters for their aristocratic patrons, and by the *machi-eshi* ('town painters'), the more plebeian artisan-painters who were to form the backbone of this popular art.

In accord with the tastes of the times, the shunga depictions of the Edo Period (1600–1868) tended to abandon the *story* format of the prior picture-scrolls. Instead, they most often simply presented an unrelated erotic series, usually of a dozen varied scenes. In the field of shunga *book* illustration, of course, we shall often find continuous fictional works on unified themes. But in both the painted scrolls, the albums and the prints, our discussion will most naturally turn not so much to the story or subject-matter itself, as to an examination of artistic schools and styles – and of the actual artists, where known.

For the first seventy years of the seventeenth century – until the appearance of Moronobu – the names of the shunga (as well as ukiyo-e) artists are largely unknown. To be sure, we have attributions of shunga works to such academic masters as Iwasa Matabei (1578–1650) and Tosa Mitsuoki (1617–91) – copies, often, of pre-Edo-Period works; and we have already, in the absence of originals, had occasion to refer to several scrolls of this type.

Although ukiyo-e itself still frequently took its subject matter from the classical periods, in its most characteristic form it treated of the people and customs of its own immediate age. One excellent example of early seventeenth-century painted ukiyo-e is shown in plate 206, in which the raw, untamed, even crude flavour of the *206* first anonymous, plebeian Tosa/ukiyo-e masters is well conveyed. Compared either to the formal Tosa artists or to the later ukiyo-e masters, the painting is indeed 'primitive'. But there is also a wild, untutored, unsophisticated mood to such work that elevates it to a world quite apart from the usual concept of 'erotic pictures'. Its flavour is surprisingly 'Pompeian' – and the artist's aim is clearly serious sex in-struction, not eroticism *per se*.

Another typical example of the best shunga work of this period is shown in plate XXV (centre), by another anonymous seventeenth-century master, but one *XXV (centre)* whose style is more gentle and restrained, and more in the orthodox Tosa/ukiyo-e tradition. His world is not so much one of violent passion as of tender sex-romance; his figures are more like pleasant dolls, ingenuously devoting themselves to the game of life.

During the Edo Period – and even among Japanese dealers today – it was customary to ascribe *all* such ukiyo-e painting in the style of the first half of the seventeenth century to the aforementioned Tosa/early-ukiyo-e master, Matabei. We now know the actual style of the historical Matabei well enough to distinguish it from the bulk of the work formerly attributed to him; but it is quite likely that Matabei himself did several shunga scrolls on commission from his daimyō patrons. Indeed, at least two historical records of the period would seem to confirm this; and he is even recorded as having prepared an elaborate shunga scroll on commission from the third Tokugawa Shōgun Iemitsu (1603–51), for presentation to that ruler's daughter on the occasion of her marriage. Such works may well yet exist: we may still hope that when one day the hidden treasures of Japanese erotic art are made generally available to art scholars, a new and significant chapter will be added to the history of Japanese painting, by the discovery of what master-pieces indeed lie hidden in the scattered private and public collections of this fascinating land.

It was in this, the Edo Period, that erotic art came into its own as an object of appreciation by the urban populace in general, no longer merely a pleasure of the wealthier samurai and of the aristocracy. A critical element in the popularization of the shunga art-form was the expansion of woodblock printing, formerly limited to a few monastic presses, to the secular world. In this connexion, let us take a look at what was happening on the Continent about this time.

To judge, at least, from the original books and records preserved in Japan, one of the major eras of shunga publication in China was that around the Wan-li Period (1573–1620). Ming works now extant bear, for example, such dates as 1594, 1595, 1610, 1624, and were doubtless imported into Japan in limited quantities in the period during and after the Shōgun Hideyoshi's Korean Campaigns of the later sixteenth century.

Several such Ming works were even adapted and printed in Japan about this time, among them the famed *Kōso myōron* (*The Marvellous Discourse between Emperor Huang and the natural girl* – in Chinese, *Huang-Su miao-lun*).

As with printing in general, the early seventeenth-century examples of printed shunga were yet very 'limited' editions, produced by and for a restricted audience of affluent connoisseurs. Such is the case with the aforementioned *Kōso myōron* – this Japanized version of the noted Chinese sex manual having been produced, in all probability, by the famed Kōetsu Press in Kyoto.

This excessively rare book consists of some sixty-five leaves, of which the first eighteen represent a reprinting of Ming Chinese shunga, the following seven, similar illustrations in Japanese Yamato-e/Tosa style, and the final forty sheets, of a Japanese translation of the Chinese sex manual itself. The newly-drawn illustrations to the volume are in a crude mixture of the Yamato-e and primitive ukiyo-e styles. They can hardly be termed beautiful in themselves – though to lovers of incunabula they represent one of the early peaks of woodcut illustration. Their primitive quality lies partly in the relatively untutored style of the artist himself, but even more, in the yet unrefined nature of the first experiments at secular printing in the early decades of the seventeenth century.

At least five other such printed Japanese shunga books exist from this early period. They are all published in the capital, Kyoto, and all derive their texts, and some of their illustrations, primarily from Chinese sources. These books justify their existence and explain their naturalistic philosophy of sex rather explicitly:

> The Way of Male and Female is by no means a device of simple pleasure-making: sexual union has existed since the world began. Father and Mother represent Heaven and Earth; between Heaven and Earth the trees and grasses grow: between the union of Man and Woman is human life born . . .

Such philosophical declarations appear frequently as postscripts or prefaces to seventeenth-century Japanese erotica. Though it is probable that a certain part of their audience considered shunga but a titillating diversion, their major function in serious sex education cannot be denied. Indeed, throughout most of the seventeenth and eighteenth centuries, shunga books, albums and paintings took as their first aim either dutiful, or pleasureful, sex education. It was only with the later eighteenth century, with the increasingly loose morals of the times, that they became, as often as not, the overtly sensual works they at first seem.

Rakuji hidenshō (*The Secrets of Sex Matters*) is probably the last extant work of this primitively-illustrated, Chinese-derived nature, and is dated 1655. It is only shortly after this date that ukiyo-e illustration was at last to find its first true flowering, bringing forth the wit and power of this new art-form to meet the needs and demands of the rising new society of Edo.

However primitive the erotic incunabula of the early seventeenth century may seem to our eyes today – contrasting, indeed, with the relative refinement and grace of the shunga *paintings* of the period – they form a landmark in early Japanese printing and printed illustration. And the very fact that shunga found their place amidst the earliest Japanese printed illustration of a secular nature, will indicate and confirm their vital place in Japanese civilization. During those early years, wood-engraving, printing and publishing were not quite the simple matter of later times; one did not go to the trouble to engrave and publish a work unless there was a real need and demand for it. The history of Edo Period shunga is thus at the same time the history of secular printing and illustration, and, in miniature, the history of Japanese life and civilization itself.

The newly-founded 'provincial' samurai capital of Edo (the present Tokyo) was, quite naturally, slow in developing cultural devices when compared to the ancient capital, Kyoto. On top of this, in the year 1657 the Great Fire of Edo destroyed the first fruits of its material culture, so that extant Edo printing and illustration in general dates from a year or two after the conflagration. Already with the earliest post-conflagration Edo books, however, we discover a fully-blown new art of printed ukiyo-e which, practically from its inception, was to set the standard and the goal of all later 'pictures of the Floating World'.

Let us recapitulate briefly, the general history of early seventeenth-century ukiyo-e. Parallel to its extensive development in the field of painting, ukiyo-e from the second quarter of the century formed that crucial liaison with woodblock printing that was to make it world-famous – to save it, indeed, from obscure relegation as one of the minor schools of Japanese art. But where ukiyo-e *painting* – the new, genre work by already-established masters – achieved greatness practically from the moment of its birth, *printed* ukiyo-e had first to go through two generations of development at the hands of pioneer artisans and illustrators. Though among the most charming of all incunabula, the semi-ukiyo-e, general book illustration of Kyoto in the 1620s and following is indeed primitive in expression and technique.

With the mid 1650s, however, appeared three different (though anonymous) Kyoto illustrators who set the first high standards of printed ukiyo-e art. Printed shunga of this period are most rare, though various titles of works now lost appear here and there in the book-catalogues of the time. Due to their specialized nature (rather than, in Japan, to outside factors such as censorship), shunga seem to have appeared only in rather limited editions, perhaps as small as one or two hundred copies each. It must always come as something of a shock for the Western librarian to open up any Japanese publishers' book-catalogue of the seventeenth or early eighteenth centuries, and find a standard section marked 'Erotica'.

The first major development of printed shunga appeared not in the old Imperial Capital, Kyoto, but in the new, samurai administrative centre, Edo. The reasons for this may be surmised as: first, ukiyo-e itself, in its printed forms, was primarily a development of Edo artists and Edo tastes; second, unlike their compatriots in Edo, the citizens of Kyoto tended to favour traditional styles and art-forms, throughout the period maintaining a love of paintings – even though often second-rate ones – over the more mass-produced prints; and third the predominantly male population of boom-town Edo rather naturally created a special demand for erotic art. Indeed, so far as shunga are concerned, the latter factor was perhaps crucial, for as the novelist Saikaku recorded in the year 1688, Edo was 'a city of bachelors . . . rather resembling the monasteries of Mt Kōya'. It was doubtless this factor that gave the publishers the extra readership needed to make extensive, quality shunga publication possible. (It is also worth adding that, though the Osaka novelist Saikaku is the most famous of Japanese writers in semi-erotic vein, he is far surpassed by his contemporaries in the bachelor-town of Edo when it comes to erotic content and detail of expression.)

The year 1660 marks the first extant, dated shunga publication in Edo, and we may assume this the general starting-point of fully-developed shunga in its printed form. For a 'starter' it was a most impressive year: one after the other appeared shunga books and prints and printed scrolls which were never really to be surpassed by later artists. Forrest Reid's controversial declaration (*Illustrators of the Sixties*), 'Most of the masterpieces of the world are illustrations', was never truer than in ukiyo-e, and especially so in the shunga genre, whose productions were never designed for public hanging, but only for private viewing in parlour or boudoir.

The first dated ukiyo-e shunga book includes more than its share of such 'master-pieces': this is the *Yoshiwara Pillow-pictures* (*Yoshiwara makura-e*) of 1660, a shunga by-product of the literary genre called 'Courtesan Critiques' (*yūjo hyōbanki*) – guides to the elaborate courtesan-quarters of Old Japan. Most of the Courtesan Critiques (which contain, incidentally, a majority of the important mid seventeenth-century ukiyo-e designs) do not feature shunga as such, but consist of guides to the pleasure-quarters with brief critiques of the famous courtesans, and illustrations of general Yoshiwara scenes or portraits of the individual courtesans.

Yoshiwara Pillow-pictures, however, extends this genre to the more specifically erotic: it consists entirely of illustrations, each page featuring a famed courtesan of the time in a love-scene, the girl identified, obliquely, by showing her 'family crest' in one corner of the page. The illustrations range from the semi-erotic to full-fledged shunga, the latter predominating. We find in these small, flavourful illustrations the true beginning of the ukiyo-e print – the first creation of that intimate world of make-believe that has bewitched collectors the world over.

Though unfortunately anonymous, this, the first artist of Edo ukiyo-e, was a true master. Very likely he came to the field with a strong background in ukiyo-e painting. Were this master's name recognized, it would doubtless be he, rather than Moronobu, who would be known today as the 'Father of Ukiyo-e'. Indeed, it was formerly the practice to give *all* the ukiyo-e works of this early period to Moronobu, in the absence of any more convenient name. Moronobu's first signed work, however, dates from 1672, and reveals a striking personality rather different, one feels, from his predecessor – doubtless his teacher – of the 1660s.

For the moment, then, let us here give this pioneer artist a provisional name – 'The Master of Kambun' – referring to the Kambun Era (1661–73) during which his principal work appeared. Future research and findings may, indeed, prove this master himself to comprise more than one artist, or even reveal a relationship closer to Moronobu than we now suppose; but it is enough for our present purposes to assume the Edo ukiyo-e work of this crucial decade the product of one man, and certainly of one style. This style was to set the pace for ukiyo-e during the ensuing two centuries of its vivid life.

Interestingly enough, the earliest notable *non*-shunga work of Edo ukiyo-e appeared in the same year, just a month after the above-mentioned volume. This was the *Yoshiwara Mirror* (*Yoshiwara kagami*), a small volume comprising a gallery of courtesans' portraits in ukiyo-e style, probably by the same artist. Thus shunga and the Yoshiwara form the first motivation and birthplace of ukiyo-e prints.

Almost simultaneously with the first shunga book illustrations of Edo, the first prints appeared. These, too, were primarily shunga, and it is of no little interest that the shunga prints preceded the appearance of *non*-erotic independent prints by fully two generations. Clearly, the audience for expensive prints was at the beginning limited to the more affluent connoisseurs of shunga.

These prints of the second half of the seventeenth century were not, to be sure, customarily issued as independent sheets: the nature of shunga prints dictated that their format be more 'private' – either that of the album, or the scroll. In the former, a series of twelve prints were folded once and lightly mounted in book form; in the latter, they were printed or mounted laterally and rolled up when not in use.

Probably the earliest extant ukiyo-e print is that famous scroll from the Shibui Collection, the frontispiece of which appears as colour-plate 10 in our *Masters of the Japanese Print*. Only the first third of the scroll is now extant, consisting of the semi-erotic frontispiece, plus three full-fledged shunga prints, all four designs printed on a single, lateral sheet of soft paper, and hand-coloured with orange, green and yellow, in the dynamic *tan-e* manner. We are privileged to reproduce here, for the first time, one of the shunga prints from this rare scroll – which ranks, certainly, as one of the prime historical treasures of ukiyo-e.

As is frequently the case with the early shunga prints, the style is somewhat harsher than that of the contemporary book-illustrations. Most likely this factor was influenced strongly by the varying skill or talent of the engravers, who were already well trained in the detailed work of book-illustration, but at first experienced difficulty in achieving the same soft linear quality in the larger format.

In all honesty, it must also be admitted that we really know very little of this formative period of ukiyo-e, other than what the prints themselves reveal. We have grouped the pre-Moronobu Edo works of the 1660s under the aegis of 'The Master of Kambun', but that artist's style may well vary markedly under the hands of different engravers; or may even encompass the work of more than one man. More certain attribution is difficult, at the present stage of our knowledge.

Each scene of this first printed scroll approximates the format of the later small, *chūban* prints – about 7½ x 10 inches in size. Very soon, however, the larger *ōban* size (about 10 x 15 inches) made its appearance in more than one series of shunga prints, presumably by the same Kambun Master. The series illustrated here most likely appeared, likewise, in scroll-form, though it is now dismounted as single prints. The delicacy of its strong black line is impressive indication that the engravers had by now more fully mastered the larger format. As with most of the early prints, the addition of colouring is not really necessary, so strong and balanced is the basic design.

Only one or two other examples of such early print series are now extant, but they rank among the rarest and most significant of all ukiyo-e. They represent the earliest true ukiyo-e prints, and already display a dramatic beauty of powerful line and austere composition that may have been equalled, but was seldom if ever surpassed, by the coming centuries of later masters.

By the later 1660s, the period when Moronobu's early work tends to become confused with that of his master, this style has become more graceful and harmonious, if less bold and elemental. This Kambun-Period work represents the style that, consolidated and transmitted by Moronobu, was to form the basis for much of later ukiyo-e figure design. Despite its primitive austerity, there is certainly no more flavourful style in ukiyo-e, and it is only to be regretted that so few works of this decade remain – and that those extant are often of a class, shunga, that can never be very widely recognized or exhibited.

The later 1660s is also a period when the mood of the shunga books sometimes becomes a more playful one – as is the case in the *Kasenmakura* (*Pillow of the Poets*), throughout the plates of which are run punning, sexual pastiches on the ancient poets. Hardly anything – whether the Gods, the Poets, the Emperor, or Sex – was sacred to the Japanese wit. Now, with the Empire finally at peace for three full generations – following such long centuries of political turmoil – it was only natural that the citizenry should begin to long for amusement, as much as for enlightenment, in all fields.

211 (*above*) Kambun Master:
From a printed scroll of twelve
scenes (incomplete). Woodblock print with hand-
colouring; Edo, *c.* 1660

212 (*left*) Kambun Master:
A game of backgammon in
bed; detail of an illustration to
the *Makura-byōbu* (*The Pillow-
screen*). Woodblock-printed
book; Edo/Osaka, 1669; *ōbon*

Two further prints by the great
founder of Ukiyo-e shunga
print art

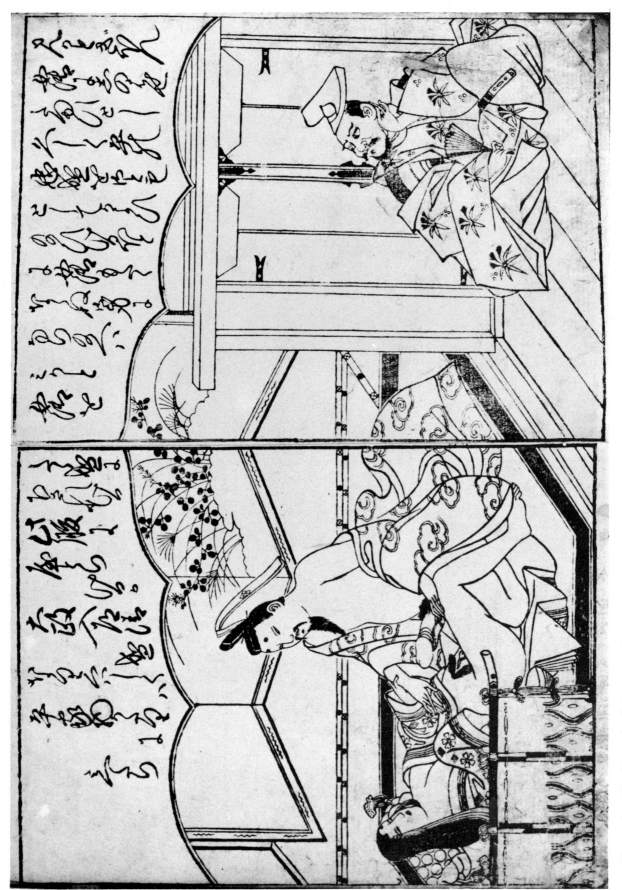

213 Moronobu: The Emperor Shirakawa, with mistress and attendant lord; illustration to the *Wakoku bijin-asobi* (*Pleasure with the Beauties of Japan*). Woodblock-printed book; Edo, c. 1672; ōbon. Signed.
A shunga book illustration in severe style illustrating a historical event, from the hand of the earliest named master of a

214 Moronobu: *A seamstress and her lover*; woodblock print with hand-colouring in *tan-e* style. Edo, *c.* early 1680s; *ōban.*
A print in the master's fully fledged gentle style

215, 216, 217 and 218 Moronobu: *Ōban* woodblock prints with hand colouring. Edo, *c.* early 1680s.
Prints from a series by the great Moronobu, illustrating the range of the master's productions.

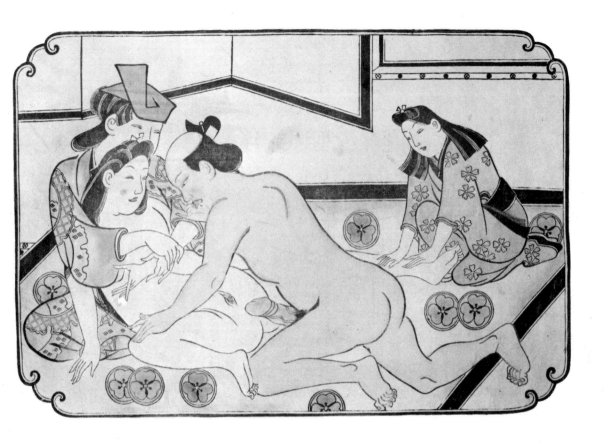

219 (*above*) Moronobu: A wealthy townsman, with mistress and attendants; illustration to the *Imayō Yoshiwara-makura* (*Stylish Yoshiwara Pillow*). Woodblock-printed book; Edo, *c.* 1683; *ōbon*

220 (*right*) Moronobu: Detail of an illustration to the *Komurasaki* (*Deep Purple*). Woodblock-printed book with hand-colouring; Edo, 1677; *ōbon*. Signed

Book illustrations by Moronobu, the *doyen* of the art during the late 17th century

221 (*right*) Kiyonobu: Woodblock print with hand-colouring in *urushi-e* style (now faded). Edo, *c.* early 1700s; *ōban*. Two different versions of this series exist, of which this is the later. The final print of the earlier series is signed. A shunga print by an artist whose primary field was theatre illustration

222 (*right*) Sukenobu: Illustration to a woodblock-printed book (title lost). Edo, *c.* 1710s; large *yoko-bon*. A shunga print by an artist who helped to modify the Ukiyo-e style in the direction of gentleness and elegance. Such treatment of the nude is rare

223 Sugimura: Woodblock print with hand-colouring in *tan-e* style. Edo, *c.* mid 1680s; *ōban*

224 Sugimura: Woodblock print with hand-colouring in *tan-e* style. Edo, *c.* mid 1680s; *ōban*

225 Sugimura: *Ōban* woodblock print. Edo, *c.* mid 1680s. The coiffure of young samurai may be distinguished from that of women by the presence of the shaven pate
Prints by the master specializing in shunga, who worked under the direct influence of Moronobu

226 Kiyonobu: *Chūban* woodblock print. Edo, *c.* early 1700s

227 Masanobu: Initiation of
a young girl into the class of
courtesan; woodblock print
with hand-colouring in
urushi-e style. Edo, *c.* 1710s; *ōban*

Characteristic works by two of
the great Moronobu's principal
followers

228 Style of Shūsui: *Ōban*
woodblock print. Kyoto,
c. 1770s. This illustrates, by comparison with the two prints
above, the effect of Harunobu's
art on the style of the Ukiyo-e
shunga print

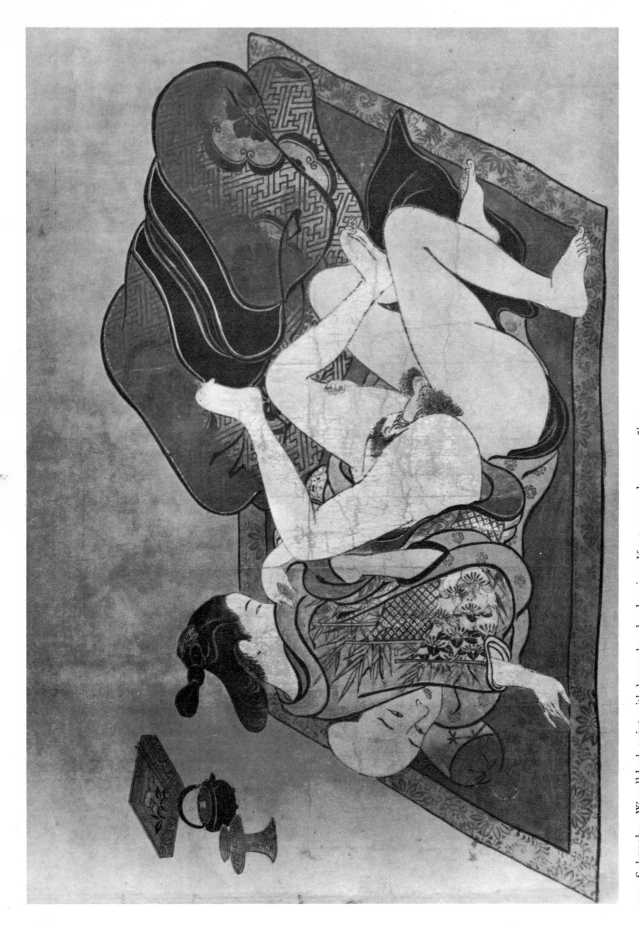

229 Sukenobu: Woodblock print with heavy hand-colouring. Kyoto, *c.* early 1710s; *ōban.*
A major work by the master who anticipated in part the stylistic revolution of the mid 18th century

230 Settei: Husband accosting his wife at morning toilette; illustration to the *Onna-shimekawa oshie-fumi* (*Erotic Instruction for Women*). Woodblock-printed book; Kyoto, *c.* 1750s; ōbon.
A book illustration by the master who attempted to combine the power of Moronobu's lines with Sukenobu's gentleness

231 Masanobu: The young warrior Yoshitsune receives initiation into the Arts of Love from a female *tengu*; illustration to the *Genkurō-gitsune sembon-zakura* (*Yoshitsune and the Thousand Cherry Trees*). Woodblock-printed book with *benizuri-e* (colour-printed) frontispiece; Edo, *c.* 1750; *yoko-bon*

232 Anonymous: Husband and wife at the kitchen hearth as their little son plays with *yajirobei* balancing-toy; illustration to the *Banzei chiwa konotama-kagami.* Woodblock-printed book in Kabuki-text style; *c.* early 1760s; *hanshi-bon.* Alternate version published Edo, 1765, under the title *Fūryū sandai-makura.*

A beautiful example of shunga book illustration with a domestic setting

We cannot here delve very extensively into the relations between Art and Society in the Edo Period. Yet we may comment that the peculiar dichotomy of Edo society – all political and legal power in the hands of the samurai, yet effective financial power in the grasp of the merchant class – must certainly have affected the direction of the arts.

Thus, art for the theoretically all-powerful samurai featured increasingly hollow formalism; and art for the wealthy but legally 'right-less' merchants tended towards hedonism and ostentation. The products of the best artists of either world – a Tsunenobu or a Kōrin – were yet of a very high standard indeed, but it must be admitted that art of mediocre quality tended to predominate. It was in the gap between these worlds that ukiyo-e rose and flourished, an art at once anti-samurai, yet at the same time only semi-bourgeois. The ukiyo-e print artists were supported by a basic throng of semi-educated but tasteful townsmen, neither rich nor poor – a thriving middle class which was to prove the vital force of Edo Period culture.

In an age when neither effectual militarism nor devout religion any longer possessed much vitality, attention tended to turn to more worldly pastimes of every kind, among which sex played a major part. With sex no longer simply a physical function or merely a procreative act, interest came increasingly to be focused on its 'recreational' aspects. Sex in Japan had always been recognized as a basic human right, a form of mental hygiene, a valid means of human catharsis. Now, however, the feudal Tokugawa government seems to have perceived that some outlet must be provided for the affluent townsmen; this they furnished by various means of 'official leniency'. In the world of public amusement, the courtesan-quarters were permitted to flourish; in the arts, erotic literature and art were allowed to come into widespread fashion.

Not all, of course, of the erotically inclined were able to take advantage of the social organs provided for sex-release: many men lacked the nerve, or the taste, or the funds to initiate liaisons with the licensed houses, or with the lower, unlicensed prostitutes. And although it is difficult to gauge their exact numbers or buying-power, this audience of the sexually underprivileged – including also the nominally celibate priesthood, and the thousands of sexually-repressed ladies of the Shōgun and daimyō harems – must surely have formed one of the sustaining sources of patronage to the shunga artists and publishers.

To these groups may be added that considerable body of 'customary purchasers' of shunga for educational, social, or superstitious reasons – as customary presents for brides and newlyweds, and even, sometimes, as magical amulets thought to bring prosperity, or to ward off fire and termites. Doubtless the latter well-defined class of habitual customers accounted for enough of a dependable audience – perhaps even one half of the total – to remove the 'speculative element' from shunga publication.

Of the remainder of shunga's audience we cannot be so specific: they doubtless consisted of men (and to a lesser extent, of women) of all classes, who found pleasure in artistic depictions of the erotic. We need neither glorify nor condemn their taste: they tended towards a generally healthy and uncritical enjoyment of sex and of erotica, and were fortunate to be catered to by a group of artists who must surely form the largest single body of true masters of the erotic to be found in any land.

Moronobu

213

At what exact point Hishikawa Moronobu (d. 1694) made his appearance, we cannot say. His first signed work of 1672 already reveals a fully-developed style, closely related, and not necessarily inferior, to that of the Master of Kambun. Moronobu's earliest signed shunga book illustrated in plate 213 dates from just about this juncture: in style it is rather more refined and balanced than its predecessor's; it retains the strong black line but adds to it that dramatic 'juxaposition of bodies' that is so characteristic of Moronobu.

We have already cited shunga books that depicted samurai, the nobility or courtesans *in flagrante delicto*, or sexually parodied the classical poets. In this early Moronobu work, we find one of that numerous class of shunga that provide an erotic and popular, but essentially sober view of History. Compared to the lubricious distortions of history prevalent in nineteenth-century ukiyo-e, the approach is surprisingly serious: deprived of its illustration, the text-caption could stand as a sober 'footnote to history', of prurient interest only to repressed schoolboys:

> The Emperor [Shirakawa] had taken to visiting privately with the Court-Lady Gion, and on these visits always took with him his trusted attendant Taira no Tadamori. The Lady before long became of a condition that could no longer be suppressed, and thus the Emperor bestowed her as wife upon this same Tadamori. The child which she bore in her womb was none other than the subsequent Prime Minister and tyrant, Kiyomori. The details of this matter will be found in the *Tales of the Heike*.

Chosen, almost at random, from the dozens of such plates in the book, this scene reveals an all-too-human facet of Imperial life, and in the humorous, vaguely melancholy figure of the Emperor's noble attendant, exposes more of the true flavour of Court politics than does any history-book we know. This is clearly the work of a master – both of dramatic design, and of the psychological insight that distinguishes the great illustrator from the merely competent.

Moronobu's work has yet to be fully catalogued in any of its varied aspects. But in the two decades from 1672 up to shortly before his death in 1694, he produced some one hundred and fifty separate sets of book illustration – volumes that were to form the source-book for his own followers, and for the future generations of ukiyo-e artists. Of this vast library of consummate designs, perhaps one fifth are shunga – about average for the erotica output of an ukiyo-e artist. Among the latter will also be found some five series of shunga-print albums or scrolls – featuring, on the average, ten shunga plus two 'cover prints' of only semi-erotic nature.

Moronobu's shunga lie principally, however, in the realm of picture-books, works most often consisting of two or three volumes each, comprising a total of fifty or sixty pages of illustrations in black and white. Perhaps the predominant format is that of the examples cited in plates 213 and 219 – a series of unrelated 213/219 erotic tableaux, each one a double-page spread devoted to some hero or heroine of history, fiction, or of the author/artist's imagination. The books are liberally sprinkled with non-erotic illustrations as well; an element designed to provide variety and 'eye relief', but also some indication that the attraction of the volumes was not prurient.

More often, the story is briefly told in flowing calligraphy printed above the illustrations; and – although research has yet to be attempted on the authorship of these early texts – there is a good possibility that the artist often prepared this literary material as well. Other typical shunga books feature romantic or erotic verses as their text; and a small portion of them revert to the original function of shunga, by comprising artistic guides to the specific varieties and positions of sexual intercourse.

To his loss so far as posterity is concerned, the larger print-series were not in great vogue during Moronobu's most productive years. Thus, the work of his follower Sugimura, who concentrated more on the larger format, sometimes tends to overshadow Moronobu's, among collectors and critics who eschew book illustration. It is only from a few series of album-plates, produced during the final part of his active years – the mid 1680s – that Moronobu is known abroad. The semi-erotic frontispieces to these albums grace the museums of the world, though the lesser-known shunga contents are by no means inferior in dramatic design or intrinsic appeal.

As we have noted in our Preface, the seventeenth-century Japanese attitude was surprisingly modern in its concept that sex alone was neither good nor evil, such being determined only by its employment. Interestingly enough, this attitude became more liberal with the coming of the famed Genroku Period – historically, 1688–1704, but in cultural history, including the decades before and after as well. Thus, the authors' prefaces and postscripts to the shunga books of the 1680s and following tend more to the theme: the purpose of sex is for pleasure, and shunga books such as this one will provide the knowledge and the *savoir-faire* necessary to permit the ultimate enjoyment of such pleasures.

We should like to think, even, that we can discern the effect of this gradual mutation of philosophy in the changing artistic styles of the period. Thus, where the oeuvre of Moronobu in the 1670s resembles in basic attitude (if not necessarily in style) the work of his anonymous master of the prior decade, the work of this same artist, Moronobu, looks almost like that of a different man, with the mid and later 1680s.

Interestingly enough, Moronobu's greatest period of all lies between these two extremes: from about 1682 to 1685 he achieved his most fully realized style, retaining the moral vigour of the earlier age, yet married to a lovely, half-voluptuous manner inspired, one surmises, by the 'wide-open', hedonistic attitude of the new generation.

It is perhaps unusual to witness these three artistic facets, of tradition, change, and first decadence, all within the space of a decade: yet we see the same features in the work of Moronobu's late rival Sugimura – as well as in the popular literature of the period – and must suspect it results as much from the influence of the times, as from any coincidental change or decline in the individual artist's powers.

To sum up, the work of Moronobu presents a comprehensive universe in itself, the first really complete and definitive oeuvre to be produced by an ukiyo-e artist. No brief sampling of this work can do more than scratch the surface of his fertile and resplendent genius.

Followers of Moronobu

Where Moronobu's oeuvre encompasses the total range of ukiyo-e publication – as well as painting – in his lifetime, the work of his follower Sugimura Jihei is both narrower and more flamboyantly impressive, within its limitations.

Sugimura (*fl. c.* 1681–96) was, it happens, that rare ukiyo-e artist who devoted himself almost exclusively to the erotic: nearly all of his ten known sets of a dozen prints each, and at least half of his dozen or more illustrated books, feature shunga. Further, at least half of his commissions fell in the realm of the large, erotic-print albums, which grew in popularity during his peak years of the mid 1680s. By this coincidence Sugimura, during his two or three ultimate years, achieved a most impressive achievement in the print world. His work after this brief flowering declined markedly – a phenomenon due as much, doubtless, to the loss of his inspiration and mentor, Moronobu, from the active scene, as to a natural decline in his brilliant but ephemeral creative powers.

Whatever the fleeting nature of his genius, Sugimura at his best marks one of the peaks of the shunga print. His flamboyant, voluptuous style contrasts with the powerful austerity of his master Moronobu, and is clearly better suited to the depiction of outright eroticism for its own sake.

Significantly, Sugimura's shunga are at their best in the 'group scene', where three or more figures give him full scope for expressing his flair for complex erotic patterns. Quite by coincidence, our choice of Sugimura's finest prints to reproduce here displays this feature most strikingly. Coincidentally, again, these all feature scenes of 'triorism' and multiple sex-play which are typical both of Sugimura, and of Genroku eroticism in general. The basically didactic element of much of the earlier shunga is here discarded entirely; the aim becomes pure delight in the erotic *per se*.

In short, Sugimura's passionate figures are immersed in sex as an end in itself. In that sense, he typifies the growing decadence of his period, so different from the generation that preceded. But in his ability to communicate a sense of the vibrantly erotic, Sugimura ranks with Utamaro as one of the principal shunga masters.

Of Moronobu's immediate pupils, the finest was doubtless Moroshige (*fl. c.* 1684–95) – an unassuming artist who, in a half-dozen sets of shunga prints and book illustrations, followed the direct Moronobu tradition in his own quiet manner. Such lesser followers as Ryūsen, Morohira, Suiō and Miss Ryū also did notable shunga work in either the prints, or hand-painted ukiyo-e. The continued popularity of the hand-painted shunga-scroll among the more affluent connoisseurs is worth recording here, in passing. Such were doubtless 'prestige items', considered, due to their cost and exclusiveness, intrinsically superior to printed ukiyo-e, and thus still in occasional demand among collectors, and as gifts to brides or to one's superiors.

Moronobu's rival in the *Kyoto* art-world, Yoshida Hambei (*fl.* 1664–90) may also be mentioned here, in passing. Hambei's shunga works consist principally, however, of small illustrations to the erotic novels and sex encyclopedias of the time, and never reach the level of general appeal to be found in Edo ukiyo-e.

The latter half of the seventeenth century clearly belongs to Moronobu – and to the anonymous Kambun Master who broke the ground for him. To these men ukiyo-e owes its foundations.

12 Later 'Primitives' and the Golden Age of Ukiyo-e

Artists of the early eighteenth century

Although the few years following the death of Moronobu in 1694 marked an ebb in ukiyo-e's fortunes, already by the end of the seventeenth century strong new forces had begun to appear, both in Edo and in Kyoto.

Torii Kiyonobu (*c.* 1664–1729) founded that school of ukiyo-e which devoted its major production to the lively Kabuki theatre. Yet Kiyonobu himself was also a master of the erotic. Interestingly enough, his shunga show far more the influence of the secondary artist Sugimura than of the prime master, Moronobu. This quirk of artistic fate was doubtless due more to the tastes of the time than to any other factor: the ebulient, hedonistic 'Genroku mood' flavoured the popular spirit of the 1690s, and Moronobu's powerful austerity and restrained, immaculate draftsmanship doubtless seemed, for the moment, old-fashioned.

It is thus the voluptuous, fleshy figure that dominates in Kiyonobu's shunga – works in which the overpowering corpulence often tends, indeed, to diminish the erotic effect. Though he also produced numerous illustrations to the erotic novels of the 1690s, Kiyonobu's major shunga work consists of some seven series of larger album-prints, and four series of smaller ones, dating from the first decade of the eighteenth century. (These include at least one set devoted to pederasty with the young actors. This was a subject natural enough in view of Kiyonobu's intimate relation to the Kabuki theatre, but one most commonly seen inserted, for variety, amidst a group of heterosexual scenes, rather than treated in such extended detail.)

Kiyonobu's shunga are undoubtedly impressive works of art – though one may find it a trifle hard to love them. Somehow, his people seem so selfishly engrossed in their own pleasure that it is difficult for the outside viewer to 'identify'. Doubtless, however, this was a feature that attracted one impassive segment of his patrons at the time; and the massive, decorative appeal of Kiyonobu's best work can hardly be denied.

Another Edo master, Okumura Masanobu (*c.* 1686–1764), took his style from his senior, Kiyonobu, during the first few years of his career at the commencement of the eighteenth century. But when he founded his own style shortly thereafter, it proved to be based more on the solid foundation set by Moronobu a generation before.

Masanobu was a master of the album format in general, and his nine or more sets of erotic album-prints are of generally uniform quality, if lacking in the striking 'show-stoppers' sometimes found in the work of Sugimura, and even Kiyonobu. Masanobu's later shunga-work – after the institution of government censorship – is most often in the format of small, lateral book illustrations. These little-known works (of which he did some two dozen, often featuring frontispieces in primitive colour-printing) mark one of the quiet peaks of erotic art in Japan, and one of the principal pleasures of mid eighteenth-century shunga.

Oddly enough, the most devoted follower of the seventeenth-century pioneer, Moronobu, was not an Edo artist at all, but an indirect pupil in Kyoto, Nishikawa Sukenobu. Sukenobu (1671–1750) had first studied under the classical Kano-Tosa masters, but of his own volition chose ukiyo-e as his métier, and as his stylistic master, Moronobu. Like his illustrious predecessor, Sukenobu was primarily an illustrator. He produced some two hundred separate volumes of illustration in his long lifetime, of which perhaps a fifth were shunga. Sukenobu transmitted Moronobu's austere vigour to a graceful, quiet charm most typical of the ancient capital, Kyoto. Though almost exclusively an illustrator, Sukenobu also did at least three series of larger prints – all in the shunga genre – a sample of which we include here. Needless to say, his gentle yet elegant figures stand a world away from the work of his Edo contemporary Kiyonobu, and mark a low-keyed revival of the manner with which ukiyo-e prints found their first major flowering under Moronobu, three decades earlier.

It was just in the midst of Sukenobu's prime period as a shunga artist that, late in the year 1722, the Japanese government at last began to take a somewhat more strict, official view towards erotica. But though the new edicts themselves seemed to ban erotica in name, in actual fact their aim, in most cases, was principally to enforce government regulations regarding sedition, lèse-majesté, luxurious editions, and the publication of books or prints without government licence. In theory the official, imported Confucian moral concepts of the Tokugawa government condemned erotic literature and art (as well as Kabuki and various other popular pleasures). But in actual practice, such laws were seldom enforced unless the offence were compounded by some crime of a more heinous nature to the state – for example, lèse-majesté (more toward the samurai rulers than the Emperor) or suspected sedition. Thus, for the main part, such edicts, even when making specific reference to erotica itself, were of but temporary effectiveness – as was equally true of the 'reform' governments that, from time to time, enacted them. During the long periods of relaxation, shunga books seem even to have been sold openly in book stalls.

Nevertheless, it must be conceded that the mere existence of such punitive laws could hardly but have had psychological effects upon both publisher, artist, and audience. Thus, the practical disappearance of the larger and more impressive shunga album-prints during the second quarter of the eighteenth century may well have been a result of this factor. (Though it might also be pointed out that the print, in general, tended to the smaller sizes during this period – influenced, most likely, by the concurrent anti-luxury edicts, which seem to have been more enforced than those against erotica.) And the psychological effect of banning on the *audience* will be noted in a later paragraph.

After Sukenobu, the major artist of erotica in West Japan was Tsukioka Settei, an Osaka master who produced two or three sets of prints and some two dozen shunga books, in addition to a number of hand-painted erotica.

Settei (1710–86) evolved a style that attempted to combine the powerful linear quality of Moronobu's designs, with the *Kamigata* (West Japan) flavour of the more gentle Sukenobu. His work, both in book illustration and the hand-painted scroll, found much favour among the connoisseurs of Kyoto and Osaka, and his shunga were even so highly regarded that magical powers were attributed to them. To some modern viewers, however, when compared to the really major artists of ukiyo-e shunga, Settei is lacking in that refinement of mood that induces optimum enjoyment. In comparison, even, with his own *non*-erotic work, Settei's shunga-figures are sometimes wooden and almost gross – contrasting strikingly with both Sukenobu, and with his Edo contemporary Harunobu.

Settei's followers were legion, and many of them produced shunga, particularly in the type of smallish book illustration favoured by the connoisseurs of Kyoto and Osaka in the later eighteenth century. Sukenobu's late follower Shimokobe Shusi did notable shunga work, and the anonymous master of plate 232 – bearing affinities to Masanobu, Settei, Minkō and Toyonobu – will serve to indicate another of the more noteworthy artists of this transitional period.

As we have already indicated in passing, despite the overwhelming predominance of printed shunga, the *hand-painted* picture-scroll continued to find favour among the more affluent connoisseurs throughout the Edo Period. Most of the ukiyo-e masters, from Moronobu, Kiyonobu and Sukenobu on, did occasional work in this genre. Even such specialists in the large *kakemono* as Chōshun and the Kaigetsudō artists are known to have executed shunga scrolls, though such are rarely extant today in the originals.

Censorship and abuna-e

Actual cases of censorship were infrequent, despite the government edicts of 1722 and following; yet the mere fact that these edicts were issued tended to make the publication of shunga more surreptitious and, necessarily, somewhat less numerous. At the same time, contrary to its intent, the official banning of artistic sex display seems to have had, rather, a *stimulating* effect – creating, one might almost say, a popular demand for the *semi*-erotic that had hitherto hardly existed. This demand was soon met by the production of the so-called *abuna-e* (a punning compound implying 'dangerous-pictures') prints or paintings in which were featured the semi-nude, hitherto a form hardly considered erotic at all.

The *abuna-e* represent both the nearest approximation to the Nude in Japanese art, as well as the closest thing to shunga of the more commonly-known ukiyo-e, and they have been collected and published widely both in Japan and abroad. Although the *abuna-e* exist in nearly all the shapes and forms of the ukiyo-e of their times, they are seen most frequently in the long, vertical 'pillar prints', and usually feature, not love scenes as such, but bathing, boudoir or toilette tableaux, or other opportunities (such as windy and rain scenes, and pictures of diving-girls, breast-feeding, summer 'cooling off', and the like) for displaying the semi-nude female form.

Such pictures usually stop short of showing the actual pubic hair or sex organs – indeed, this 'minor' feature would seem to form the dividing line between shunga and *abuna-e*. (A point that might be illustrated, incidentally, from the

XXV (*top and centre*) From shunga scrolls of twelve scenes. Colours on paper, *c.* mid 17th-century; (*top*) in Muromachi style, (*centre*) early ukiyo-e school
XXVI (*overleaf left and top right*) Harunobu. Woodcut colour prints. Edo, late 1760s; *chūban*

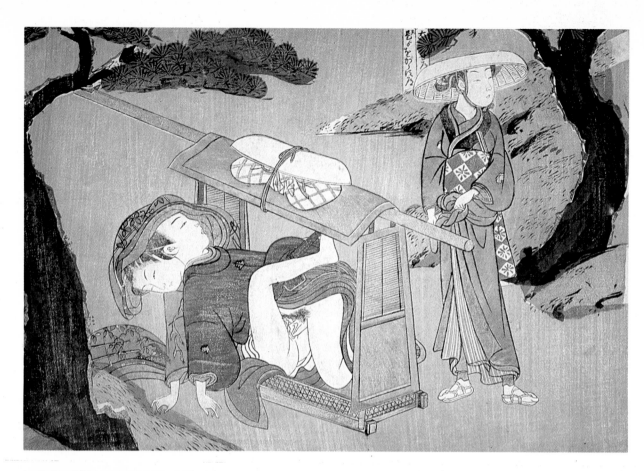

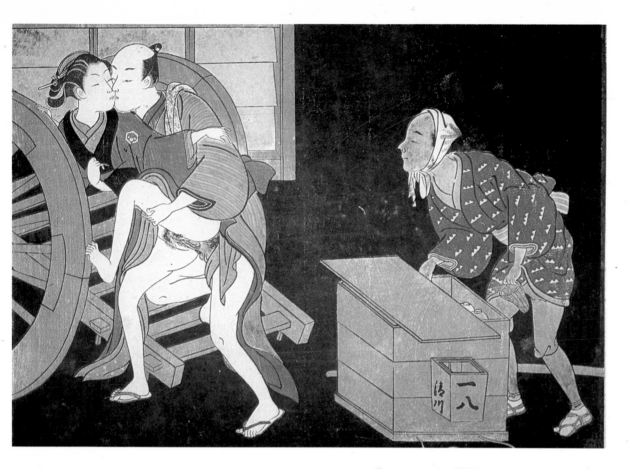

Utamaro album, *Uta-makura,* which, viewed alone, is barely past the borderline of *abuna-e* – though when considered in the context of the total album, is nearer to the erotic than it would appear to the casual viewer. Another famous print from the same album [J. Hillier, *Utamaro* plate VII] is, though somewhat subdued in tenor, more decidedly shunga, since actual sexual intercourse is suggested – both in the design, and in the accompanying metaphorical verse: 'His bill encased so firmly in the clam's shell,/No longer can he rise in flight,/this snipe: at dusk-filled evening.')

Perhaps the best-known artists of the *abuna-e* (which flourished particularly from the 1750s through the 1770s) were Toyonobu, Kiyomitsu, Kiyotsune, Harunobu, Koryūsai, Shunshō and Shigemasa. Numerous examples were found also in such earlier masters as Masanobu, Shigenaga and Kiyohiro; and the form was continued, as well, in works by later artists such as Kiyonaga, Shunchō, Utamaro and Eishi – on through Eisen, Kunisada, Kuniyoshi, and Yoshitoshi.

In its broader sense, of course, the term *abuna-e* applies also to any print or painting of an erotic scene which stops 'just short' of becoming shunga – and as such, forms one of the major categories throughout the history of ukiyo-e. During the first century or so of ukiyo-e, such tableaux appeared mainly as frontispieces, or for variety and change of pace amidst shunga scrolls or albums. In the later ukiyo-e, however (particularly, from Utamaro on), the semi-erotic seems to have become a more self-conscious form, its aim more specifically eroticism for its own sake.

The nude, as a conscious form in Japanese art, will be seen to have developed as a direct consequence of the official censorship of shunga. In any but the most primitive of civilizations, to be sure, the nude can hardly be considered a form divorced very far from the erotic. But it will be clear that the Japanese nude developed on a quite different basis from that in, say, Indian, or European, art. (Which is not to say that, in speaking of 'European art', we suppose the Greek nude, and the Renaissance nude, to have produced anywhere near the same effect on contemporary viewers.)

Thus the *abuna-e* reflected a newly widespread popular curiosity in sex, and in the nude as 'pin-up' – a polite version of shunga. Its conventions were, therefore, those of shunga, and its attention was directed not so much to the balanced harmony of the nude form, as to focusing erotic attention on the pubic regions.

Despite their great talent in the depiction of the nude, oddly enough, such masters of the *abuna-e* as Torii Kiyohiro and Ishikawa Toyonobu seem to have done relatively little shunga work as such. Perhaps, their devotion to the semi-erotic consumed whatever creative interest they might have had in the more boldly erotic.

If the four decades between the government edicts of 1722 and the rise of Harunobu seem to represent a quiescent eddy in the development of ukiyo-e shunga, this is doubtless the case. For the specialist, the books do exist, and in considerable actual numbers. But it cannot be denied that major works are lacking, and that the field in general was passing through a stage of dormancy.

XXVII (*preceding page bottom right*) Koryūsai: Woodblock colour print. Scene in a Buddhist nunnery. Edo, *c.* 1770; *chūban.* Signed
XXVIII (*above*) Koryūsai: The woman praises the little girl for her festive garments. Edo, *c.* 1773; *chūban.* (*below*) Woodblock colour print. Edo, mid 1770s; *ōban.* Signed

The great revival of ukiyo-e in all categories came with the mid 1760s, which mark one of the great epochs of the print. The corrupt, free and easy ways of such Shogunal 'Court-favourites' as the Tokugawa adviser Tanuma Okitsugu (deposed in 1787), played a background role in this rebirth of the popular arts, as did, on the technical side, the development of the first full-colour prints. Once again, we find the artists (such as Harunobu and Koryūsai) openly signing their shunga prints with their true names.

During the early 1760s several masters vied for predominance in the print field, among them, the aforementioned Toyonobu, and Torii Kiyomitsu (*c.* 1735–85). The latter artist stood as one of the last figures in the great school founded by Kiyonobu at the turn of the century. Despite the varied shunga activity of the founder, erotic work by these Kabuki-oriented artists is relatively rare. The great figure of the new age was an artist whose works were to mark one of the true summits of ukiyo-e – Suzuki Harunobu.

Harunobu (*c.* 1725–70) appeared at a fortunate time, for his true genius lay exactly in this dream-like world of the full-colour print, which he helped develop. His dozen albums of colour-prints in the smaller, *chūban* format mark, indeed, one of the peaks of ukiyo-e shunga, as do, in a lower key, his nearly equal number of illustrated shunga books.

The mid 1760s constitute a turning-point in the history of ukiyo-e, with Harunobu as the predominant catalyst. A glance at the prints of his period will reveal immediately the revolution that occurred in the development of a more fully-realized background, and in the bold employment of opaque yet delicate, variegated colouring. The foreground figures remain relatively unchanged, but the world in which they act and play has expanded and been filled with a mood, an atmosphere, wholly new to the genre. This innovation of Harunobu's period was to flavour all of the later century of ukiyo-e – but seldom with the richly compelling effect of its remarkable innovator.

In the warm richness of colouring that suffuses Harunobu's finest works, shunga reached a level of quality and atmospheric effect that was seldom if ever to be repeated in ukiyo-e. To view a complete Harunobu shunga album of twelve (sometimes, even twenty-four) of these lovely colour prints is to enter into another world, to be seized by a narcotic dream sometimes too beautiful to be borne: like the visitor to Xanadu, one can return only with regret to the mundane outer world.

With Harunobu's lovely figures, gone completely is the roughness of the Kambun Master, the austerity of Moronobu, the self-centredness of Kiyonobu: at their root, doubtless, lies the gentle otherworldliness of Sukenobu, but here married to a mood and colouring that advances them to the very limits of erotic art. Whatever the boldness of his subject-matter, the gross and the extreme are completely strained away by the genius of this evocative, gentle master.

Yet even the most precious of dreams are but fleeting: Harunobu's lasted less than a decade. His own fully-developed style was cut short in its sixth year, with his sudden demise in 1770; within three years, the work of his followers had already turned to the ever-new fashions and innovations that lay, intrinsically and inescapably, at the root of ukiyo-e's destiny.

Harunobu's leading pupil and follower was Isoda Koryūsai (*fl.* mid 1760s–1780s), an artist of samurai origins. At its best, the early work of Koryūsai is distinguishable from Harunobu only by experts. Indeed, Koryūsai's contribution to ukiyo-e shunga was a colourful, ingenuously hedonistic flavour that, in some cases, renders his work even more effective than his master's in the creation of an emotional, erotic mood. An analogy with Moronobu and his follower Sugimura in the previous century is most apt: the earlier pioneer set the firm foundation which his pupil followed – but extended to a higher level of erotic atmosphere. In both cases, the original master grew to maturity in a more austere age, and entered the newly-born atmosphere of hedonism only in his last decade. Thus both Moronobu and Harunobu stand as peak figures in the history of ukiyo-e: but in one field, the erotic, their pupils Sugimura and Koryūsai sometimes excel them, through being more emphatic to the new, erotic age in which they worked.

Possibly, this element of a sharply defined, old-fashioned 'moral fibre' has a good deal to do with the high position we accord to Moronobu and Harunobu in art history. And the relatively lower rank of their pupils may well have as much to do with this indefinable factor, as with the more abstract element of artistic genius. Nevertheless, the pupil often excelled his master in this one field, the erotic.

From around 1773 – three years after Harunobu's passing – ukiyo-e styles commenced to change from that master's replete, miniaturized dream-world to the rather larger, more gross world of the adult. Plate XXVIII (above) shows a *XXVIII (above)* Koryūsai print produced just at this juncture: the lovely fantasy of Harunobu's ideal is seen just at the point of resolving into the larger concept of the coming age. The format is still the smaller, *chūban* size, and the colouring is only slightly modified, to a more transparent hue. But the figures have commenced that trend toward the monumental that we see in more full development in plate XXVIII *XXVIII (below)* (below) of but a few years later.

From this period on, the prints tended, further, to the larger, *ōban* or *aiban* sizes, and the figures expanded in impressiveness of physique to fill the format. Gone is the intimacy of the Harunobu period; in its place we find a certain grandeur of scale and colour-massing – but at the loss of this intimate mood that characterized the 1760s.

Koryūsai's shunga oeuvre comprises a half-dozen sets of small or medium-sized album prints, a dozen or more sets of very small prints (*koban* – about 5 x 5½ inches), and an equal number of illustrated books. With this period we also find occasional use in shunga of the size called *hashira-e* ('pillar-print' – about 39 x 5 inches), both in vertical and horizontal format. The horizontal employment of this curious, narrow format in erotica is easy to imagine; the vertical use, however, must be seen to be believed, and to that end we may cite plate 237. This *237* example will also serve as another indication of transitional ukiyo-e trends in the mid 1770s – a style found also in the shunga work of Shigemasa, Kyōden (Kitao Masanobu), and the early Kiyonaga.

To return again, briefly, to the time of Harunobu's predominance, mention must be made of several other followers whose early work was clearly in the Harunobu manner.

That strange genius Ippitsusai Bunchō (*fl.* 1760s–1770s), though primarily a Kabuki specialist, produced at least three remarkable sets of shunga prints at about the time of Harunobu's death. Plate 236 shows the cover-sheet to one of these series, which, it must be admitted, suffer somewhat from that curious, restrained, *shibui* characteristic of Bunchō's work – usually, one of his principal charms, but hardly conducive to that mood of intimacy we find in the most effective shunga.

Another notable Harunobu follower was Kitao Shigemasa (1739–1820), in whose early work we discern a 'lesser Harunobu' – and whose later designs are rather in the manner of the Koryūsai already shown in plate 237. Prints by this artist are rare, but he produced at least a dozen sets of shunga book illustrations. In the work of his maturity, Shigemasa's style is sometimes strikingly similar to that of his confrère Shunshō – with whom, indeed, he sometimes collaborated. Shigemasa's precocious pupil Kyōden (Kitao Masanobu: 1761–1816) also produced one or two shunga print series, and a half-dozen shunga books, which have yet to be fully differentiated from those of his master.

Parallel with Koryūsai, Bunchō and Shigemasa, among the most notable followers of Harunobu was Katsukawa Shunshō, who founded his own school of realistic Kabuki depiction (and was the teacher of Hokusai).

Shunshō (1726–93) produced few of the larger erotic prints, but was a master of shunga book illustration, over twenty separate works being known by him. His compositions are more crowded than those of Harunobu, but they succeed well in adding, unobtrusively, that element of detailed realism that was to find its culmination in the work of Utamaro and Hokusai, a generation later. Those interested in investigating the inspiration of some of these later artists' early shunga designs would do well to study first the book illustrations of Shunshō – as well as Shigemasa.

In his final years Shunshō seems to have been stimulated and inspired by the fierce competition in the ukiyo-e world of the later 1780s. The album-plate of plate XXIV for example, is surely one of the shunga masterpieces of this period. As erotica, to be sure, it conceals more than it reveals – though the protagonists' conversation conveys much of what the design obscures. Most adroitly, however, the arched back of the angry cat performs the phallic function that the quilting hides. And the annoyed comments of the animal ('What a noisesome pair! And when I was having such a good nap!) add a curiously cinematic, recollective quality to the print – recreating vividly the scene as it must have appeared but a moment before, as man and girl sat primly within the quilts of the brazier, on top of which tabby slumbered happily – dreaming, perhaps, of feline sexual conquests of its own. While not, visually speaking, by any means among the most readily perceptible of compositions, this print surely represents ukiyo-e shunga wit at its peak.

Needless to relate, the landscape and shunga were not, generally, compatible forms. Here and there in the early *uki-e* ('perspective-prints'), however, we find attempts to marry these two disparate genera – as in the unusual work of Utagawa Toyoharu (1735–1814) shown in plate 234.

Just as the perspective-prints themselves received their basic inspiration from the importation (however limited) of Western art, so must it also be remembered that this was a period when Western science was being introduced for the first time. Sugita Gempaku's famed *Kaitai shinsho* ('New Text on Anatomy') – an adaptation of Dutch medical texts – had been published in 1774, and must have

XXIX (*above*) Style of Kiyomitsu: Woodblock colour print. Edo, mid 1760s; *chūban*.
(*centre*) Shunchō: Woodblock colour print, from the series *Kōshoku-zue jūni-kō*. Edo, mid 1780s; *ōban*. (*below*) Rekisentai Eiri: A Yoshiwara courtesan and her lover. Woodblock colour print; Edo, *c*. 1800; *ōban*

exerted more influence on depictions of the human form by Japanese artists than has generally been conceded.

Indeed, the rather general mutation in figure styles and ideals in the later 1770s might well be traced directly to such outside sources. For artists of talent are ever sensitive to innovation, and the new world of occidental learning suddenly opened to them by this book, and by the European engravings imported at this period, may well have been enough to effect such a change. The realistic work of the classical Kyoto master Maruyama Ōkyo (1733–95), for example, clearly documents this influence, and it is more than likely that the coming 'Golden Age' of ukiyo-e took something at least of its surface inspiration from this current of change introduced from abroad.

Lastly, it is a well-known fact that the fad among connoisseurs for colour-engraved New Year's prints, from the year 1765 and following, had a near-revolutionary effect on the technical development of the full-colour print, under Harunobu's direction. While the scattered historical references to shunga need not necessarily be taken as representative of major trends, it is interesting to note that these record that the exchange of erotic calendar-prints as New Year's greetings was, for several years, the rage in Court circles. Examples of these – scrapbooks collected by the nobility of the period – are still extant today.

Erotica were also, evidently, considered eminently suited as gifts to one's superiors, among the samurai and court nobility. Of course, this custom doubtless depended a good deal upon the taste of the actual recipient, and presumably tended to utilize the more prestigious painted scrolls, rather than prints or books. In general, however, the role of the upper classes in patronizing the more luxurious of the shunga throughout their history can hardly be denied.

The Golden Age of Utamaro

To Torii Kiyonaga (1752–1815) is usually given credit for introducing the robust, 'wholesome, magnificently normal' female figure to ukiyo-e design. It is thus with interest that we turn to his half-dozen sets of shunga prints, to see to what degree his (to quote the praise of the early Western critics) 'Grecian perfection' proved effective in this form.

While admitting that personal taste must intrude strongly here, we do not feel Kiyonaga to have been one of the great shunga artists. His designs are impeccable, his colouring excellent. But to us, at least, there is a certain statuesque, immobile quality that seems ill-suited to this genre. 'Static' art is just not the most effective manner for the graphically erotic.

With Kiyonaga's close follower Katsukawa Shunchō, however, this style found most remarkable expression in the shunga genre. Shunchō (fl. late 1770s–1790s) – actually, a pupil of Shunshō – brought a combination of wit and variety to shunga that was to prove one of its saving graces in this, the 'Golden Age' of ukiyo-e.

Of Shunchō's half-dozen or more sets of erotic album-prints, one example must suffice to show his masterly extension of the Kiyonaga manner to the emotional needs of true shunga. Some of his best series (such as this one), indeed, derive their

347

XXX (*above*) Utamaro: A Yoshiwara courtesan and her lover. Woodblock colour print. Edo, *c.* 1800; *ōban.* (*centre*) Shunchō: Woodblock colour print. Edo, late 1870s; *ōban.* (*below*) Hokusai: Woodblock colour print from the album *Ehon tsuhi no hinagata* (*Models of Loving Couples*). Edo, *c.* 1810s: *ōban.* The man is dressed in festival regalia for the 'Lion Dance'

inspiration directly from similar work by Kiyonaga. But in Shunchō there is always that added breath of life that makes him – while not a great creative genius – one of the most consistently enjoyable of the shunga artists.

With the great Kitagawa Utamaro we come to the next major watershed of ukiyo-e's development. Only, in this case, it was the beginning of the end so far as the figure print, and shunga, was concerned.

Utamaro (1753–1806) was known even from his own times as the leading Japanese shunga artist – and his prints are said even to have been exported as far as China. First studied by Edmond de Goncourt in the late nineteenth century, he is probably the best-known, abroad, of the Asian masters of the erotic.

Unlike most Japanese artists, who worked primarily from experience and intuitive imagination, Utamaro is said also to have employed an artist's model – his own younger sister – in sketching the preliminary designs for bodily positions in shunga. In his diligence of early studies and sketching, he far excelled most of his contemporaries, and it is no wonder that his genius took the decade of the 1790s by storm.

Utamaro's most impressive shunga are found in his half-dozen sets of album-prints in the medium sizes, *ōban* and *aiban*. Interestingly enough, his most noteworthy single erotic work was one of his first, the *Song of the Pillow* (*Utamakura*) album of 1788.

By the time of this work, Utamaro was already an established artist, a firm master of all the techniques of ukiyo-e. Thus, it is not surprising that he should have been able to concentrate his creative genius so intensively in this, his first major effort with the shunga print.

The *Song of the Pillow* is not really typical of Japanese shunga: its content is too varied, too realistic – in a sense, even, too anti-erotic. Its effect is highly memorable, even violent; but by that very token, its aphrodisiac effectiveness is diminished – a factor that may well account for its only minor popularity in its own time, and its relative rarity in extant copies today. It represents the great *tour de force* of ukiyo-e erotica, but is so intellectualized, so much a showcase of the 'artist's artist', that its true erotic effect is relatively small.

XXIII   Of its masterpieces, our plate XXIII is that most in the line of the earlier shunga– the scene is reminiscent of Shunshō, a somewhat similar work of whose we saw
240   in plate 240. But here predominates, nevertheless, a fascination with the grotesque
247   that is Utamaro's unique creation. With plate 247, however, the artist is no longer simply playful: unlike the usual ukiyo-e depictions of the type, this is a most uncompromising scene of rape: the maiden has no intention of yielding, the brute, no mind to giving up. Only the sexually immature would find this scene priapic. Again, in Utamaro's *Uta-makura*, the scene of the jealous mistress despite its lovely colouring is too fierce and realistic to move the viewer erotically: 'Hell hath no fury like a woman scorned'; and this, too, is hardly an occasion for erotic stimulation.

In short, the *Song of the Pillow* is a remarkable compendium of sex fantasies and sex fears; yet it defeats its own erotic purpose in the violence of its execution. It ranks, thus, as one of the undoubted masterpieces of ukiyo-e, but marks a curious, impressive deviant in the lineage of shunga *per se*.

Utamaro's subsequent erotica fall more into the regular shunga tradition, and include much of the finest work of this period. It is remarkable how, in a print like
XXX (above)   plate XXX (above), for example, such an open, 'clinical' view can be rendered so
348   inoffensive and appealing by this master. His art, to be sure, is frankly sexual – gone

forever is the dreamlike childishness of Harunobu's age. But there is also a very high level of taste encompassed in Utamaro's shunga – without, however, the least attempt to cover up the 'facts'.

Utamaro's remarkable shunga oeuvre of some two dozen illustrated books has tended to be neglected in favour of his larger album-prints. Despite their smaller size, however, the varied plates of these volumes reveal an amazing fertility of inventive imagination, in which scene after scene of fresh insights into human erotic life strike the eye. Utamaro is never satisfied merely to present the erotic alone: every element of the tableau is gauged, most skilfully, both to attract us to the central scene, yet distract us with the fascinating secondary theme. Plate 246 well illustrates this striking combination of opposing forces and complex *246* variety – Utamaro's supreme achievement in the art of book illustration.

Government censorship of erotica, seen first in 1722, raised its head fully twice during the reign of Utamaro – in the years 1790 and 1804 – and once again during the subsequent generation in 1842. Its effective target was, however, again primarily sedition and lèse-majesté. When Utamaro, the leading Japanese master of erotica, was, indeed, confined briefly for breach of the publishing laws in 1804, it was for the unauthorized publication of a set of prints that offended the government by their satirical inferences, not from any erotic content.

Utamaro literally dominated the shunga-world during much of the last two decades of his life. Such noted contemporaries as Shumman, Toyohiro, Eishi, Eishō, Eiri, Chōki and Gabimaru produced limited numbers of shunga prints or books – as did Utamaro's own pupils Kikumaro and Utamaro II – but these artists all worked in the shadow of the great master.

At their best, however, these lesser figures of the late eighteenth-century shunga world produced prints or illustrations of great charm. They were not, to be sure, capable of the striking power of Utamaro's oeuvre, but featured a more low-keyed manner which revealed, nevertheless, their own unique, if smaller, talents in this field. As examples of this quiet if fascinating eddy in the shadow of Utamaro, we have chosen two notable followers of Eishi.

Rekisentei Eiri (*fl.* 1790s) forms a kind of 'lesser Chōki', for his prints exert something of that strange, other-worldly quality that represents, doubtless, a throwback to Harunobu. Eiri adds to this his own peculiar 'beauty of lassitude': his figures seem, often, too frail and devitalized to be able to support life, much less the exertions of sex. Yet with all these manifestations of feeble decadence Eiri's shunga are among the most fascinating of their class.

The artist of our plate 251 presents something more of a scholarly problem. In *251* Japan, this series has long been famed as the work of Eishi's pupil Chōkyōsai Eishō (*fl.* 1790s). We somewhat question this attribution, and might suggest, rather, that the mysterious artist Chōkyōsai Eiri (sometimes supposed to be the early name of the aforementioned Rekisentei Eiri) may be somewhat nearer to the mark. Though much indebted to Utamaro, this series of prints constitutes, at any rate, one of the most notable products of later eighteenth-century shunga, and will serve to typify the work accomplished by his lovely, if unequal, followers.

Utamaro may often have been equalled, and sometimes even surpassed, by his contemporaries in the non-erotic print. But in the shunga genre he stands as the artist par excellence of his age.

13 The Final Century of Shunga

Hokusai and Eisen

Japanese erotica, during most of the first century and a half of ukiyo-e's flourishing, tended to retain much of the original, elemental force of the early shunga. From the 'Golden Age' of Utamaro and on, however, decadent elements came gradually to predominate, and the innocent sexual curiosity of the earlier years was increasingly replaced by a manifestly prurient, near-pornographic interest. This mutation is seen, in one form or another, throughout much of the art and taste of the later Edo Period.

The figure-print, indeed, had reached its final culmination in Utamaro, and it was perhaps too much to expect it to proceed in the same direction much further, under the masters who followed. The nineteenth century was not to prove a major age of figure design, but, rather, of the landscape. Since shunga were, after all, only one form of figure-print, it was natural that their fate but followed suit.

These allegations would not, however, be agreed to by all collectors and connoisseurs. In Japan, particularly, there is a large class of collectors who take their principal delight in the later figure-work of Eisen and Kunisada. We ourselves have no intention of slighting these artists; yet in viewing the long history of ukiyo-e, we cannot fairly claim that even the best of the later figure-prints equal the mere average of the masters who went before.

If an exception were to be made, it would be in the work of Katsushika Hokusai.

Hokusai (1760–1849) had, to be sure, already been designing prints, paintings and illustrations from the 1780s; but his shunga activity seems mainly to fall in his middle years, the 1810s. His best-known work is undoubtedly the *Models of Loving Couples (Ehon tsuhi no hinagata)* of just this period, an album of twelve remarkable colour prints.

Recent research has suggested that the text of this album may be by Hokusai's noted fellow-artist Eisen, and that Hokusai's own daughter, O-ei, may well have had a hand in the illustrations themselves. The story of O-ei's assisting her father in his shunga work has long been known, of course. Whatever her part in the collaboration, for our present purposes it is enough to describe this album as probably the finest single shunga work of the nineteenth century.

Nothing else of the period can match the kaleidoscope of brocade-like colours *XXX (below)* enriching the print of plate XXX (below). The 'nervous line' of Hokusai's manner is here employed to create a totality of complex pattern that is matched by no other artist. It is, to be sure, a most perilous manner: in lesser hands it would drop instantly to a tasteless, designless, gaudy splotch of crude colouring.

The album as a whole is of a remarkable consistency and variety, of which plate

233 (*above*) Toyonobu: Illustration to a woodblock-printed book (title missing). Edo, 1750s; *yoko-bon*.
A shunga work by a master whose principal field was abuna-e

234 (*left*) Toyoharu: Woodblock colour print. Edo, *c.* 1776; *ōban*.
An unusual example of the *uki-e* 'perspective-print' in semi-Occidental style, in shunga

235 Koryūsai: Woodblock colour print. Edo, early 1770s; *chūban*. In another version, signed.
A work by Harunobu's principal follower, who excels in the depiction of mood

236 Bunchō: Woodblock colour print. Edo, *c.* 1770; *chūban.* Another impression of this print bears the artist's seal

237 (*left*) Koryūsai:
Woodblock colour print.
Edo, late 1770s; *hashira-e*.
Signed
238 (*right*) Buncho:
Woodblock colour print.
Edo, *c.* 1770; *chūban*
(Matsukaze, the legendary
salt-gathering girl,
masturbates with dildo
tied to a pine-branch,
embracing her cap and
robe as though they were
a man)

239 (*right*) Buncho:
Woodblock colour print.
Edo, *c.* 1770; *chūban*.
(At the right the legendary
Shojo—the Japanese
Bacchus—sips from a
huge saké cask.)
Plates 238 and 239 are
from a series of prints
representing erotic puns
on well-known classical
or mythological scenes—
the text consisting of
pertinent conundrums.
These illustrate further
aspects of the traditional
Japanese acceptance of
the erotic

240 Shunshō: A maiden's fearsome dream – a scene continued from previous page of book; illustration to the *Ehon kaname-ishi* (*Eros' Foundation Stone*). Woodblock-printed book; Edo, 1782; *hanshi-bon*. This exemplifies the variety of expression possible in shunga

241 Courtesan with a monk; from an illustrated book. Mid-18th century. A popularly accepted fact of life

242 Style of Shigemasa: Illustration to the *Ehon kai-kasen* (*Poets of the Vulva-shell*). Woodblock-printed book; Edo, early 1770s; *hanshi-bon*. Each scene features a different bivalve shellfish – symbol of the vulva and of coitus – with appropriate erotic verse and tableau.

This work expresses a total innocence of attitude, and illustrates the common Japanese use of symbolism

243 Shigemasa: Parents distracting baby with an array of festival toys; illustration to the *Neya-no-hana tori-dasuki* (*Boudoir-flowers of Brocade*). Woodblock-printed book with unusual colouring in mixed woodblock and hand-coloured style; Edo, c. 1776; ōbon. This book has also been attributed to Shunshō. Here the domestic naturalness of sex is beautifully conveyed

246 (*opposite*) Utamaro: Illustration to the *Ehon koi no ōgi* (*The Mysteries of Love*). Woodblock-printed book; Edo, 1804(?); *hanshi-bon*. Little boy: 'Hey, what are you trying to do to my sister? You bum, you bum, you bum!' The Girl: 'I really must catch some fireflies to take back home to my parents—or else how can I explain where I have been?' This print illustrates the great Utamaro's mastery of pure line

244 Kiyonaga: A Yoshiwara scene, from the series *Imayō jūni-kagami*. Woodblock colour print. Edo, early 1780s; *aiban*

245 Kiyonaga: Woodblock colour print. Edo, mid 1780s; *aiban*

Two superb shunga by one of the supreme masters of the Ukiyo-e

247 (*opposite*) Utamaro: An illustration of a legend concerning a mythical water creature, the Kappa, which is said to ravish the Awabi-fisher girls. Woodblock colour print from the album *Uta-makura*; Edo, 1788; *ōban*

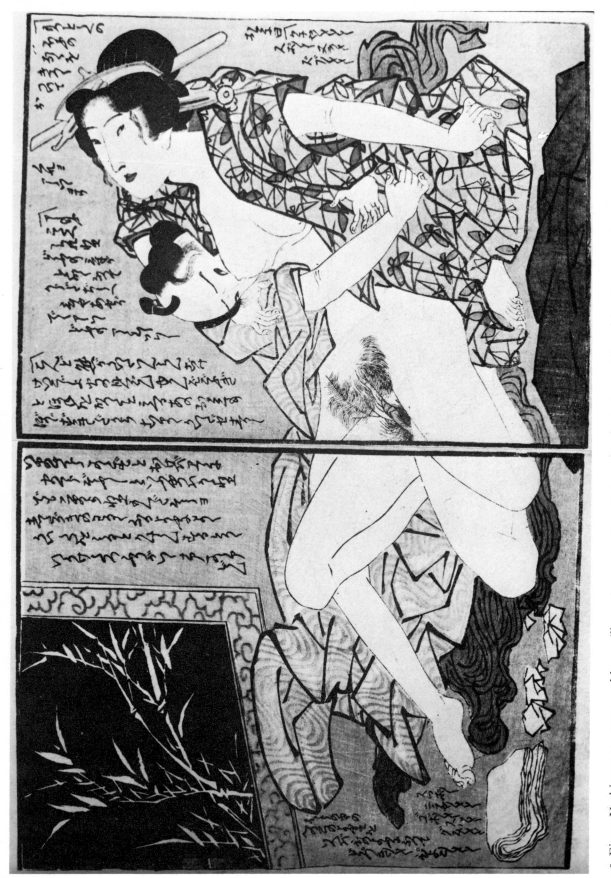

248 Eisen: Yoshiwara courtesan and lover; illustration to the *Ehon Fuji no yuki* (*Erotic Snows of Fuji*). Woodblock colour-printed book; Edo, 1824; *hanshi-bon*. Signed.
A splendid work by one of the major masters of the later Ukiyo-e

249 Kunisada: Illustration to the *Shiki no nagame* (*Views of the Erotic Seasons*). Woodblock colour-printed book; Edo, *c.* 1827; *ōbon*. At the back, the shunga-scroll's box; on the right, a smoking-stand with filed love-letters. This illustrates one of the major social purposes of the traditional type of shunga scroll, both in China and Japan

250: (*above left*) Kyōsai: Tengu-demon attacking a Japanese girl. One of a set of twelve small *surimono* prints, mounted back-to-back in pairs. One side shows a detailed shunga tableau in straight, late Utagawa ukiyo-e style; the other side, as here, shows a more impressionistic scene in semi-Shijō manner. Woodblock colour print; Edo, *c.* 1860s; narrow *koban*. Signed

251 (*above right*) Chōkyōsai Eiri (?): Woodblock colour print, from the series *Fumi no kiyogaki* (*Calligraphy Models*). Edo, *c.* 1800; *ōban*.

252 (*below*) Hokusai: Woodblock colour print, from the album *Ehon tsuhi no hinagata* (*Models of Loving Couples*). Edo, *c.* 1810s; *ōban*. The courtesan's secret lover wears a tobacco-case held by a *netsuke* on his belt.
This work of the world-famed eccentric master shows him as a powerful traditional artist

253 (*above*) Kuniyoshi: Illustration to the *Chimpen shinkeibai*
(*The Pillowed Boudoir*). Woodblock colour-printed book; Edo,
1839; *hanshi-bon*. Signed. Inset on the left shows interval
at a Kabuki theatre. The book is a parody on the Ming
erotic novel *Chin-p'ing-mei*.
A shunga print by an artist much collected in the West

254 and 255 (*right*) Kinkasai: Two octopi and two ground-
cherries; from a picture-scroll in colours on paper, with
twelve scenes depicting the erotic-comic aspects of still life
and animal postures. Shijō School, mid-19th century. Signed
This exemplifies the Japanese fondness for the allegorical
metamorphosis of the natural world

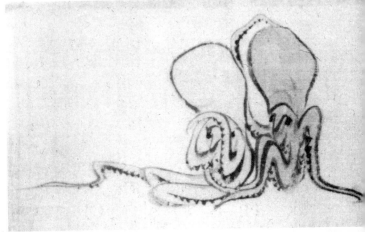

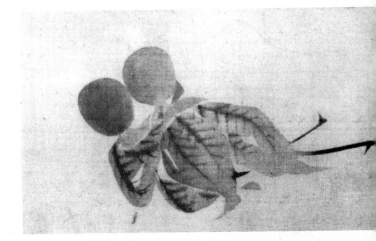

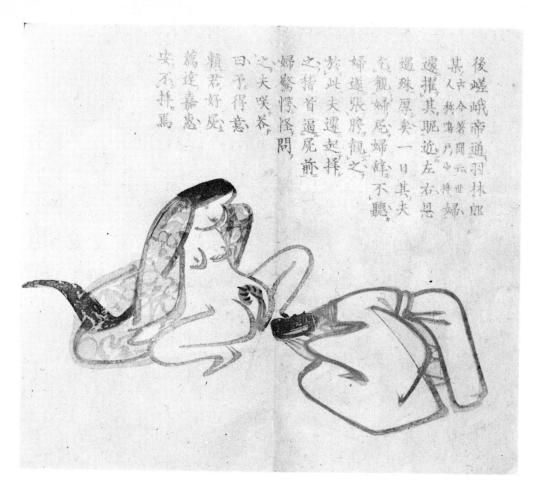

256 (*left*) Hōshū: Illustration to the *Daitō keigo* (*Boudoir-tales from the East*). Woodblock-printed album; Nagoya, 1867; narrow *chūbon*. A courtier's wife was beloved of the Emperor Go-Saga, who thenceforth bestowed great honours upon her husband. Here, the cuckolded husband is seen paying homage to the source of his worldly success. The original designs for this album were attributed to Taigadō (1723-76); the album illustrated here is signed by the Nagoya *bunjin-ga* artist Shibata Hōshū (1840-90)

258 (*opposite*) Meiji Ukiyo-e School: Yoshiwara courtesan with lover; from the album *Yakumo no chigiri* (*Poetic Intercourse*). Twelve woodblock colour prints; Tokyo, *c.* 1899; *ōban*. The illustrations are ascribed to Tomioka Eisen and his pupil Hamada Josen

257 (*above*) 'Tennō Kabura': The Empress Kōmyō dallying with her lover, the abbot Gembō; from a picture-scroll in colours on silk, by a *bunjin-ga* artist of the mid 19th century—after the original Taigadō designs of the *Daitō keigo* (see plate 256). Signed. Plates 256 and 257 represent a survival of the traditional narrative scroll style, in its erotic mode

259 (*opposite*) Modern Ukiyo-e School: Scene from an album of twelve paintings. Colours on paper, *c.* late 1920s; large *ōban*. By a skilled master in the tradition of Kiyokata, possibly an Osaka artist

will offer another less complex, but powerfully-designed sample. These prints, 252
produced perhaps a decade after Utamaro's death, fittingly constitute the last great
landmark of the Japanese figure-print.

Aside from his two or three such sets of larger shunga album-prints, Hokusai
designed over a dozen picture-books, among which are contained some of his
most powerful and varied work. The print of the two octopi is justly famous. Its
inspiration derives, probably, from a book-illustration (in rather lower key) by
Hokusai's master Shunshō; nevertheless, it marks a peak in the aesthetically-
grotesque in Japanese sexual art. For its type, it stands with Utamaro's famous
underwater scene of plate 247 – and excels it in power of design, and sheer exoticism. 247
Whether such a design rates inclusion under the aegis of 'normal' erotic art, we
cannot say; but certainly, it ranks among the most remarkable of all shunga.

After Hokusai, undoubtedly the most striking figure among the later shunga
artists is Keisai Eisen.

Eisen (1791–1848) was to prove one of the most prolific of all ukiyo-e shunga
masters. His several sets of larger album-prints are well known, and he produced
more than three dozen different shunga books as well – mostly, signed with his
erotica pseudonym, 'Insai Hakusui'. Like Moronobu, Masanobu and Harunobu
before him, Eisen was a skilled writer, and is thought to have written the texts,
as well, for many of his shunga picture-books and novelettes.

Eisen's first shunga productions are yet confused with those few works of his
master Eizan, but by the early 1810s he had already begun publishing characteristic
work of note. There is little doubt that, had Eisen been born a generation earlier,
he would have ranked near Utamaro as one of the great figure-print designers of
ukiyo-e. This, however, the times did not permit: the general decline in taste on
the part of publishers and patrons, and the unnatural conventions of design and
concept which were forced upon the artists, combined to reduce the work of
Eisen to a much lower level of quality than he should otherwise have achieved.

In his shunga, however, Eisen produced not only some of his very best work,
but, for that matter, some of the rarely fine figure designs of the later Edo Period.
The album illustrated in plate XXXI, for example, ranks both in colouring and XXXI
design on a level not far below that of Eisen's ultimate mentor, Utamaro.

Eisen's principal contribution to ukiyo-e lay in that sense of typically late-Edo
iki (smartness, chic) which so delights Japanese connoisseurs, but may sometimes
seem a trifle silly or overdone to the outsider. The late-Edo concept of *iki* serves
to indicate, however, a new and decadent attitude towards life and towards sex –
an increased absorption with purely physical stimulation, and an endeavour for
ever-increasing variety in such stimulants. This changing attitude was not, of
course, Eisen's invention – he was but mirroring the declining tastes of his times.

It must always be remembered that ukiyo-e was an essentially *popular* art-form:
primarily, it produced just what the public wanted. When (as with Sharaku) an
artist of vision originated a new manner which neither met current demands nor
created fresh ones, he simply ceased to get commissions, and turned to something
other than art for a living. There was no 'art for art's sake' in ukiyo-e.

Plate 248 reveals another, perhaps more typical phase of Eisen's work, a colour 248
illustration to an erotic novel. The design is a striking one, and the idea of both
protagonists looking so keenly at the *reader* is certainly an unusual one for ukiyo-e.

260 Yamazaki Kō: Two Girls. Water colours on paper, double-*ōban* size; *c.* 1964. From a
series of shunga sketches by a leading modern illustrator (b. 1921)

Doubtless, Eisen's success at such illustrated novels lay, in part, in his intimate connexion with the texts as well. His erotica possess a unity of concept that was far more difficult of achievement when author and artist divided the work.

Decline of shunga

Together with Hokusai, one of the leading figure-print designers of the later eighteenth and early nineteenth centuries was Utagawa Toyokuni. Like Hokusai, Toyokuni (1769–1825) seems to have produced little in the way of shunga during the period of his finest work in the *bijin-ga* ('girl-picture') genre – the 1790s. Indeed, his half-dozen shunga books seem largely to have been a product of his final few years – the early 1820s – and as such, are readily confused with the work of his immediate pupil and successor Utagawa Kunisada (Toyokuni III). It was to this pupil that the mantle of the Utagawa-School figure-print fell, and with it, a predominant position in nineteenth-century shunga.

In the shunga field, Kunisada (1786–1865) worked almost exclusively in illustrated books, some four dozen being known. Most often, these are signed with one of his erotic pseudonyms, e.g. 'Fukiyō Matabei'. It must be added that, with Kunisada, the distinction between the book illustration and the album-print is *XXXII/249* sometimes a very fine one: such books as that illustrated in plates XXXII and 249 feature more elaborate colour-printing than any but the most luxurious of prints; they must have cost, complete in several volumes, the price of two dozen or more individual colour prints.

XXXII Plate XXXII represents Kunisada at his best: an impressively decorative scene, most overpowering in colour, in which attention is not drawn too closely to his *249* over-formalized figures. Plate 249, from the same elaborately-printed book, will serve as an example of the shunga 'frontispiece' – in which an only *semi*-erotic tableau is presented, to lead more gradually into the erotic extremes to be presented further on.

We include the latter plate here in part, however, for its content. The young hero is seen employing an early, painted shunga scroll as they were used in the days of the Han dynasty in China to remove inhibitions, and overcome a girl's resistance. Whether for bridegrooms or seducers, this was one of the 'customary' functions of shunga, mentioned earlier. The pictured scroll itself seems to be a typical example of pre-ukiyo-e Yamato-e work, featuring its own frontispiece, which straightway leads into a second, more frankly erotic scene. (Aside from making manifest the format, and one of the uses, of the shunga scroll, the activities depicted in this plate may also serve to indicate why so few of these scrolls remain extant today in anything like mint condition.)

Equal in rank with Kunisada – and in some ways a more unique and interesting artist – was his confrère, Utagawa Kuniyoshi.

Kuniyoshi (1798–1861) has long been a favourite of Western collectors, and it is surprising that so little has been said or published of his erotic work. His shunga are principally in the form of books illustrated in colour – the erotic novels of the period. He executed at least three dozen separate works in this category, usually signed profusely with one of his erotica signatures, 'Ichimyōkai' or 'Hodoyoshi'. Another of his 'signatures' is the omnipresent sleeping cat that he so loves to position somewhere in his erotic scenes.

Kuniyoshi's shunga have a special flavour of their own, found in no other artist of the period. But other than to the true Kuniyoshi devotee, his designs are interesting rather than beautiful, and he cannot really be considered one of the masters of Japanese shunga.

Although Kunisada and Kuniyoshi are customarily considered, with Eisen, the leading shunga artists of their generation, to us at least, their work lacks that spark of erotic excitement that distinguishes the *oeuvre* of the latter master. As with most of the nineteenth-century artists, to be sure, their illustrations suffer when detached from context, and shown in monochrome. For much of their charm lies in the excellent colouring, and in the total impression of the book they illustrate. As independent designs, however, they seldom equal the work of the seventeenth- and eighteenth-century masters.

The contemporaries and followers of Kunisada and Kuniyoshi are legion, and it is their countless works that are most commonly seen, and purchasable, in Japan today. A check-list of these lesser nineteenth-century masters would include such Kunisada and Kuniyoshi contemporaries, pupils and followers as Hiroshige, Kuninao, Kunimaru, Kunimori, Shōzan, Kunisada II, Sadatora, Sadafusa, Sadahide, Yoshikazu, Yoshiiku, Kunichika, Chikanobu and Kyōsai; and such Hokusai pupils and followers as his daughter O-ei, Hokuba, Hokkei, Taigaku, Kanenari, Goshiehi and Shigenobu.

Of the mid nineteenth-century masters in the Kunisada manner, Koikawa Shōzan was certainly the most prolific – fully five dozen shunga books by him being known. Shōzan's name is thought to be a pseudonym of the minor novelist Ryūsuitei Tanekiyo (1822–1908), in which latter capacity he wrote most of his own texts. We have yet to see any *non*-shunga works by this artist, so that he may well be considered a rare specialist in the field. His works extended on into the Meiji Era and, with his great productivity, it is as often as not his books that are seen most commonly on the market today.

The most unusual of the later shunga masters, however, was Kawanabe Kyōsai (1831–89), a sample of whose work we have chosen to show the comic, fantastic view of sex that prevailed as one facet of late-Edo erotica. This print features one of the same water-demons we saw in the Utamaro print of plate 250; but the spirit *250* here is that of grotesque comedy – and the style, more that of the Shijō school, to be noted subsequently.

In short, the shunga print followed the destiny of the figure-print in general: it reached a peak with the last quarter of the eighteenth century, thence declining gradually until, by the middle of the nineteenth century, it was a rare artist or publisher, indeed, who could design or issue a print anywhere near the level of the earlier masters, the earlier publishers. The fault was largely that of the age: the public, stagnant after too-long centuries of seclusion from the outer world, had lost its taste for figure-prints of grace and lovely harmony. No publisher ever rose to counter this decline in taste, nor, very likely, could such have had any lasting success.

By the time of Commodore Perry's arrival with his fleet in 1853, Japan's artistic traditions were all too ready for a shock and a renaissance – even if the stimulus needs must come from a civilization quite alien to their own, a civilization whose fruits would, eventually, kill off whatever yet lingered of the Old Japan.

Erotic art in other fields

As we have noted earlier, the painting of shunga was but one of the many normal functions of the Japanese artist. Even aside from shunga commissions from their patrons, however, the artistic impulse to sketch and paint erotica was equally strong among certain members of the more austere, non-ukiyo-e schools of the Edo Period. In this terminal note we shall briefly record their shunga activity, as well as attempting to indicate something of the trends of Japanese erotic art in modern times.

Over ninety per cent of the shunga production of the Edo Period consisted of the prints and printed books of the popular, ukiyo-e school. But a survey of the remaining ten per cent – i.e. the hand-painted shunga of the Edo Period – reveals that nearly all types and classes of artists at one time or another painted such works, for their own amusement, or on commission from their patrons. Even the most austere of Confucian scholars were not exempt from shunga connexions: we have an historical record, fore xample, that the great Ogyū Sorai (1666–1728) was requested to write an appreciative, prefatory inscription for an erotic scroll, and responded with this apt paean to shunga (or to sex itself): 'O Mystery of Mysteries: Gateway to All Wonders'.

A detailed study of the shunga *oeuvre* of the non-ukiyo-e masters is rendered difficult by the relative scarcity of extant works. Such were, of course, seldom issued in printed form – and even in manuscript were less apt to be seen and copied by pupils than were a master's more 'presentable' works. Despite this paucity of reference material, we shall attempt to illustrate and discuss here at least a few of the extant works of the neo-classical artists.

It is worth recording that, to judge from the literary sources of the time, a surprising number of the great names of the eighteenth- and nineteenth-century *Bunjin-ga* and Shijō schools were known for their shunga. These include such artists as Taigadō, Ōkyo, Genki, Soken, Goshun, Miss Shōran, Chikuden, Bunchō, Kazan, Aigai, Yōsai, Kyōsai and Miss Shōhin.

The *Bunjin-ga*, or Literati School of Japanese art, had risen in the eighteenth century under predominantly Chinese influence, its artists, as often as not, gifted amateurs. Their subjects were primarily Chinese landscapes and Chinese sages, but they did sometimes turn to shunga, in such witty, stylized depictions as we *256/257* see in plates 256 and 257. Their significant contribution to the field was a humorous, almost sex-less view of the erotic, most charming in its near-childish denial of the harsher facts of sex.

Somewhat related, was the work of the Shijō School artists, who in the early nineteenth century, developing after the lead of Ōkyo, brought an impressionistic approach, and sure brush-stroke, to the traditional subject matter of Japanese art. Though in itself not primarily a *popular* school, Shijō influence on the later

XXXI Eisen: Yoshiwara courtesan holding a saké-bowl. Woodblock colour print; Edo, *c*. late 1810s. This illustrates the phase of the Ukiyo-e shunga print in the early 19th century after the death of Utamaro

ukiyo-e masters was great. Shijō figure-work itself sometimes turned perceptively to shunga subjects. We have also, already (plate 203), cited a notable semi-Shijō *203* print-album composed on the model of classical shunga subjects. This school was often at its best, however, in the still-life, the animal or plant sketch, and one of its finest extant contributions to shunga, shown in plates 254 and 255, is indeed in *254/255* this latter witty vein.

While our concern here has been primarily with pictorial and graphic art, it may be useful to survey briefly Japanese erotic art in other genres of the seventeenth century and following.

The Edo Period was clearly not a great age for sculpture, nor was monumental sculpture ever suited to the decorative needs of the Japanese home – even of the mansions of the wealthy aristocracy. The production of certain religious statuary of a sexual nature continued, but it is, rather, in the miniature carvings and earthenware figurines, ceramics and metalwork, that we find the principal (if minor) masterpieces of this genre, whether in erotic or non-erotic fields.

The numerous, small *netsuke* carvings in wood, bone or ivory represent one of the principal Japanese achievements in erotic art of this nature – a three-dimensional, miniature art-form that must really be examined in the palm of the hand for true appreciation. The sexual implements (e.g. *harikata* – dildos) of the Japanese boudoir also sometimes featured bas-relief, erotic carving of incredible intricacy. And metalwork of phallic or erotic nature is also often seen – including, interestingly enough, the metal fittings for the samurai sword. This latter feature might, at first, strike one as but an extension of the medieval practice of placing a shunga scroll in one's armour-chest, as both phallic and magic charm. But with the peaceful centuries of the Edo Period, the samurai penchant for such erotica seems likely to have been a more human taste, typical of the male in any country.

Other crafts or folk-arts featuring the erotic were ceramics (saké-cups with shunga designs being best known); the famed Hakata Dolls (the base of which often featured an erotic bas-relief); the *oshi-e* – silken doll-figures in relief, featured on the battledores used in New Year's games, or sometimes seen mounted on screens; as well as erotic paintings or embroidery done on tobacco-cases, purses, and the like.

Shunga and the nude in modern Japan

The history of modern Japanese erotic art lies outside our main line of inquiry, and we shall attempt to describe only a few impressions here.

In modern Japan, shunga as such have had only a minor role, and this, in the hidden shadows of art. During the Meiji Period (1868–1912) the final generation of ukiyo-e artists – despite strong government censorship – played their last role, and sometimes produced shunga work of merit, such as the famed *Poetic Intercourse* (*Yakumo no chigiri*) of plate 258. *258*

The neo-ukiyo-e artists, though deprived of an audience for the prints, have continued their work of romanticizing Old Japan in the form of hand-paintings of old customs, and their occasional work in shunga is a bright spot on an otherwise

373

XXXII Kunisada: Night cherry-blossoms; illustration to the *Shiki no nagame* (*Views of the Erotic Seasons*). Woodblock colour-printed book; Edo, *c.* 1827; *ōbon*.
Here the multi-colour print reaches a high point of technical elaboration and density of form and colour during the third decade of the 19th century

barren landscape. The unfortunate fact is, however, that the lover of Old Japan collects early shunga; and the lover of the modern, collects erotica in European style.

For shunga – as with ukiyo-e in general – the demand ceased, for all practical purposes, when the convenience, the cheapness and the modernity of Western civilization came to be fully realized by the Japanese. Whatever steps Japan takes in the future, they will not be in a backward direction.

Finally, as a kind of supplement to our principal inquiry, it may be of interest to note here the difficult reception which Japan accorded the nude in art, with the widespread introduction of Western cultural forms in the later nineteenth century.

At the time Japan was opened to foreign civilization in the 1860s and 1870s, there were many artists skilled at shunga, but none at depiction of the nude *per se*. The new fad for all things Occidental naturally included Western art. To put it bluntly, the predominant position of the nude in European art came as a rude shock to the austere Japanese leaders of Westernization – much like the effect of an Occidental's first view of shunga itself. For a time the early shunga were even used as textbooks for the study of nude art, and it took several decades – including the experience of study abroad by leading Japanese painters – to convince even the artists themselves that working long hours from a living, nude model was not something immoral and obscene.

Among educators, statesmen, officials and critics unfamiliar with the conventions of Western art, opposition went even further, encompassing the extreme view that it was simply improper to view the naked body, whether in the flesh, or through art. The problem came to widespread public attention in the year 1889, with the reproduction of a nude painting in a supplement to the newspaper *Kokumin no tomo,* and the appearance of suggestive nude frontispieces in the novels *The Butterfly* (*Kochō*) by Yamada Bimyō (the design by Watanabe Shōtei, after an earlier painting by Kikuchi Yōsai), and *The Elegant Buddha* (*Fūryū-butsu*) by Kōda Rohan (illustrated by Hirafuku Suian). By this time the Japanese government had become involved in the controversy, and in November of the same year summarily banned the nude from all publication.

Further public controversy was aroused in 1894 and 1895 when the leading artist Kuroda Seiki (1866–1924) – who had returned recently from ten years of study in France – displayed a striking nude painting at exhibits in both Tokyo and Kyoto. (This particular painting had already been exhibited in Paris, on the recommendation of Kuroda's mentor Puvis de Chavannes.) The exhibits themselves went untouched, but the various reproductions that appeared of the painting were promptly confiscated by the police.

The conservative view towards the nude in art remained unchanged throughout the later nineteenth and early twentieth century. In the words of the influential newspaper, *Miyako shimbun*: 'If public morals must be sacrificed lest the advance of oil painting be hindered, then let that advance cease!' And, 'The Nude is only one step removed from Shunga.' Criticism of nude art reached an even more extreme degree in another leading newspaper of the time, the *Nippon shimbun*: 'Nude art is the lowest of the low. It bears hardly anything to distinguish it from Shunga. Indeed, it is even *more* degraded than Shunga!'

In the Tokyo Autumn Art Show of 1901, official censure extended even to the exhibition hall: on all the nude paintings and sculpture the police draped brown cloths – in the famous *Koshimaki* ('Loincloth') Affair. In the Exhibit of two years later, nude works were placed in a restricted, Special Room – much as pornography is treated in print cabinets today – a custom that was followed for some years, in order to lighten the hand of official censure. Yet despite this concession, some of the work of the sculptors was not considered suitable for even limited exhibition: Shinkai's 'Two Nudes' had papier-mâché fig-leaves glued over the genitals; and Asakura's noted male nude 'Darkness' had its modest phallus removed by a police saw.

Such censorship extended even to the specialized publications intended for artists and art students – where, through most of the later Meiji Era, nude art was customarily deleted by the police authorities prior to, or banned after, publication. This ban extended, to be sure, to ukiyo-e itself, where even reproductions of old *abuna-e* prints showing but the nude torso were confiscated.

Although tolerance towards the Western-style nude increased during the following Taishō and early Shōwa eras, the latter was not really freed of official restrictions until Japan's defeat in the Pacific War. And even today, one may doubt that a fair segment of the Japanese population understands the real difference between the nude and shunga – except that the one is foreign and therefore admirable: the other, native and therefore contemptible.

To the Occidental reader, perhaps, our digression on the trials of nude art in the Meiji Period may seem somewhat unrelated to our major theme. To us, however, it is significant in indicating both the difficulty the Japanese had in distinguishing the nude from shunga; and the rapid yet illogical prejudice against *both* shunga and the nude that developed with the Westernization of the country. It may also, possibly, provide some key to understanding the function of shunga in Old Japan.

They will, we think, be seen to represent a fascinating eddy in the mainstream of world art – a predominantly serious, artistic glorification of the erotic, as far removed from phallic-religious significance as it was from snickering prurience. It was a clean and open art-form, enjoyed, without guilt, by a race to whom the full pleasures of sex were considered but one of the natural rights of mankind.

Select Bibliography

of books in European languages, translations, or texts with substantial introductions in European languages.

INDIA M. R. Anand, *Kāma Kalā*, Geneva, 1958.

Anon., *History of the Sect of Maharajas*, London, 1865.

W. G. Archer, *The Loves of Krishna*, London, 1957.

A. Avalon (pseudonym of J. Woodroffe), *The Principles of Tantra*, London, 1914-6.

A. Avalon (pseudonym of J. Woodroffe), *Shakti and Shakta*, Madras, London, 1929.

A. Avalon (pseudonym of J. Woodroffe), *The Serpent Power,* 3rd ed., Madras, 1931.

A. Avalon (pseudonym of J. Woodroffe), translated, *Karpurādistotram*, Calcutta, London, 1922.

A. Avalon (pseudonym of J. Woodroffe), translated, *Ānandalaharī*, Madras, 1924.

Bhagavatapurāṇam, translated by J. M. Sanyal, Calcutta, New Delhi, nd.

Agehānanda Bharati, *The Tantric Tradition*, London, 1965.

F. D. K. Bosch, *The Golden Germ*, S'Gravenhage, 1960.

Brahmavaivarta Purāna, translated, R. N. Sen, Allahabad, 1920-2.

G. W. Briggs, *Gorakhnath and the Kānphaṭa Yogīs*, Calcutta, 1938.

M. Carstairs, *The Twice Born,* London, 1957.

S. K. Chatterji, *Origin and Development of the Bengali Language,* Calcutta, 1926.

W. Crooke, *An Introduction to the Popular Religion and Folklore of Northern India,* Westminster, 1896.

S. B. Dasgupta, *Obscure Religious Cults,* Calcutta, 1946.

S. B. Dasgupta, *Introduction to Tantrik Buddhism,* Calcutta, 1950.

A. David-Neel, *Initiations and Initiates in Tibet,* London, 1931, 1958.

A. David-Neel, *With Mystics and Magicians in Tibet,* London, 1931.

Sri Mad Devi Bhagavatam, translated by Swami Vijñanananda, Allahabad, 1921-3.

M. Eliade, *Yoga: Immortality and Freedom* (recommended especially for its bibliography which includes references to numerous periodicals), London, 1958.

Max-Pol Fouchet, *The Erotic Art of India,* London, 1959.

L. Frederic, *Indian Temples and Sculpture*, London, 1959.

R. Gnoli, *The Aesthetic Experience according to Abhinavagupta,* Rome, 1956.

Guhyasamāja Tantra, Baroda, 1931 (Gaekwad's Oriental Series LIII).

Hathayogapradīpika, translated by B. Bhaba, Bombay, 1889 (other editions also).

R. E. Hume, translated, *Thirteen Principal Upanishads*, London, 1921: Oxford, 1934.

The Hymns of the Rig Veda, translated by R. T. H. Griffith, 2nd ed. Benares, 1896.

C. G. Jung, Works: Passim; especially *Psychology and Alchemy*, translated New York, London, 1953: *Symbols of Transformation,* New York, 1956.

Kokashāstra, translated with introduction by Alex Comfort, London, 1965.

S. Kramrisch, *The Hindu Temple,* Calcutta, 1946.

Love Songs of Vidyāpati, translated by D. Bhattacharya, London, 1963.

J. J. Meyer, *Sexual Life in Ancient India*, London, 1930.

Nishpannayogāvalī, Baroda, 1949 (Gaekwad's Oriental Series CIX).

J. C. Oman, *The Mystics, Ascetics and Saints of India,* London, 1903.

Sāṅkhyakārikā of Īshvarakrishna, translated by S. S. Suryanavayana Sastri, Madras, 1948.

D. C. Sen, *Chaitanya and His Age,* Calcutta, 1922.

D. C. Sen, *History of Bengali Language and Literature,* Calcutta, 1911.

M. Shahidullah, *Les Chants Mystiques de Kānha et de Saraha: les Dohakosa et les Carya,* Paris, 1928.

Shivasamhita
Gherandasamhita } translated by Sris Chandra Vasu, Allahabad, 1914.

The Shiva Sūtra Vimarshiṇī of Kshemerāja, translated by P. T. S. Iyengar, Allahabad, 1912.

S. H. Sinha } *History of Prostitution in India,* Bengal Social Hygiene Association,
N. K. Basu } Calcutta, 1933.

D. L. Snellgrove, *The Hevajra Tantra,* London, 1959.

P. Thomas, *Kāma Kalpa,* Bombay, nd.

Kāmasūtra, translated by R. Burton, introduction by W. G. Archer, London, 1963.

E. Thurston, *Tribes and Castes of Southern India,* Madras, 1909.

H. Zimmer, *Myths and Symbols in Indian Art and Civilisation,* New York, 1946.

H. Zimmer, *The Art of Indian Asia,* Washington, 1946.

CHINA

Woo Chan Cheng (pseudonym of J. Pampaneau), *Érotologie de la Chine,* Paris, 1963.

R. H. van Gulik, *Sexual Life in Ancient China,* London, 1961.

R. H. van Gulik, *Erotic Prints of the Ming Period,* Tokyo, 1957.

Chou Yi Lang, 'Tantrism in China', *Harvard Journal of Asiatic Studies VIII,* 1945, pp. 241-332.

H. Maspéro, *Le Taoisme,* Paris, 1950.

H. Maspéro, 'Les procédés de "nourir le principe vital" dans la religion Taoiste ancienne', *Journal Asiatique,* April-June, July-September, Paris, 1937.

J. Needham, 'History of Scientific Thought', Vol. II of *Science and Civilisation in China,* Cambridge, 1956.

ISLAM

R. Burton, *Love, War and Fancy, Writings on the Arabian Nights,* London, 1964.

R. Burton, *The Book of the One Thousand Nights and One,* Benares, 1885 ff.

JAPAN

Anon. (Julius Kurth (?)) *Japanische Erotik,* Munich, 1907.

Marianne Densmore, *Les Estampes Érotiques Japonaises,* Paris, 1961.

Charles Grosbois, *Shunga: Images of Spring,* Geneva, 1964. (Cf. our detailed review in *Ukiyo-e Art,* No. 10, 1965.)

François Poncetton, *L'Estampe Érotique du Japon,* Paris, 1927.

Kōzō Hara, *Nihon kōshoku bijutsu-shi (History of Japanese Erotic Art),* Tokyo, 1930.

Yoshikazu Hayashi, *Empon kenkyū-Kunisada; Utamaro; Utamaro Pt. 2; Shunshō; Kuniyoshi; Harunobu; Toyokuni; Hiroshige and Utamaro; Eisen* 9 vols., to date, Tokyo, 1963-6.

Nihon empon daishūsei (Compendium of Japanese Erotica), Tokyo, 1954.

Kiyoshi Shibui, *Genroku kohanga shūei* ('Estampes Érotiques Primitives du Japōn'), 2 vols., Tokyo, 1928.

Ars Erotica, Tokyo, 1930.

Ukiyo-e naishi (Secret History of Ukiyo-e), 2 vols., Tokyo, 1932, 1933.

Shoki hanga ('The Primitives'), Tokyo, 1954.

Tetsu Takahashi, *Takahashi Tetsu Collection,* 2 vols., Tokyo, 1962, 1963.

Hihō emaki-ko ('Secret Heirloom Picture Scrolls'), Tokyo, 1965.

Ukiyo-e, 26 vols. to date, Tokyo, 1962-6.

Teruji Yoshida, *Ukiyo-e abuna-e,* 3 vols., Tokyo, 1963.

Ukiyo-e higa, Ukiyo-e enga (Ukiyo-e Erotica), 2 vols., Tokyo, 1961, 1963.

Ukiyo-e jiten (Ukiyo-e Dictionary), 2 vols. to date, Tokyo, 1965.

Joseph E. De Becker, *The Nightless City, or the 'History of the Yoshiwara Yūkwaku,'* Yokohama, 1899.

Howard Hibbett, *The Floating World in Japanese Fiction,* New York and London, 1959.

377

Richard Lane, 'Saikaku and Boccaccio: the Novella in Japan and Italy'. *Monumenta Nipponica,* Tokyo, 1959.

 Masters of the Japanese Print: Their World and Their Work, New York and London, 1962.

 'The Banning of Fiction in Genroku Japan', *Monumenta Nipponica*, Tokyo, 1966.

 Kana-zōshi, Los Angeles, 1966. (Earlier version in *Harvard Journal of Asiatic Studies*, Cambridge, 1957.)

 Studies in Japanese Literature, Los Angeles, 1966.

GENERAL G. Bataille, *Eroticism*, Paris, 1957; London, 1962.

 H. Benoit, *The Many Faces of Love*, London, 1956.

 R. Briffault, *The Mothers*, London, New York, 1927.

 E. Crawley (ed. T. Besterman), *The Mystic Rose*, London, 1902, 1927.

 M. Delacourt, *Hermaphrodite: Myths and Rites of the Bi-sexual Figure in Classical Antiquity*, London, 1961.

 R. Graves, *The White Goddess,* London, 1948.

 J. Hastings (ed.), *Encyclopaedia of Religion and Ethics,* especially see articles on 'Phallism', 'Marriage'.

 S. Lilar, *Aspects of Love in Western Society*, London, 1965.

 R. B. Onians, *The Origins of European Thought,* Cambridge, 1951.

 N. M. Penzer, in *The Ocean of Story*, Appendix to R. Tawney's translation, *On Sacred Prostitution*, privately printed, London, 1924.

 H. M. Ploss
 M. & P. Barteks } *Woman*, English ed., London, 1935.

Index

Note: Book titles are given in italics, usually in their original language.

Temples are usually listed under the appropriate town.

Italicised figures refer to black and white plate numbers, not pages; Roman numerals refer to colour plates.